# Legends & Narratives
## of Islam

### The Biblical Personalities

Dr. Khaled Sanadiki

# Legends and Narratives of Islam
## The Biblical Personalities

Khaled Sanadiki, M.D.

Registered at the Library of Congress no. TXu 917-261

Book cover designed by Chuck Knapp, illustration from Tunisian folk art representing Noah's ark; artist unknown.

ISBN: 1-930637-17-9

5/03

Distributed by:

Kazi Publications, Inc.
3023 West Belmont Avenue
Chicago IL 60618
(T) 773-267-7001; (F) 773-267-7002
email: info@kazi.org and catalog at www.kazi.org

Say: " We believe in God and what has been sent down to us, and what was send down to Abraham, Ismael, Isaac, Jacob, and his children, and what was given Moses and Jesus, and what was given the [other] prophets by their Lord. We do not discriminate against any one of them and are committed [to live] in peace with Him."

-Qur'an 2:136

# Foreword

## What is a legend?

Legends are types of literature, such as a tragedy or comedy, which usually, but not always involve God and miracles. Most of the legends are not supported by what we term "historical fact" because much of the past did not survive into the history books. Legends with miracles are not supported by our strictly defined physical laws, but the realm of physics incorporated phenomena which are even more strange and absurd than simple miracles. For example, there are four or more dimensional spaces, black holes, expanding universe, pinpoint universe, and worm holes. The personalities of legends sometimes act out of the norm of what we define as a normal human response, perhaps acting in a puerile manner or in an unexpected one. But people behaving normally do not make it into the list of legends. In legends, God or gods sometimes act in a strange way, unlike the God whom we think we know, and this is because we like to give God human like characteristics, and God, by definition, is not a human.

A legend is as real as any other story we hear of. It may be different and you do not expect everyone to believe it, but that is true of every kind of story. Legends as stories stand on their own, supported by the faith of the believers. In legends we come face to face with the history of the human search for its own existence and being, human behavior and its ethical values and the constant drive of the human soul to seek his creator. Legends are one of the constituents of the human psyche and this manifests itself in the human behavior, belief and ambition.

What is meant by "legend" in this book is a story which lived in the memory of a nation for a long time and was accepted by them as a true story, and only under these circumstances a story can be called a "legend." A legend, like any story, could be a true historical event, fictional or a combination of the two.     As a child I used to listen to my father and grandmother telling me the Islamic stories of the great prophets, and their miracles have fascinated me since.  When I was ten years old I found a Bible in my father's library, and after reading it, came to the realization about how much the differing faiths have in common.  Since that time, I have dreamt about writing a book encompassing both the Islamic and Biblical versions of these stories, but it was not until I was in my fifties that I completed my Arabic book and in 2000, finished this English version.  Many English books have been written in the past twenty years covering all aspects of Islam: political, historical, social and demographic.  But no one has, until now, tackled this aspect of religious stories and legends.  Although these stories make up between twenty and thirty percent of the Qur'anic verses, authors have perhaps felt that the subject is not vitally important for the introduction of Islam to English readers.  But this is not the way I felt.  Rather, this subject is something Moslems share with both Christians and Jews, and it will proffer a unique perspective that may reveal that these religions can respect and accept each other peacefully.  The problem of writing such a book is that Moslems find it difficult to separate this subject from the  different aspects of Islam, i.e law, ethics and traditional values. In the first book of Islam, the Qur'an did not separate these issues, they were combined with other teachings, and the books of Tafsir, (the commentary of the Qur'an) followed the same direction.  The components of these stories have different religious certainty in the mind of the Moslem believer, and while the Qur'anic part is absolutely true and without dispute, the writings of the sahaba (companions of the Prophet) can be debated according to the rules of Islamic criticism. On the other hand, those portions coming from Jewish lore or Arabic legends are mostly considered for entertainment value. I did my best, when I wrote these stories to acknowledge which are Qur'anic and which are reported by sahaba and what are complementary stories.

These stories are a compilation of many diverse and shorter stories which may not be completely compatible with one another, so it should be no surprise to the reader to find some discrepancy in the larger stories.

I did all the English translation from the Arabic sources, but for the Qur'an I used mostly the translation of T.B. Irving, 'The Noble Qur'an,' and 'Abdullah Yusuf 'Ali, 'The Meaning of the Holy Qur'an.' and I would like to emphasize my appreciation for the courtesies of T.B. Irving and the publisher of the Yusuf 'Ali translation. The Arabic language of the Qur'an can be translated in many different ways, depending on the subject you want to emphasize in the translation, and because most translations of the Qur'an try and emphasize the totality of that Book, I chose to concentrate on the stories–which made it necessary to look for the appropriate wording and used both the aforementioned books as well as using my own translation. The Yusuf Ali translation used archaic terms such as 'thou,' and 'dost,' which I changed to more contemporary phrasing with permission from the publisher. I did the same thing in quoting the Bible and used the King James Version with some modernization. For the Pseudepigrapha references I used the remarkable book edited by James H. Charlesworth and published by Doubleday. For most of my Hebrew references, I used the inimitable book 'The Legends of the Jews.' by Louis Ginzberg. There were other notable English books on this subject although I made every effort to check with the original Hebrew text. The English translation of the 'Book of Yasher,' published in 1840 by M.M. Noah in New York, was invaluable, and the footnotes on Yashar reflect both the original source and the English text.

I also would like to thank the famous Arabic poet Lamia A. Amara for her roll in reviewing all the Madaeans referrals; Mrs Amara, Manda'i by birth, is an authority on Mandaean religion and books.

My sincere appreciation to Shelagh Campion for her assistance in the writing of this book.

For the Moslem readers who may not be familiar with the biblical parallels (written to the side of the text), I would like to say that this is a common procedure in works of this kind.  It means that there is a similarity between the text and the referred part in the Bible.  This similarity can be caused by the influence of one book on the other, or that both of them were inspired from one source, or it could be that they developed in two different time, independent of each other.  When it comes from a common source, it is usually the divine origin of all books of revelation.

## Explanation of typographical and reference systems

When referring to the Bible I used chapters and verses separated by a colon.

When referring to the Qur'an I used the number of the sura and verses separated by a colon.

Verses which were taken from the Qur'an translation are written in Dauphin script and the referral comes immediately after the verse.

When the Qur'anic translation is not word to word, I left it in the Times New Roman script and the letter 'Q' was used for the Qur'an before the referral numbers.

Italics in the text were used for Arabic words as well as to stress certain passages. The marginal references are limited to significant parallels of the Bible and certain Gospels.

In the footnotes I did not use any diacritical marks in writing Arabic names, as was done in the main text. I also underlined the names of Hebrew books to be identified and not be confused with Arabic references.

## List of abbreviations

Arabic books

| | | |
|---|---|---|
| Ara-Tha | *'Arāyis ul-Majālis* | by *Al-Tha'labī* |
| Taf-Tab | *Tafsīr ut-Ṭabarī* | |
| Taf-Bagh | *Tafsīr ul-Baghawī* | |
| Taf-Khaz | *Tafsīr ul-Khāzin* | |
| Tar-Kath | *Tarīkh Ibn Kathīr "Al-Bidāyah wan-Nihāyah"* | |
| Tar-Mak | *Akhbār Makkah* | by *Al-Azraqī* |
| Tar-Kham | *Tarīkh ul-Khamīs* | by *Ḥusayn bin Muḥmmad Ad-Diyārbakrī* |
| Tar-Tab | *Tareekh ut-Ṭabarī* | |

| | | |
|---|---|---|
| Qis-Kath | *Qiṣaṣ ul-Anbiyā* | by *Ibn Kathīr* |
| Qis-Kis | *Qiṣaṣ ul-Anbiyā* | by *Al-Kisā'ī* |
| Sah-Bukh | *Ṣaḥīḥ ul-Bukhārī* | |
| Sah-Mus | *Ṣaḥīḥ Muslim* | |

Abbreviation of Bible books and Gospels

| | |
|---|---|
| Gen. | Genesis |
| Exd. | Exodus |
| Lev. | Leviticus |
| Num. | Numbers |
| 1Sam. | 1 Samuel |
| 2Sam. | 2 Samuel |
| Lk. | The Gospel of Luke |
| Mt. | The Gospel of Matthew |
| Jn. | The Gospel of John |
| Inf. Thom | The Infancy Gospel of Thomas |
| Prot. James | The Protevangelium of James |
| L.O.J. | Legends of the Jews, by Louis Ginzberg. |
| L.O.B. | Legends of the Bible, by Louis Ginzberg. |
| O.T.P. | The Old Testament Pseudepigrapha, edited by James H. Charleworth |

Other abbreviations

| | |
|---|---|
| Rep. | Reported |
| Pub. | Published |

# Table of Contents

# 1     The Story of the Stories

*We relate the greatest stories to you.*

The religious stories of Judaism, Christianity and Islam reflect an extremely strong and unanimous belief that what they depicted were actual historical events. In his book 'Antiquities,' Josephus collected all biblical stories, as did Arab historians such as *Ibn Kathīr,* and both began the history of the world with the story of Adam and Eve. There was much competition and argument among the scholars of all three religions, which centered around who had the most historically accurate information, for this would portend the attainment of the actual words of God, whose words were inviolable. However, by the early nineteenth century, the examination of these stories had moved from the study of history into the study of methodology, and historical accuracy became less of an issue and would be replaced by another measure of evaluation: originality. And only if the religious story was originated by its own believers would it be considered valuable. Many writers became entrapped in their zeal to defend the originality of their stories, and lost or ignored the religious nature of these narratives which represented thousands of years of a tremendous amount of faith. This faith is what gives the stories strength and beauty, and any attempt to interpret or understand their significance without considering this aspect of faith would be comparable to evaluating religious paintings on technical merit alone.

In many of the stories presented in this book, the issue of originality is, at best, vague. The story of Noah and the flood goes back in antiquity to Mesopotamia and most probably, a few thousand years before that through oral tradition. Many of what are termed 'universal myths' originated in many cultures throughout the world, not by diffusion but by separate cultures seeking to explain their own origins.

Islamic scholars evaluated the stories by their content, such as, what kind of ethical and philosophical doctrine the stories pointed to and what was their source of inspiration; what was to be learned from them? These scholars accepted those stories that were judged in a positive light by the above mentioned criteria, even when there was a contradiction. They also modified certain stories to fit their standard in a favorable light, as can be seen in the story of Job and the story of David's sin, as altered by *Wahb bin Munabbih*. Muslim scholars are proud to defend these modifications, and that in itself may manifest a degree of Islamic originality. The aim of modification of these stories is to accommodate Islamic theology. These changes have been considered a 'purification' process designed to return such narratives to what had been their original inspiration, and Muslims are not the first to introduce changes in these narratives. All of these stories were redacted time after time before they reached their final version in the Torah/Pentateuch which we read today.

Islamic narratives encompass much more than the stories of biblical personalities. They also include stories from the life of the prophet Muhammad and other non-biblical Arabic prophets, as well as pre-Islamic Arab legends and stories of Islamic saints. When the orientalists first translated the Qur'an, they commented that the stories were a corruption of biblical ones, and attributed this to Muhammad who did not obtain these stories from knowledgeable sources. But the biblical stories are the result of many generations of inspired narratives, and their various oral versions have changed with the passage of time. Though stories written in a book or on a tablet are permanent and hold to specific period in time, oral versions will continue to propagate and change with time. Some stories have both multiple written versions and many oral ones, and as more and more of the old texts are discovered, translated and analyzed, scholars realize that what was thought of as corrupted stories are heretofore unknown versions of the same stories.

Northern Arabia is a vast land with great distances between tribes, and literacy was rare in pre-Islamic times. But these nomadic people developed a strong oral tradition in which stories were recounted. It was not unusual for the Arab storytellers to recite from memory thousands lines of poetry.  These storytellers traveled between villages and developed reputations as entertainers, some of whom are known to this day, like *Sa'd al-Qarqara* who performed under the reign of *An-Nu'mān bin al-Mundhir* and is still spoken of, as is *An-Naḍar bin al-Ḥārith,* who made his mark by encouraging the people of Mecca to fight Islam and the Prophet Muhammad, by narrating the legends of the Persian kings Rostam and Esfandyiar. Two other story tellers of note are *Tamīm bin Aws ad-Dārī*, who accepted Islam and imparted his stories at the mosque of Medina, and *Al-Aswad bin Sarī' as-Sa'dī,* who recited at the Al-Basra mosque. The pre-Islamic poets incorporated the lives of biblical personalities into their poems and this, along with their other work, if read at the pan-Arabian convention at *Suk 'Ukāzh,* would promise great popularity and the guarantee that their poems would become ubiquitous throughout the tribes and villages.  The story of Adam and Eve was mentioned by *'Uday bin Zayn al-'Ubādī* and *Umayya bin Abis-Ṣalṭ,* the latter of whom also spoke of Noah, Moses, David and Lot.  *Al-A'shā* talked of Noah and Solomon, *Al-Ja'dī* spoke of Noah's Ark, *Al-Afwah* mentioned Noah's sons.  *Ṭurfa bin al-'Abd* talked about David and *An-Nābigha* spoke of Solomon and all the preceding examples occurred before Islam.

## MODIFICATION OF THE BIBLICAL STORIES
### I. Purification of the 'Idea of the Divine.'
Pre-Islamic Arabic legends were to a large degree influenced by their original belief in one God, the God of Creation, and many lesser gods.  But these early legends did not survive intact, and what remained were the purified legends in which there is almost no mention of any lesser gods. However, in the story of Noah as reported in the Qur'an, there is reference to the  people rejecting his teachings of worshiping only one God but not the lesser gods, and here we find the names of these lesser gods are actually names of Arabic pre-Islamic idols "*Wadd, Siwā', Yaghūth, Ya'ūq* and *Nisr,* " and this most probably reflects a pre-Islamic adaption of the story of Noah.

The stories of the Bible were written a long time before the Qur'an, and the 'idea of the Divine' changed over that time. The Yahweh of Genesis lied to Adam when He told him, "For the day that you do eat from it, you shall die" Gen.2:16-17. And on the return of Moses to Egypt, "the Lord met him and tried to kill him." Ex 4:24. Yahweh seems forgetful, changes His mind and very often the punishment is harsher than the severity of the crime. Interpreters of the Torah devised all manner of comments to elucidate the meaning of the real God of Judaism. Christianity, which has adopted the Hebrew books, has had to comply with their explanations. But Islam rewrote these stories to represent the strong belief of an omnipotent God, which resulted in a God of the most exalted status.

## II. Liberation of the 'God-believer' relationship.

The doctrine of the 'chosen people' put severe restrictions on God's relationship with believers beginning with Shem, son of Noah, down to Jacob, the father of the Israelites. God chose one son over the others and He chose the people of Israel over other nations. This doctrine was rejected later by St. Paul who argued that the blessing which was given to Abraham should include Gentiles. Gal. .2:9, 2:14 and "in Jesus Christ all believers are children of God through faith." Gal. 3:26. In Islam, we find, *"O mankind, we created you from man and woman and we made you into different tribes and nations that you may know each other. The most honored of you in the sight of God is the most righteous of you."* 49:13.

## III. The rehabilitation of public figures, biblical patriarchs and prophets.

For Muslims, all the personalities mentioned in this book are 'prophets of God,' they commit no sin, and are the best examples of what the human race can produce and what others should strive to emulate. So it should come as no surprise that Muslims rejected the story of the Prophet Lot's incest with his two daughters under the influence of wine, as well as the story of David's adultery with Bathsheba. Islam also changed the names of some biblical personalities for linguistic reasons;  hence, *Mūsā* instead of Moshe, but names were also altered to purposely convey to the believers that Islam had brought enlightenment to the venerable but often heard stories, as well as to new personalities seen in a uniquely Islamic light.  These changes are evidenced in changing the name Jesus from *Yasū‘*, son of God, to *‘Īsā*, the Prophet of God,  and changing the name of King Saul, who killed eighty five priests of God, into King *Ṭālūt*, a prophet without sin.

## STAGES OF ISLAMIC RELIGIOUS STORIES
### I. The Pre-Islamic Arabic Era
There is evident an abundance of work in the oral tradition in northern Arabia, consisting of poems, histories of tribal wars, histories of other nations, stories of jinn and demons, stories of extinct tribes and towns, as well as the narratives of the biblical personalities.  This era is well known today because of the extensive studies done by Arab scholars at the beginning of the Islamic Arab caliphate, when Muslims collected and preserved their pre-Islamic heritage.
### II. The Era of Qur'anic Revelation
In 610 C.E. the Prophet *Muḥammad*, peace be upon him, received the first of many divine revelations at the cave of Hira near Mecca, which was followed by a series of revelations over a span of twenty-two years until his death in 11/632.  As paper was unknown in Arabia at that time, the prophet's scribes would record these revelations on thin sheets of stones or on the delta-shaped stems of palm tree leaves. More telling than this process of preservation were the fervent beliefs that were kept alive in the hearts of the believers. They memorized these divine words  and kept the accuracy of them by listening to the prophet reciting them during the morning, sunset and evening prayers, augmented by the special sessions which were made for that purpose.  As the years progressed and the size of the revelatory teachings increased, it became obvious that most people could not memorize all the known revelations, and it fell to a few hundred of the most dedicated followers to take up the task of

memorizing both the known and the new revelations. They stayed close to the prophet, listening to him at least three times each day during the prayers. The death of the prophet *Muḥammad* brought with it the end of the revelations, and when war erupted between the Islamic central government under *Abū Bakr* and tribes who wanted to secede from the first Islamic pan-Arab union, seventy of those who had memorized the Qur'an, the total revelations of Muhammad, were killed at the battle of *Yamama*. Worried about what effect this would have on the preservation of the Qur'an, *Abū Bakr*, the first caliph, commissioned *Zayd bin Thābit*, one of the prophet's scribes, to write the whole revelation "Qur'an" on stone plates. *Zayd*, who had memorized the verses, was not to rely on his memory alone, but would use a document, written in the presence of the Prophet, and this in turn would be confirmed by two others who were qualified to recite the Qur'an. Once *Zayd* had successfully completed this duty, the plates were held at the home of the caliph. However, prior to this and immediately after burying the Prophet, a cousin and son-in-law of Muhammad, *'Ali bin Abī Ṭālib,* secluded himself in his home for 6 months. During that time he wrote  the Qur'an in a book of parchment. This book, however, was not well received by the caliph, probably for political reasons. Other  Qur'anic scholars such as *Ibn Mas'ūd* wrote their own Qur'an for their own use.

At the time of *'Uthmān,* the third caliph, the Islamic empire had expanded and Muslims in distant lands began to disagree about Qur'anic recitation. In 25/645. *Uthmān* formed a committee with *Zayd bin Thābit, 'Abdullāh bin az-Zubayr, Sa'īd bin al-'Āṣ* and *'Abdur-Raḥmān bin al-Ḥārith* as its members, and they were entrusted with making copies on parchment of the Qur'an compiled by *Abū Bakr,* which were to be dispersed throughout the Islamic empire. After the committee borrowed the written Qur'an from *Abū Bakr's* daughter *Hafṣah,* and copies were made, *'Uthmān* then ordered that every other written revelation should be burned, and even the Qur'an of *Ibn Mas'ūd* met this fate. Any Qur'an in use after that can be traced to that of *Abū Bakr,* the holy book of Muslims and considered by the believers to be the actual words of God.

The Qur'an speaks to many subjects. Dr *Fathi Osman,* who translated the Qur'an in concepts, grouped its verses into topics including: 'Faith' which describes God and His attributes and the eternal life to come; 'Creation', which included the creation of the universe, life on earth, humans, angels, jinn and devils; 'Worship', including prayer, fasting, the giving of alms, hajj and other acts; 'Moral Value and Manners'; 'Islamic Law'; 'The Stories of the Prophets'; and 'The Stories of the New Islamic Community and its Guidance' are all discussed. The topics in the Qur'an change every few pages or verses, and *mufassirun*[1] attempted to connect these topics using logic. But in most instances it is the idea of 'multiple religious experiences,' which is the intention of the changes, and reading even a few pages of the Qur'an manifests this. The Qur'an is unevenly divided into one hundred and fourteen suras, the longest–Sura 2–having two hundred eighty-six verses, while the shortest–Suras 102 and 108–have only three verses each. The written Qur'an of *Imam 'Ali,* compiled after the death of the Prophet, was arranged according to the date of revelation, but the *Abū Bakr-'Uthmān* compilation which is the standard, arranged the suras according to length, with the longest sura being the first, and concluding with the sura having the fewest verses, though there are a few exceptions. The Qur'an is renowned for its eloquence, and Arab critics consider it a unique work with no rivals, and a miracle of Islam.

Narratives in the Qur'an account for approximately twenty to thirty percent of the total verses, and certain stories such as that of Joseph, The Elephant, Al Khadir and the People of the Cave are presented in one sura only, while others like that of Moses are spread over more than seven suras. The inclusion of a small part of a story in a sura along with other topics confirms the idea that these stories are cited for contemplation and not for historical purposes. After the conversion of Arabia to Islam, the Muslim Arabs had for the first

---

[1]- Mufassirun is plural for mufassir, a scholar who works on commenting on the Qur'an and interpreting its ambiguous verses.

time a 'book of truth', which included a specific version of the stories of what the Christian literature calls 'the biblical personalities.' This was adopted later by Muslims of all nations. Oral versions which contradicted the official Qur'anic text were repudiated, while those which corroborated it were used for expanding and giving detail to the accepted book.

### III. The Era of Oral Tradition, The 'Ḥadīth.'

The Prophet and the early Muslims felt it was imperative to expedite the documentation of the revelations in order to preserve unaltered the word of God as well as keep separate the divine revelations from the preaching or chronicles of the Prophet. But those who followed the Prophet memorized his words and, though not as significant as the revelations, his words were kept alive and are known as 'hadiths,' which means a talk. Early on, only those who had heard the Prophet's own words were considered competent to repeat those hadiths, but when that generation died it became acceptable to keep his words alive by speaking first the name of the person they heard it from who had heard it directly from the Prophet and then communicating the text of the hadith. In time, the names of these intermediaries increased, sometimes numbering five or six, and every hadith was divided in two parts; the series of intermediaries connecting the speaker to the Prophet 'As-Sanad,' and the original text or 'Al-Matn.' The expansion of the Sanad ceased when the hadiths were eventually published. The Prophet's companions, 'Sahāba' [1] and their disciples 'Tābi'un' [2] were also quoted in regard to Qur'anic interpretation. Al-Bukhārī, for example–who had perhaps the best and most accurate hadiths taken from the oral tradition–published 503 hadiths in a chapter on that subject, quoting

---

[1] - The term 'sahaba' a plural for 'sahabi' is a title used for early Muslims who had a proven company to the Prophet Muhammad.

[2] -Tabi'un is plural for tabi'i the second generation Muslim scholars who had been taught by sahaba.

the Prophet and famous Qur'an commentators in the early years of Islam. We will mention some of them here:

1- **'Abdullāh bin 'Abbās**, known as *Ibn 'Abbās*, was born three years before Hijra[1] and was a cousin of the Prophet. Taught by the Prophet himself, until age thirteen when the Prophet died, he was then tutored by the *sahaba* and became the most knowledgeable person on the Qur'an, even at an early age. He was an authority on pre-Islamic poems which helped him to adduce and interpret the uncommon words of the Qur'an. Although he introduced some biblical stories into the Islamic *tafsīr*[2], he was conscientious and meticulous so as to contradict neither the Qur'an nor its narrative spirit. He died 68/687, at the age of seventy, and all *mufassirun* who came after him considered him an unparalleled interpreter of any ambiguous verse in the Qur'an, and he was given the title of "the supreme scholar of the nation."

2- **'Abdullāh bin Mas'ūd,** known as *Ibn Mas'ūd*, was one of the early Muslims, at a time when Islam was preached secretly. After the Prophet, he was the first one to recite the Qur'an at a public site in Mecca, where he was persecuted by the people. *Ibn Ms'ūd* was very close to the Prophet, and attended to him to such a degree that some thought he was part of the Prophet's household. Because of the oppression in Mecca, *Ibn Mas'ūd* fled first to Abyssinia, then returned and fled with the Muslims of Mecca to Medina. *Ibn Mas'ūd* was promised by the Prophet – depending on divine knowledge – that he would be one of the paradise dwellers.

*Ibn Mas'ūd* was quoted, "For every verse in the Book of God, I know where and for what it was revealed. And if I learn of anyone who is more knowledgeable in the Book of God, and he can be reached, I will seek him." He was known as the most erudite of all

---

[1]- Hijra is the flight of the Prophet from Mecca to Medina in 620 C.E. Muslims used that year as the start of their Hijra Calendar and most dates in this book are written in Hijra and Common Era dates separated by slash '/' the first number is the Hijra one, the second number is always C.E.

[2]- Tafsir is the science of commentating and interpretation of the Qur'an.

the *sahaba* of the Book, and comprehended both its clear and ambiguous parts, understood its legal teachings, its stories and parables and the reason behind every revelation. He read and followed the instructions of the Qur'an, and was familiar with the Prophet's traditions. He died 32/652.

3- *'Alī bin Abī Ṭālib*, known as *Imām 'Alī*, the Prophet's cousin, who later became his son-in-law and the forth caliph. After the Prophet, *Imam 'Alī* is accepted as the most knowledgeable man with respect to Islam in general and the Qur'an in particular; the Prophet referred to him in the quote, "I am a city of knowledge and Ali is its gate." But many of *Iman 'Alī*'s hadiths were lost, ignored or disregarded because of rivalry among the sects and, in 40/660 at age 63, he was assassinated.

4- *Ubay bin Ka'b bin Qays al-Anṣārī*, was, before accepting Islam, a Jewish scholar who, in time, became one of the Prophet's scribes and wrote the revelations. He was referred to by 'Umar, the second caliph, as "the most honorable of Muslims," and his work on Qur'anic study and interpretation is both impressive and extensive. The date of his death is unclear, but most probably he died 30/650.

5- *Sa'īd bin Jubayr al-Asadī*, known as *Ibn Jubayr*, and was one of the second generations of Islamic scholars in Mecca and a disciple of *Ibn 'Abbās*, whom he frequently quoted. His honesty was recognized by later publishers of the hadiths who accepted his sayings with no criticism. He was killed, at the age of forty-nine, in 95/713, by the notorious governor of Iraq, *Al-Hajjaj*.

6- *Mujāhid bin Jabr*, born in 21/641 and known as *Mujāhid*, was another second generation Qur'anic scholar of Mecca and disciple of *Ibn 'Abbās*. He often reviewed the Qur'an with his tutor and was diligent in the contemplation of its meanings, and this assiduous study led to both praise and the publishing of his hadiths. Died 104/722, at the age of eighty-three.

7- *'Akrama* of the Berber, known by his first name. A disciple of *Ibn 'Abbās*, who hailed from the Berber area of North Africa and was recognized by all publishers of hadiths and received mostly praise from the critics. Died 107/725.

**8- '*Aṭā bin Abi Rabāḥ*,** known by his first name, was a black man having a weak arm, weak leg, and only one eye. But in spite of these infirmities he persevered and studied under *Ibn 'Abbās, Ibn 'Umar* and other *sahaba,* and holds a place in Islamic history as a second generation scholar of Mecca. He became an authority on Islamic law and was held in high esteem by the publishers of the six books of the hadiths. Died 114/732.

**9- *Abul-'Āliya, Rāfi' bin Mahrān Ar-Riyāḥī*,** known by his first name, was a second generation scholar of Medina who accepted Islam two years after the death of the Prophet. His mentors were *Imam 'Ali, Ibn Mas'ūd, Ibn 'Abbās, Ibn 'Umar, Ubay bin Ka'b* and other *sahaba.* He was recognized by the six books of hadiths. Died 90/708.

**10- *Masrūq bin al-Ajda'*,** a second generation of Islamic scholars from Iraq who studied under '*Uthmān, Ibn Mas'ūd, Ubay bin Ka'b* and others, had the recognition of all the publishers of the hadiths. Died 63/682.

**11- *'Āmir al-sha'bī*,** was known by his second name and was a second generation scholar. He became a judge of Kufa and quoted '*Umar, 'Alī, Ibn Mas'ūd* indirectly and also cited *Abū Hurayra, 'Āyishah, Ibn 'Abbās* and *Al-Ash'arī*. Recognized by all of the hadith publishers, he was born in 20/640, and died in 109/727.

**12- *Al-Ḥasan al-Baṣrī*,** known by his first name and a second generation scholar form Iraq, he earned praise from the critics and was recognized by the hadith publishers. Died 110/728 at the age of eighty-eight.

**13- *Qutāda bin Da'āma as-Sadūsī*,** yet another second generation Iraqi scholar from Al-Basra who quoted '*Akrama, 'Atā* and others, and developed his reputation as an authority on Arabic poetry, the history of tribal wars, Arab genealogy, and was considered an expert in the study of the Arabic language. He was celebrated for his sharp memory, praised by the critics and recognized by the hadith publishers. Died 117/735 at the age of fifty-six.

**14- *'Abdullāh bin Salām*** began his life as a Jew in the city of Medina and converted to Islam after the Prophet's arrival there. He was not only learned in the study of the Qur'an, but also in the Torah and other Jewish books of note. He introduced stories from the Torah into Islamic writings. His work was extolled by *Al-Bukhārī*, and the Prophet conferred upon him the promise of becoming a dweller in Paradise. Died 43/663.

**15- Ka'b bin Māti'**, known as *Ka'b al-Aḥbār*, was a Yemenite Jew who accepted Islam when *'Umar* was the caliph. He began his work in Medina. Then, under the caliphate of *'Uthmān,* he journeyed to Homs in Syria, where he died in 32/652, at the age of one hundred and four. His sources included *'Umar , Ṣuhayb* and *'Ayishah* and was himself quoted by *Mu'āwiya, Abū Hurayra, Ibn 'Abbās* and *'Atā.* Known as an authority on both Qur'anic and Hebrew literature, he was criticized for his excessive borrowing from Hebrew writings, though he was accepted by the early hadith scholars such as *Abū Dāwūd, Tirmidhī* and *Nisā'ī.* More recent Muslims, i.e. *Aḥmad Amīn* and *Rashīd Riḍā,* have cast aspersions upon his work, for the introduction of much Jewish lore into the Islamic stories.

**16-Wahb bin Munabbih**, the Yemenite who was known by his first name, quoted *Abū Hurayrah, Ibn 'Abbās, Ibn 'Umar, Anas, Jābir* and others and was himself recognized by *Al-Bukhārī, Muslim, An-Nisā'ī At-Tirmidhī* and *Abū Dāwūd.* He was knowledgeable of the history of Yemen, and authored a book about the kings of *Himyar,* a Yemenite royal dynasty. He understood both Persian and Greek besides Hebrew, and introduced many biblical stories into Islamic literature. Born 34/654 and died 110/728.

**17-'Abdul-Mālik bin Jarīj**, Known as *Ibn Jaiīj,* and was a Byzantine Christian before accepting Islam and was the first to write a book in Arabia. He often quoted *Ibn 'Abbās* and was recognized by *Aṭ-Ṭabarī* in his tafsirs, though many authorities of the hadiths did not acknowledge or accept his sayings. Born 80/699 and died 150/767.

**18-Muḥammad bin as-Sā'ib al-Kalbī,** known by his last name, was born in Kufa and lived in Basra, Iraq. He became the mufassir of Basra when its mayer offored him that position. Quoted *Al-Sha'bī* and others, recognized by *An-Nisā'ī, Abū dāwūd, At-Tirmidhī* and *Ibn Māja.* Died 147/763 in Kufa.

**19-*Ismā'īl bin 'Abdur-Raḥmān As-Siddī*,** known by his last name, was a great mufassir and scholar of the hadiths. He also wrote books on the pre-Islamic tribal wars. He originally was from Arabia but lived in Kufa. He quoted *Anas, Ibn 'Abbās* and others, and was recognized by *Muslim, Abū Dāwūd, At-Tirmidhī* and *Ibn Māja*, but criticized because he quoted people indirectly, and accused of being Shi'a. His commentary was used in many later tafsir books. Died 128/745.

**20-*Abū Hurayra*,** is actually a nickname meaning 'the owner of a small cat,' but was used extensively as we are unsure of his true name. He became a Muslim at age 30 and stayed very close to the Prophet Muhammad for the last four years of the Prophet's life. He devoted his time to the study and memorization the words of the Prophet and reported more hadiths than any other sahabi despite spending a relatively short time in his company. He explained his extensive collection of hadiths by saying that he was the only one who dedicated himself exclusively for that purpose and because of the Prophet's prayers for his not forgetting anything of what he had learned. He died in the year 58/677, in the reign of *Mu'āwiya*, the first Umayyad caliph. The legacy of *Abū Hurayra*, aside from his hadith collection is his verbatim accounts of the words of the Prophet

### V. The Era of Book Publishing

It became evident to Muslim scholars that, after generations of passing down the Prophet's words solely by word of mouth, it was necessary to record them for posterity, and this required that the true hadiths be isolated from those words that were false and had been invented for political purposes. This gave rise to the development of a 'science of hadith criticism' called '*At-Tajrīḥ*'. The imams[1] first gathered all kind of hadiths from those who had memorized it in all parts of the vast Islamic empire and their words were written down. In-depth research was done on those involved in the chain of the *sanad* and the provenance of the hadiths. Their lives were analyzed

---

[1]- Imam is a great religious leader.

and they were held to strict codes in their beliefs, their ethics and behavior. If there was even a slight variation from the standard, the entire hadith failed and was rejected. The transmission of hadith between any two people of the *sanad* should be accepted if they lived in the same town at certain time. This safeguard was successful in preventing many false hadiths from reaching publication. Those hadiths which were deemed worthy were judged according to the reliability of their accuracy in a scale of 'accurate, acceptable, & suspicious.'

This era produced six books of canonical hadiths authored by *Al-Bukhārī*, died 256/ 869; *Muslim*, died 261/874; *At-Tirmidhī*, died 279/892; *Ibn Mājah*, died 273/887; *An-Nisā'ī*, died 303/915; *Abū Dāwūd*, died 275/888; and the Shi'a book of hadith, 'The Referrals of the Four Hundred' which was written by the year 148/765. This last book did not survive although it was copied in later books. All these books were celebrated for being beyond reproach. Another significant work of this era was *As-Sīra*, a biography of the Prophet written by *Ibn Hishām*, who died 213/828. It should be emphasized that many books were written before this era but did not survive; such as the hadith books of *'Abd bin Hamīd*, died 249/863; *Ādam bin 'Alī*, died 220/835; *Yazīd bin Hārūn as-Salmī*, died 117/735; *'Abdur-Razzāq bin Humām*, died 211/826; and *Wakī' bin al-Jarrāh*, died 197/812. Pre-dating even the above, it was found that the Umayyad caliph *'Abdul-Malik bin Marwān*, who died in 86/705, had commissioned *Ibn Jubayr* to write a book of tafsir encompassing the entire Qur'an. The book was kept in his archives until its discovery by *'Atā bin Dīnār* who utilized the work in his lectures.[1] The following are four books from that era, that were used extensively in research for this book.

**1. Tafsīr At-Tabarī** known as *"Jāmi' al-Bayān Fī Tafsir al-Qur'an"* by *Muhammad bin Jarīr at-Tabarī*, born 224/838 and died 310/922. He left his home in Tabarestan, Persia, to study under scholars in

---

[1]- At-Tafsir wal-Mufassirun, by Muhammad Husayn Al-Dhahabi, I:141; pub. by Dar al-Kutub al-Hadithah, Cairo.

Egypt, Syria and Iraq. He lived in Baghdad until his death and in addition to the tafsir, was the author of *"Tarīkh ut-Tabarī"*, a history which still survives and other tomes which did not. His tafsir is considered important because it is the oldest surviving text on the subject, completed in 306/918, and includes all the early mufassirun commentaries. He expanded his tafsir by stories traced to *Ka'b, Wahb, Ibn Jarīj, As-Siddī* and anonymous Christian writers. He was assiduous in including the '*sanad*' before each hadith he wrote, and because of his research many lesser known stories survive.

**2. *Tafsīr Al-Tha'labī,*** known as *"Al-Kashf wal Bayān 'an Tafsīr al-Qur'an."* His full name was *Ahmad bin Ibrāhīm Al-Tha'labī* and he was born in Nishabur, Persia. His other works included *" 'Arāyis ul-Majālis,"* a collection of stories of the prophets. But as he relied heavily on both Christian and Jewish sources, his accomplishments were met with criticism. Died 427/1035.

**3. *Tafsīr Al-Baghawī,*** known as *"Ma'ālim ut-Tanzīl."* Born in the city of Bagh in Khurasan, his full name was *Al-Husayn bin Mas'ud al-Baghawī*. He wrote his tafsir which contained almost every known story using Christian and Jewish sources as well as books on hadiths and a biography of the Prophet. Died 516/1122.

**4. *Tafsīr Al-Khāzin,*** titled *"Lubāb at-Ta'wīl fī Ma'āni at-Tanzīl,"* was authored by *'Alī bin Muhammad bin Ibrāhīm* who was known as *"Al-Khāzin,"* and who was born in Baghdad in 678/1279 and died in Aleppo in 741/1340. *Al-Khazin* actually copied *Al-Baghawī* on his comments on the biblical figures and did not add anything to what *Al-Baghawī* already said.

**5. *Sahīh Al-Bukhārī*.** This is the most famous book in the collection of hadiths written by *Muhammad bin Ismā'īl Al-Bukhārī* from Bukhara. This book contains 9082 hadiths, though some are repeated, chosen from six hundred thousand testaments. Every hadith came with its *sanad* which contained sometimes up to six or seven intermediaries. His book was praised by every scholar and was considered second only to the Qur'an as a reference on Islam. He reported his hadiths from more than one thousand scholars, and as many as seventy thousand men heard and copied this book directly from him. He died in 256/869 in Bukhara at the age of 62.

**6. *Ṣaḥīḥ Muslim*,** the second most famous book of hadith, written by *Muslim bin al-Ḥajjāj*, from Nishapur. He made his collection of hadiths from thirty thousand oral testaments. He died in 261/874 at the age of 57.

The following are other works which discuss biblical stories and personalities we use in this book.

**1-*Tārīkh aṭ-Ṭabarī*.**

**2-*Tārīkh Ibn Kathīr*,** *also known as "Al-Bidāyah wan-Nihāyah"*, authored by *Ismaʿīl bin ʿUmar bin Kathīr*, who lived in Damascus and died in 774/1372. He also wrote a book of tafsir known as *Tafsīr Ibn Kathīr*.

**3-*ʿArāyis al-Majālis*,** was written by *Al-Thaʿlabī*, and has previously been mentioned.

**4- *Qiṣaṣ al-Anbiya*** "The Stories of the Prophets" by *Ibn Kathīr*, which is a concentrated version of what had already been written in his books of tafsir and tarikh.

**5- *Qisas al-Anbiya*,** by *Al-Kisāʾī*, was written in the eleventh century C.E. This book was written with the intention of making a great story rather than an accurate one from the Islamic point of view. The author added many details and connected the phases of the story under one theme with increasing tension so as to keep the reader interested until the end. The book is part of Arab story telling as opposed to Islamic narrative and, as such, I made minimal use of it.

Because of continuous changes and additions to the Islamic narratives over the centuries, some of these stories changed and expanded over time and to represent the early Islamic narrative I have restricted my sources to the Qur'an, the books of hadith, the early Islamic tafsirs (*Aṭ-Ṭabarī, Al-Baghawī* and *Al-Khāzin*) and, from the books of *Qisas,* I used *Ibn Kathīr* and *Al-Thaʿlabī*. These books compliment each other and do not contradict each other to any great degree.

**Contemporary Tafsir**

*Imām Muḥammad 'Abdo* (1849-1905 C.E.) was the impetus behind the era of contemporary tafsir. His legacy of tafsir writing comprises work to the fifth part[1] of the Qur'an, which he began during his exile in Beirut, Paris and Tunis, and continued after returning home to Azhar University in Cairo, where he died. He was followed by *Shaykh Muhammad Rashīd Riḍā*, (1282-1354 C.E.) who was described by Imam Muhammad as "united with him in belief, thought, ideas, ethics and work." His work began at the beginning of the Qur'an and ended with his death, his work having reached the thirteenth part. One aim of the work of *Muhammad 'Abdo* was to separate tafsir from Jewish and Christian legends, even if their removal would leave the Qur'anic stories incomplete or ambiguous.

The attitude that the inclusion of Jewish and Christian lore alters the spirit of Qur'anic stories was not new, and from the time of *Ibn 'Abbās* until the present, mufassirun differ on how much of the biblical stories should be recognized. The Qur'an accepted the Torah and the Gospel as Books of God, and Muslims found no fault in quoting from them, but they did not have a reliable Arabic translation for these texts, and they were suspicious of the authenticity of those books. This idea was expressed by *Ibn Kathīr*: "The existing translations of the Torah are corrupted and full of mistakes, as not everyone can translate properly from one language to another. This is particularly true if he is not fluent in Arabic as well as not understanding the original book. For this reason there is much corruption of the words and mis- understanding in the meanings."[2]

As a result, most mufassirun advocated that a biblical source can only be used if there was no contradiction with the Qur'an. Functions such as finding names or places in the Bible which were not mentioned in the Qur'an, or explaining specious detail, were received with some deference. But the controversy arose when attempts were made to use the Bible to expand on Islamic narrative,

---

[1]-The Qur'an is divided into 30 equal 'parts '.
[2]- Qis-Kath I: 22

particularly in a way which does not have the Islamic style or spirit. Objections to the tainting of Islamic verse have long plagued scholars, and we see this phenomenon in *Tafsir Ibn Kathīr*, who commented on the story of "Moses and the Cow" by saying that the story was borrowed from Jewish books, which was not considered a problem; however, he wrote, the story itself should be neither rejected nor accepted, but recognized only if the elements concurred with the Islamic truth. But the idea of leaving part of the Qur'an ambiguous did not catch on and *Shaykh Riḍā* used some biblical sources in his tafsir. Recently, *Abul A'la Al-Mawdūdī* in his tafsir '*Tafhīm ul-Qur'an*,' was the first Islamic scholar to refer to biblical sources directly. For example, in his commentary of Q3:38 and Q3:46-47 he referred to the Gospel of Matthew 3, 9 and 14; and Mark 1 and 6. And commenting on Samuel and David he referred to 1Sam7:15, 8:4-22, 12:6-23. *Al-Mawdudi* also referred to the Talmud when he commented on Abraham's imprisonment and burning.

*Ibn Khaldūn*, in his famous "Introduction," written in 490/1096, stated that it was the curiosity of the human spirit, combined with the dearth of literature, except for the Qur'an, which made the *mufassirun* turn to Christian and Jewish sources in their tafsir writings. Further, *mufassirun* were susceptible to the whims of their readers, and in utilizing biblical stories which temporarily took their audience away from the staid and serious roots of Arabic grammar and composition, it conferred popularity on their works. Though these stories were not a part of the earliest Islamic narrative form, in time they became a cohesive force in the books of tafsir, and became an integral part of the lectures given in mosques which boasted enormous support from the people. While not considered "Qur'anic," the stories are "Islamic," and though some contemporary Islamic writers are calling to expunge them from Islamic texts, I am of the opinion that we should not reject our past.

# 2     The Story of Creation

*He is the One Who created heaven and earth in six days*
—Qur'an 11:7

## God of Muslims

"*He is the First and the Last.*" 57:3 He is the First for whom there was no 'before,' and nothing can be before Him. He is the Last for whom there is no 'after,' so that nothing can be after Him. He is the Eternal with no beginning and no end. "*There is nothing like Him.*" 42:11 Nothing can be compared to Him in Essence, Attributes or Actions. He has no adversary, no opponents and does not in any way resemble His creations. He is the Living, the Self-Subsisting' "*slumber does not overtake Him, nor does sleep.*"2:255 "*There is no Deity but Him.*" 2:255 "*He begat not, nor is He begotten.*" 112:3 "*God has the power over all things.*" 2:20 "*God will not be thwarted by anything in the heavens or on earth.*" 35:44 Nothing can happen unless He allows it. His decree cannot be blocked. His judgement cannot be distracted. His command cannot be defeated. Praise is due to Him whose worth cannot be described by speakers, whose bounties cannot be counted by calculators and whose claim to obedience cannot be satisfied by those who attempt to do so, whom the height of intellectual courage cannot appreciate and the most deep understanding cannot reach.[1]

---

[1]- Nahj ul-Balaghah. Sermon 1.

**His First Creations**

The first thing God created is the Holy Throne / *al-'Arsh*, the most wondrous and the greatest of all His creations. It cannot be described to any comprehensible degree but nevertheless the Prophet, in one of his hadiths, discusses its features. According to tradition, the distance between its four legs is equal to the distance a bird can fly in thirty thousand years. It is carried by four angels but this number will be increased to eight on the Day of Judgement. The Throne is covered with seventy thousand different colors of light which change every day and is located above the seventh Heaven, separated from it by seventy thousand veils of alternating light and darkness. No one can gaze upon the Throne or they will perish.[1]

The Chair / *al-Kursi*, the next of God's great creations is larger than the earth and all the Heavens but is still negligible in comparison to the Holy Throne.

Then God created the Protected Board and the Holy Pen. The Protected Board, *'Al-Lawh ul-Mahfuzh,'* is made, according to tradition, of white pearls, inlaid with rubies and is of such tremendous size as to be indescribable. The Pen, *'al-qalam,'* according to tradition is made of diamond, and it is as long as the distance which a man can walk for one hundred years. After their creation, when God commanded the Pen to write on the Board, it shook with fright and emitted a thunderous roar and then proceeded to write. It wrote with a pure light emanating from its tip as if it was ink flowing from an ordinary pen and compiled all that happened and all that will happen until the Day of Judgement. When the Pen had finished its composition, it ran out of its ink of light.

**The Primordial Water**

Before God created the heavens and the earth, His Throne was, *'on the water.'*[11:7] This ambiguous Qur'anic verse does not say either what kind of water it was or what the relationship was between

---

[1]- Rep. by *Ja'far bin Muhammad*, pub. by Taf-Bagh 40:7 and Taf-Khaz 2:255.

the primordial water and the water on this earth. Many early imams tried to put the primordial water in a comprehensive creation doctrine, and I will mention here Imam Ali's study as he explained it in one of his sermons:

"Then God created the space, and in the space God created water which was contained by wind; He then sent another wind into the water which intensified its motion and dispersed it far and wide. He ordered the wind to raise up deep waters which escalated the severity of the waves; the winds churned the primordial oceans as cream is churned to make butter, until the surface was raised and covered in foam. The Almighty raised the foam in the space and made from it seven heavens."[1]

## Creation of Heavens

God created the heavens and earth in six days.[2] But these are not earth days, rather each day is equal to one thousand years of our time. He first created the primordial universe and on the second day separated the heavens from the earth which were still in primordial form. He then bestowed His blessing on earth, and planned its vital features such as the location of the mountains. God then soared to heaven which was nothing more than haze, and commanded the primordial earth and heaven to develop, either willingly or unwillingly. They acquiesced and developed willingly. God determined that there should be seven heavens and they were made within two days, and He inspired its own order in every heaven and the lowest heaven was beautified with stars. Q 41:9-12.

God made the sun the bright indicator for the day and the moon the gloomy indicator for its night. He then put them in motion in their orbits and ordained their pace of movement through the stages of their paths in order to distinguish, with their help, the

---

[1]- It is amazing how much Imam Ali's doctrine matches modern scientific theories if the word 'water' is replaced with 'subatomic particles' and the 'wind' with 'radiation.'

[2]-This phrase recurred seven times in different suras of the Qur'an. In Gen.1, God created heavens and earth in six days and rested on the seventh day.

difference between night and day, and in order that the reckoning of years and calculations may be known by their fixed movements. Then He hung in its vastness its sky and put therein its decoration consisting of small bright pearls and lamp-like stars in motion on their appointed routine and made them into fixed stars, moving stars, descending stars, and ascending stars.[1]

## Creation of Earth

After He separated the heavens from the earth in primordial form, and planned the earth's vital features, He then brought these features into being; thus the springs flowed, the rivers ran, the grass and trees grew and the mountains were put into place. Q 79:30-32 "For the parts of earth which are not reached by the springs and rivers, He sent to them rain clouds to bring life therein and brought up vegetation."[2]

## Creation of Angels

"God, praise and glory be to Him, created angels to inhabit His Heavens. He filled Heavens with them, He created them in different shapes and with diverse characteristics. They have wings and they glorify the sublimity of His honor. They do not appropriate to themselves His skill that shows itself in creation, nor do they claim they created anything in which He is unparalleled. But they are rather honored creatures who do not take precedence over Him in uttering anything and they act according to His command." Q 21:26-27 He has made them the trustees of His revelations and sent them to prophets as holders of His injunctions and prohibitions. He has immunized them against the waves of doubts. Consequently, no one among them goes astray from the path of His blessing.[3]

God made angels into many classes. The first class, eight in number, are the bearers of the Throne on the Day of Judgement.

---

[1]- Nahj ul-Balaghah. Sermon 70.
[2]- Ibid
[3]- Ibid..

Q 69:17. The second class of angels were placed around the Holy Throne. Q 39:75. There are one hundred thousand angels encircling the Throne and around them another one hundred thousand angels standing`in place. All the angels are praising God but in different ways[1] as well as praying for humans to be blessed and protected. Q 40:7-9. A third class of angels dwell in the seven Heavens that constantly praise God and each day seventy thousand of them make their one time pilgrimage to the Heavenly shrine of *Al-Bayt ul-Ma'Mūr.* Yet another class of angels work to maintain heavenly paradise for those who will enter it, and another are the protective angels who protect humans from indiscriminate harm until the time of their inevitable death. Lastly, there are the watchers, who observe humans and register their deeds, both the good and the bad. Q50:18 Gabriel and Michael, *Isrāfīl* and *Izrā'īl,* are the most familiar of the angels for Muslims and are part of Islamic belief and theology.

### ARCHANGEL GABRIEL, *(Jibrīl, Jibrā'īl)*

Mentioned by name in the Qur'an 2:98, he is the Angel of Revelation who descended with God's revelations to all the prophets including the last, Muhammad, who saw him for the first time in the cave of *Hirā* as he made his descent carrying sura 96, the first Qur'anic revelation. Gabriel, the Trustworthy, continued bringing revelations to Muhammad for twenty years until the entire Qur'an was revealed. Though Gabriel usually remained unseen to everyone but the Prophet, there were occasions when he would present himself as a man and would be seen by the Prophet as well as his companions. It was Gabriel who attended Muhammad during his ascension to the seven Heavens until they reached the *'sidra,'* near the end, where the Prophet saw the angel in his true shape. Gabriel is mentioned in the Old Testament by name, in Dan 8:16 and 9:21 when he appeared to Daniel and explained Daniel's vision and told him of the coming of the Messiah. In the New Testament, he announced to Zachariah that a son, John, would be born to him but

---

[1]- Rep. by Wahb, pub. by Taf-Bagh 40:7.

certainly as the plethora of works of art attest to, it is his appearance in the Annunciation where Gabriel is most often found. Gabriel was described in the Qur'an as *"Most honorable Messenger, endowed with power, with rank before the Lord of the Throne. With authority and faithful to His trust."* 81:19-21 Gabriel explained to the Prophet Muhammad how this honor was granted. "I was sent to the four towns of Sodom and Gomorrah with four hundred thousand warriors in each town, not including the children. I extirpated their town, and raised them with their inhabitants to the sky until the dwellers of Heaven heard the sounds of chickens and the barking of dogs. I then hurled them to the ground."[1] Gabriel was described in a hadith of the Prophet, "His radiant light, when compared to other angels is like day and night. He has twenty four green wings encrusted with pearls and rubies."[2]

### ARCHANGEL MICHAEL (*Mīkāl, Mīkā'īl*)

Mentioned by name in the Qur'an 2:98 and in the Bible, Dan.10:13,21;12:1 Michael described by the Prophet Muhammad as the undisputed custodian of rain and plants. According to Jewish and Christian tradition, Michael is the hero of the first war against Satan and the angels who revolted and who were expelled from Heaven. He is the angel who gave Moses the Tablets and the Jews consider him their guardian angel. It is said he annihilated one hundred and eighty-five thousand men of the army of the Assyrian King Sennacherib who threatened Jerusalem in 701 B.C.E.

### THE ANGEL OF DEATH

Known in the Qur'an as the Angel of Death, traditionally Muslims call him *'Izrā'īl* and he is responsible for the collection of the souls of every human being at the predetermined time of their death.

---

[1]- Bihar ul Anwar 59.
[2]- Ad-Durr ul-Manthur I:91.

## THE ANGEL OF THE HORN, *Isrāfīl*

This angel will blow the horn which will end all life on earth, and on his second blow the dead will be resurrected. Israfil will be waiting under the Throne for this noble task which he will fulfil assiduously and attentively.

Other angels named in Islamic traditions are: *Munkir* and *Nakīr* who question those who have died recently about their beliefs. *Raḍwān*, the Angel of Heaven. And *Mālik*, the Angel of Hell.

### Creation of *Iblīs* and the Jinn

*Iblīs*, the devil and the jinn are mentioned many times in the Qur'an. The jinn were created, not from clay like man, but from smokeless flame. Q55:15. The devil *Iblīs* was considered one of the angels of Heaven, though he was actually one of the jinn. Q18:50. But there is no one story that coalesces these two verses as there is for the creation of man. This gap was bridged by the story tellers of Islam and from them it reached the early tafsir books. I will present the story as related by *Ibn 'Abbās*:

"God created the jinn from smokeless flames of fire. They were housed on earth and for a long time worshiped God until they succumbed to temptation and committed all manner of sin. This prompted God to send His attendant angels with *Iblīs* as their leader and oust them from their homes and banish them to remote mountains and distant islands. *Iblīs* and the attendant angels were then allowed to inhabit earth and praise God, both on earth and in heaven; however *Iblīs* became very proud of his position and thought himself above the other angels which caused his fall from grace when God created Adam."[1]

---

[1]- Rep. by *Ibn 'Abbas*; pub. by Taf-Tab, Taf-Bagh and Taf-Khaz 2:30, Tar-Kath I:55.

# 3     Adam and Eve

*He has created you from single soul; then made its mate from it.*

–Qur'an 39:6

## Introduction

The story of Adam and Eve is one of many Creation epics which flourished in Mesopotamia, the cradle of civilization. Unlike the Memphite theology from the first Egyptian dynasty, the Akkadian epic, 'Enuma elish,' or the Phoenician epics, this legend is unique because it involves only one God. The oldest written form of this story is in the Book of Genesis and according to the biblical scholars it was redacted from two sources, the first source 'J' which probably was written before 900 B.C.E., and source 'E' which was written a century later. These two sources probably came from one source which the biblical scholars call source 'G'. The last redaction of the Book of Genesis occurred during the reforming activities of Ezra and Nehemiah when the Jews returned from exile, and that made the story of Adam and Eve the official story of Creation for those who returned to Jerusalem after seventy years of captivity, with new dreams and a new monotheistic religion.

But this story was also known in Arabia where it became the dominant Creation epic in that part of the world. Though the people of northern Arabia were nomadic and illiterate and left no writings, their culture survived in the poems of pre-Islamic poets, including the story of Adam and Eve. The poems that were born of this oral tradition reflect some biblical influence brought by Arab Christians

and Jews and this multicultural mixture formed an amalgamation of
Arabic-biblical versions as evidenced by the poet *'Uday bin Zayd ul-
'Ubādī*, whose rendition of Adam and Eve includes even the serpent.

> He made the creations in six days and on the last He
> created man.
> He called him Adam and he became alive after blowing the
> spirit into the body which He had formed.
> He housed him in Paradise and created a wife for him from
> his rib.
> His Lord prohibited him from only one tree–to not eat nor
> even smell the fruit.
> The Serpent, a great creation like a camel, seduced them.
> Because of Eve, they ate from the tree which they were
> prohibited from.
> They both made their dress from fig leaves.
> God punished the Serpent for seducing His creation.
> The Serpent crawls on its stomach and eats dirt.[1]

The biblical influence is paramount in this poem, but the description
of the serpent as a creation like a camel is in the Arab tradition.
*Umayya bin Abiṣ-ṣalṭ*, a monotheistic poet with no known religious
affiliation, writes of both the serpent and the devil which he refers to
as 'the Jinn,' who were in pre-Islamic legends a name for the Devil.[2]
Adam is an Arabic word from '*adama*' which means dirt or earth,
while '*Hawwa*' or Eve comes from the word '*hayah*,' meaning life.
The two names were used by pagan Arabs before Islam as evidenced
by the name *Adam bin Rabī'a bin Al-Ḥārith bin 'Abdul Muṭṭalib*, an
enemy of the Prophet, and '*Hawwa*' the grandmother of '*Amr bin
Ma'ādh*, a companion of the Prophet.

Qur'anic revelation confirms the Adam and Eve story as the
official creation story for the new Islamic believers, but it was devoid
of some pertinent details such as the creation of Eve. These were
clarified with the *hadiths* of the prophets and with the further

---

[1]- Al-Hayawan, *Al-Jahizh* 4:197.
[2]- From Diwan *Umayya bin Abis-Salt*.

incorporation from both biblical and rabbinical sources. Over the centuries the interaction between the Islamic and biblical Adam and Eve continued and reached its zenith in Spain where, under strong Arab influence, both Jewish and Muslim scholars worked together in a cultural exchange and produced a universal Adam and Eve albeit with many different details.

The story of Cain and Abel was unknown to the Arabs before Islam, yet still developed into a story that took on Islamic detail.

# The story of Adam and Eve

## The Arguments of Angels[1]

When the Lord wanted to create the first man He said to His angels: *"I am placing an overlord on Earth,"* and they said, *"Will You place someone there who will corrupt it, and shed blood while we sing hymns which praise and sanctify You?"* God said, *"I know what you do not know"* 2:30

## Collecting Adam's Mud from Earth

God revealed to earth that He was about to make a people from earth itself, and those people would be judged according to their obedience. Those who would obey His will would go to Paradise, while those not obeying would end in Hell. Earth asked, "Are You creating people from me who may be placed in Hell?" When God

---

[1] - The Bible did not mention any discussion between the Lord and His angels regarding the wisdom of the creation of man, but Hebrew literature mentioned that the angels had a disagreement over the creation of man. Angels of love welcomed the new creation because he would be a loving entity full of emotions, but the angels of truth were not happy. They believed man would be of a deceiving nature who would lie; the angels of justice liked man as they thought he would practice justice, but the angels of peace thought he would be violent. When the angels let God know of their trepidations God said, "Why do you think I created the birds of the sky and the whales of the ocean? They will be meaningless without the creation of man." ( Tosifta Soloh 6.5; Berashit Rabbah 8.3-9; Tehillim 1,23; Tanhuma Introduction 154; Yerushalmi Berakot 9.12d). Midrash Konen 26-27 mentioned the objection of the angels but in a more violent fashion. The first group of angels who objected to Adam's creation were destroyed except for their leader Michael. The second group was also destroyed save their leader Gabriel and the third group after witnessing the fate of the others announced their joy at man's creation, and they pledged to help him. From L.O.J. I, 53-55 and endnotes Adam 12 and 13.

confirmed this, Earth cried and the water burst forth from its springs as tears flow from the eyes.[1]

God asked Archangel Gabriel to bring him a fistful of dirt from the four corners of the earth to be used for the creation of the first man, Adam. The dirt should include both black and red, both clean and filthy dirt from its plains and mountains. When Gabriel went to collect the dirt, earth said to him, "By God's grace, do not take any part of me which might end in Hell later on." Gabriel could not find it in himself to force earth and went back empty handed, and explained to the Lord what earth had said. God then asked the Archangel Michael to acquire the earth's dirt, but Michael also returned with the task unaccomplished. God then asked the same of *'Izrā'īl*, the Angel of Death. After hearing earth's reluctance to cooperate, the Angel of Death said, "By the grace of God, I will not defy His order." And he took a fistful of dirt from the four corners of the earth and proffered to the Lord."[2]

The pollution of earth's dirt occurred when the Devil Iblis walked on earth; wherever he stepped the ground beneath him became unclean, and man's ego–the confinement of evil–was created from that contamination, whereas the prophets were created from dirt which was clean and had not been defiled.[3] The dirt which comprised Adam was procured from all parts of the world. The dirt of Jerusalem created his head while Iraq's dirt produced his chest, and his backside was made from the dirt of Babylon. Dirt from the area of *Ka'ba* in Mecca was used for his right hand while dirt from Persia was used for his left, and finally his legs and feet were comprised

---

[1]-Rep. by Wahb. Pub. by Taf-Khaz. 2:30.

[2]- This story was reported by *As-Siddi* and he attributed it to *Ibn 'Abbas* and *Ibn Mas'ud* and other sahaba. Pub. by Taf-Tab 2:30; Ara-Tha 22; Qis-Kath I:39. A similar story appeared in Hebrew writings in Midrash Yerahmeel 15 and Konen 27. Gabriel was sent to bring dirt from the four corners of the earth, but earth refused to give any part of her to the angel because later it would be cursed by man. God, when He heard the earth's objection, took a fistful of dirt by His own hand. From L.O.J. I, 55 and endnote Adam 14.

[3]- From Tar-Kham I:37.

from the dirt of India and the land of Gog and Magog. It is because of this geographic diversity, and the different colors and quality of the dirt, that Adam's descendants come in all colors, shapes and personalities.[1]

### The Making of Adam's Body

When *'Izra'īl*, the Angel of Death returned with the handful of dirt, God instructed him to make it mud. *'Izrā'īl* mixed the dirt with fresh, salt, and bitter water, then left it to age for forty years until it became firm. After yet another forty years the clay became black in color and was fashioned into a shape. Forty more years were needed for the clay to dry. God made it into the shape of a body and left it on the angelic road between Mecca and Heaven. The angels who used the road on their journey to Heaven had never seen anything before like that body, and would stop and admire it. But the devil *Iblīs* did not share the angels' excitement and he kicked the body, then entered the body first through its mouth and exited through the anus, then accomplished this feat in reverse. He then addressed the body saying, "You are nothing to me, but you have been created for a very serious purpose, but if I should gain authority over you I will torture you, while if you get authority over me I shall disobey you."

In another version of this story, *'Izrā'īl* mixed together the dirt and placed it on the road between Mecca and Al-Taif. For forty years a rain from the Sea of Sadness (a cosmic sea under the Holy Throne) fell upon it. It is said that is why it is unlikely for a person to live any one day with only happiness and without some feeling of sadness in his heart.[2]

---

[1]- Tar-Kham I:38 quoting Ibn Mas'ud.
[2]- These stories were reported by *'Abdulah bin Salam* and *Ibn 'Abbas*, published by Ara-Tha 22-23; Taf-Tab 2:30. Taf-Khaz 2:30. The second version published also in Ara-Tha 23.

## The Spirit of God Breathed into Adam

God wanted to give Adam's body a soul, but the soul retorted, "It is too dark and deep to enter." He ordered it again but received the same reply. The third time God said, "Enter him unwillingly and you shall leave him unwillingly." God breathed from His Spirit into Adam's clay body.* The spirit entered Adam through his head, and Gen 2:7 and whichever part of him the spirit touched became alive. When it touched his head he sneezed, and the angel asked him to praise God; he complied and God responded by saying "God bless you Adam." When the spirit touched his eyes he saw the fruit of the trees in the Garden, and when it touched his stomach he felt hungry. He jumped to reach the fruits but could not, as the spirit had not yet reached his legs. It has been said in the Qur'an, "Man is created of haste.[1]" 21:37

## Adam Paraded through Heaven

It has been said that Adam was sixty cubits tall and seven cubits in width.[2] God perfected Adam's creation by breathing the spirit into him, dressing him in the best garments from the Garden, decorating him with all type of adornment, and then he would shine like the sun. Adam then rested in a palanquin and was carried on the shoulders of the angels through Heaven. God told the angels, "Parade him throughout My Heavens to see the wonders and strength of his faith." The angels did this for one hundred years until Adam had seen every wonder and sign in Heaven. God then brought Adam a horse with two wings, the horse created from pure musk and the wings from pearls and gemstones. Adam rode the horse with Gabriel holding the reins, Michael on his right side and Isrāfīl on his left. They ran through the Heavens with Adam greeting the angels and receiving their felicitations in return.[3]

---

[1]- Pub. by Ara-Tha 24; Taf-Tab & Taf-Khaz 2:30; Qis-Kath I:40; Qis-Kis 26.

[2]- Pub. by Ara-Tha 24; Taf-Tab 2:30.

[3]- Pub. by Ara-Tha 24-25.

### *Iblīs* **Refused to Make Obeisance to Adam**

Upon Adam's creation, God told the angels to kneel down to Adam, and every angel prostrated himself, but not so *Iblīs*, who was proud and rejected God's will. God said, "*Iblīs, what prevents you from prostrating yourself to one whom I have created with My own hands, Have you become too proud or are you the exalted one?*" *Iblīs* said, "*I am better than him—You created me from fire while you created him from clay*" 38:75-76 *Iblīs* would not show any reverence for Adam. He turned away from him and stood erect while the other angels bowed down in veneration and deference. They assumed this position for one hundred years, and when they raised their heads, *Iblīs* had still not acquiesced his stance. They bowed for a second time and *Iblīs* continued to disobey. God then banished *Iblīs* from Heaven *"You are cast away and my curse is upon you until Judgement Day."* *Iblīs* said, "*My Lord, grant me a respite until the day of resurrection.*" God did grant *Iblīs* a respite until the appointed time. *Iblīs* said, "*Thereby Your Might I will make them live an evil life. All except Your servants from among them—the purified ones.*" God replied, "*The truth is this that I speak—that I will most certainly fill Hell with you and those among you who follow you.*[1]" 38:77-85

---

[1]- A similar story is found in the "Life of Adam and Eve," the Latin text: "After blowing the life into Adam, God's likeness; Michael called all the angels and asked them to worship Adam, the image of God, but the Devil, who was one of the angels said, 'I will not worship one inferior to me, I am prior to him in creation and he ought to worship me.' And because of this, the Devil and the angels under him who had followed him and refused to worship Adam were expelled from their glory and have been cast onto the earth". Vita 12-16. Dr K. Blankinship wrote to me:

"*This passage does not occur in the extant Greek versions. One or two of the Latin manuscripts are from the ninth century and thus quite old, it is not particularly likely, but perhaps not impossible, that the story in Latin was influenced by the Qur'an. It is unlikely because of the differences in the Latin story and the greater amount of detail. The scholars of the Pseudoepigrapha suggested that this work originated in 400 C.E., or more likely by 100 C.E., and is based on a Hebrew original, and that the passage in question on the angels being called on to worship Adam is a part of that Hebrew original that has dropped out of the*

## God Taught Adam the Names

God taught Adam the names of everything, but there is disagreement between Islamic scholars about what names God taught him. *Ibn 'Abbās* said, "He taught him every name, even the cooking pot and spoon." *Muqātil* said He taught the name of every thing He created– animals, inanimate objects and other things. He told Adam, "This is an ass, a horse, a mule, until he knew them all." *Sa'īd bin Jubayr* said, "He taught him the name of every species."[1]

[God] *taught Adam all the names, presented them to the angels and said, "tell me the names of those". They said, "Glory be to You. We have no knowledge but that which You have taught us. You are the Knowing and the Wise." He said, "Adam, inform them of their names." When Adam informed them of their names God said, "Did I not say to you that I know the seen in heaven and on earth and I know what you manifest and what you hide?"* 2:31-33

## The Making of the Covenant

When God touched Adam's loin with His hand, out fell all of Adam's descendants–as small as ants, male and female, believers and non-believers, rich and poor, kings and commoners, scholars, those who had died in childhood and those who had died of old age, all those created by God until the day life ended on earth. God gave them intelligence, hearing and speech. The first group came from his right loin–sparkling white in color, and God said, "These are destined to Paradise because of their good deeds." The second group came from Adam's left side and God said, "These are destined for Hell because of their evil deeds."

*" Your Lord brought forth the children of Adam and their descendants and made them bear witness against their own souls, asking, 'Am I not*

---

*extant Greek versions."* K.Y.B.
[1]- Pub. in Taf-Bagh, Taf-Tab, Taf-Khaz 2:31 and almost all books of tafsir. In Gen 2:19-20 God, after creating the animals, brought them to Adam who gave names to them.

*your Lord?' 'Yes,' they said, 'we bear witness lest you say on Resurrection Day we were heedless of this.'"* 7:172

God presented all Adam's descendants to him and each one had a dim light between his eyes. Adam noticed that one person had a special light and asked God who this was.

"This is David, your descendant," God answered.

"How many years will he live, my Lord?"

God replied that David would live for sixty years.

"My Lord," said Adam, "take forty years of my life and give it to David."[2] But when the Angel of Death came to Adam forty years before his time Adam asked, "Do I not have forty more years of life?" The Angel of Death reminded Adam of what he had given to David but which Adam now denied. Since then, all arrangements must be in writing, signed and witnessed.

### Creation of Eve (*Hawwa*)

When Adam was housed in the Garden[3] he lived alone

---

[1]- Most Islamic scholars timed the making of the covenant after the expulsion. This story was pub. by almost all tafsir books at 7:172; it is also reported in hadiths books *'Tirmidhi; Nisa'i; Imam Ahmad*; and *Abu dawud.'* In Hebrew writings, God revealed to Adam the history and fate of mankind. With each generation He showed him the leaders, the judges, the pious and the wicked people. And told him everything about them including how long they will live. Seder 'Olam 30; 'Abodah Zarah 5a; from L.O.J. I: 61 and endnote Adam 27.

[2]- In Hebrew writings, Adam, after finding that David's life was very short, gave him seventy years from his own. Tehillim 95, 408; Pirke de Rabbi Eliezer 19; In Berashit Rabbeti 67-68 God and Archangel Metatron signed the deed of gift to Adam, from L.O.J. I: 61 and endnote Adam 28.

[3]- There is disagreement about the place of the Garden where Adam and Eve resided. Most muslim scholars believe it is in Heaven (Paradise), and they described the expulsion from the Garden as a descent down to earth. There are, however, a minority who take the biblical point of view that the Garden was on earth, and they explain the descent as simply movement between two places on earth. This view is claimed to be of *Ubay bin Ka'b; Ibn 'Abbas; Wahab bin Munabbih; Sufian bin 'Uyayna*; and mentioned in many books of tafsir including *Al-Bulati; Ar-Razi; Al-Qurtubi; Ibn 'Atiyya; Al-Mawardi* and *Al-Rummani.* The

without company until one day when he awoke and found a woman sitting beside him, whom God had created from his rib\*, and she was the most beautiful of God's creations. Adam asked her, "Who are you?" and she answered, "I am your wife, God created me so you will find rest with me and I will find rest with you." Gen 2:21-22

The angels wanted to test Adam and asked him, "Who is she, Adam?"

"A woman."

"Why is she called woman?" asked the angels.

"Because she was created from man."[1]\* Gen 2:23

"But what is her name?"

"Eve," said Adam.

"Why Eve?" the angels asked.

"Because she was created from life."[2]\* Gen 3:20

The angels asked Adam, "Do you love her?"

"I do," responded Adam.

"And you, Eve, do you love Adam?"

Eve, in spite of the extreme love in her heart for Adam, did not want to admit to this love so she said, "No, I do not." It has been said if any woman should confess the truth of her love that woman should be Eve.[3]

## Adam's Wedding

Islamic authors did not have Adam and Eve living together without benefit of marriage. *Ibn al-Jawzy* said, "When Adam wanted to make love with Eve the angels would not allow it without

---

creation of Eve was not mentioned in the Qur'an, but this story which coincides with the biblical version was reported by many Imams including *Ibn 'Abbas; Ibn Mas'ud* & other sahaba, and is published in almost every history and in the tafsir books.

[1]- In Arabic, the word "woman" *(imra'ah)* is derived from man *(imru')*; in Hebrew it is (ishshah) women vs (ish) man.

[2]- The Arabic word for life is *(hayah)* and for Eve is *(hawwa)*. The story is from Ara-Tha 25.

[3]- From Tar-Kham I:47 quoting Tafsir at-Tha'labi.

a wedding. And God made the wedding ceremony and delivered this sermon: "Praise is My grace, Grandeur is My belt, and Proudness is My dress. All creatures are My servants. O My angels and the carriers of My Throne and the inhabitants of My Heavens witness the marriage of My servant Eve to My servant Adam, the perfection of My creation and the making of My Own two hands, for a dowry of celebrating My Praise and extolling My Holiness. O Adam-live you and your wife in the Garden.[1]" 2:35

## Adam's Sin

All but the fruit of one tree[2] can be eaten in the Garden by Adam Gen 2:16-17 and Eve*. This divine decree was meant to test Adam and Eve and to bestow God's will on them and their descendants. The Devil *Iblis* attempted to enter the Garden, but the guards prevented him. He talked to the animals one at a time and asked each one to carry him into the Garden. But every animal refused to assist him until he came upon the Serpent. He told the Serpent that if she helped him gain entry she would be protected from Adam and his descendants. The Serpent put him in her mouth between her two fangs and carried him into the Garden. Once inside the Garden *Iblis* came out of the serpent's mouth and a terrible wailing began. This distressed Adam and Eve and they asked the Devil the reason for his anguish. He said,

---

[1]- From Tar-Kham quoting 'Salwat ul-Ahzan' by *Ibn al-Jawzi*. In the Hebrew 2alphabet of R. Akiba 60, the splendor of Adam and Eve's wedding was described. God gave a speech and pronounced a blessing upon the couple while the angels danced and played their musical instruments. L.O.J. I: 68 and endnote Adam 48.

[2]- The forbidden tree identified in Islamic writings as the wheat tree *"Ibn 'Abbas* and *Muqatil, "* (wheat in the Garden grew on trees); the date tree; the grape vine *"Ibn Mas'ud"*; The fig tree *"Ibn Jarij "* ; or the camphor tree *"Imam Ali"* ; pub. by Taf-Bagh 2:35; In Hebrew writings it is identified as wheat, grape, fig or apple. The Bible spoke of two different trees in the garden: the tree of knowledge and the tree of life, but Islamic writings and the holy Qur'an mentioned only one kind. The Devil, during the temptation of Adam and Eve, lied when he described the tree as "the Tree of Immortality." Q 20:120.

"I am wailing for both of you because you will die and lose dignity and favor." He then said, "Your Lord has not forbidden you this tree except that you may not both become angels or that you may not become of the immortals*." 7:20  This talk had a great effect on them, Gen 3:4 especially on Eve. When Adam asked her to satisfy his desire, she said, "No, not until we go under the forbidden tree." Once there, Adam again asked and her reply was, "No, not until you eat from that tree."[1]

In another version of Adam's sin–the peacock version–*Iblīs* waited at the door of the Garden for three hundred and sixty years awaiting news about Adam and Eve.  He at last saw a beautiful and colorful bird emerge, strutting about, and *Iblīs* asked him, "You beautiful creature, I have not seen anything from God's creation as pretty as you. Who are you and what is your name?" He answered, " I am a bird and my name is Peacock." When *Iblīs* found the bird was from the Garden he asked for news of Adam.

"Adam is well, the Gardens are maintained for his pleasure and we are his servants."

"Can you take me to him?" he asked.

"But who are you ?" asked the Peacock.

"I am one of the Cherubim Angels and have advice to give to Adam."

"Why don't you ask Angel *Raḍwān* (the garden's attendant) to let you in?"

"He refused me entry," said *Iblīs*.

"But *Raḍwan* doesn't prevent anyone from giving advice."

"That is true," said *Iblīs*, "but I don't want him to know about the advice."

"Advice is never hidden," said the Peacock.

---

[1]- The main Islamic view puts the blame equally on Adam and Eve for the sin, while the the Bible blames Eve in particular. This view was endorsed by some Islamic scholars and in a hadith pub. by Al- Bukhari. This story rep. by *Al-Hasan*; pub. by Taf-Bagh & Taf-Khaz 2:36. Qis-Kis 38-42.

"We, the Cherubim Angels, do not say anything except in private. If you will
allow me in I will teach you a prayer to prevent you from losing your beautiful colors."

Although the Peacock would not agree to this he did tell *Iblīs* that the Serpent might be able to help him. The Serpent was as big as a great camel, having four limbs made of green peridot and colored in all colors. The Peacock told the Serpent that an angel at the Garden gate had advice for Adam, and if the Serpent would admit him, they would learn of a prayer to keep their magnificent colors always. The Serpent went to *Iblīs* and said, "I can let you in but I am afraid you may cause me trouble."

"You are in my protection and on my honor, nothing bad will befall you," said *Iblīs*.

"But how can I let you in? *Raḍwān* will prevent it," said the Serpent.

"I will become wind. Place me between your fangs and I will pass through. But don't let *Raḍwān* know," said *Iblīs*. So *Iblīs* changed into wind and entered into the Garden, carried in the serpent's mouth, and was delivered to the prohibited tree. *Iblīs* then played his flute, and Adam and Eve, hearing this, soon found the source emanating from the mouth of the Serpent. *Iblīs* tried to entice them to come closer, but they were wary of being too close to the tree. They said, "God prohibited us from coming close to this tree." *Iblīs*, through the mouth of the Serpent, answered, "Your Lord has not forbidden you this tree except that you may not both become angels or that you may not become immortal." When *Iblīs* found that neither Adam nor Eve believed his words he swore to them both, "I am a sincere advisor to you." 7:20-21 He was the first to lie under oath and the first who deceived. Eve was the first to take a piece of fruit from the tree and eat it . Then she brought fruit to Adam saying, "I
Gen 3:6 saying, "I ate from it and it did not hurt me."* Adam did not eat from

from that tree for one hundred years, and during that time he saw no
ill effects on Eve.  At that time he proclaimed it safe and put the fruit
in his mouth.[1]

## The Consequences

Before Adam had a taste of the prohibited fruit, his crown was
decorated with pearls, rubies and diamonds.  He had a copious
wardrobe of 700 dresses and he sat upon a jewel-encrusted palanquin.
After Adam's disgrace the palanquin slipped from beneath him
saying, " Adam, your sorrow will be long. I feel ashamed to be a part
of any disobedience towards God." Until then, their shame was unknown to them* and covered by bright light. After Adam and Eve's   Gen 2:25
fall from grace that light disappeared and they recognized their
shame.  As Adam ran away, every tree or river chastised him, saying,
"Adam has disobeyed the Lord."  The holy *Sidra* Tree[2] caught him
and said, "Do you think you can run away from God?"  Now
conscious of his exposed part, Adam tried to cover himself with
leaves from the trees he passed, but they raised their limbs and
thereby kept them out of reach.  The trees told him, "We will not
cover who has been uncovered by God."  The fig tree felt sorry for
them and asked them to use her leaves.*But when they tried to make   Gen 3:7
use of the leaves they dried  and crumbled, and they heared a voice
saying, "Those who are uncovered by God will have no cover and
those who have rejected God will have no ally."  They prayed to God
to be covered and when they approached the fig tree again it shook
three fig leaves down to Adam.  It shook again and five leaves fell to
Eve to make her dress.  God asked the fig tree, "Why did you give
them your leaves?"  "My Lord, you don't deny Your mercy to those
who disobey you; how can I deny them my leaves?"  For this reason
God protected the fig tree from becoming firewood and protected its

---

[1]- Pub by Ara-Tha 26-27; Qis-Kis 36 with more details.

[2]- A tree in Paradise, mentioned by this name in the Qur'an, described
in a hadith that "every one leaf from it gives shades to a nation."

leaves from becoming food for the animals.[1] God criticized Adam, saying, "Why did you eat from that tree? Did I not forbid you from doing that?"   Adam said that Eve gave him the fruit ane Eve said the Gen 3:11-13  Serpent* had encouraged her to partake of the fruit. The Serpent claimed the Peacock was responsible, and the Peacock said, "*Iblīs* made me do it".

**The Penalty**

*Iblīs* 'penalties were thus: God cursed him, and transformed him into a hideous shape.  His original name of '*Al-Ḥārith*' was now *Iblīs* and he lost his place in Heaven and was dismissed to earth.  The Peacock's image was also changed and his legs shortened.  The Serpent's limbs were removed and God said, "Your sustenance will be in the dirt, you will be made to crawl on your stomach, and who-
Gen 3:14:15  ever shall see you will throw stones,* and you will die every winter."[2]
God put ten penalties on Adam:
1-God criticized Adam saying, "Did I not prohibit you both from that tree?" 7:22
2-Adam's shame was uncovered.
3-His skin was covered by a horny layer which disappeared but for the tips of his fingers and toes. This remained so as to not forget the past.[3]
4-Adam was spurned from his closeness with God.
5-Adam was separated from Eve.
6-His descendants fought each other, God addressed them saying "You will become one another's enemy." 2:36

---

[1]-The fig leaves have a certain alkaloid in them that render them inedible by animals; its wood is soft and moist, not a good  firewood.

[2]- Snakes hibernate in the winter

[3]- The idea of horny skin was borrowed from <u>Hebrew</u> <u>literature</u>. In <u>Targum Yerushalmi</u> it is mentioned that Adam was covered in a garment of light which disappeared after his sin. Both Adam and Eve were covered in a horny skin enveloped in a halo, until they sinned, when the halo disappeared as well as the horny skin, except for that on the tips of their fingers and toes. <u>Targum Yerushalmi</u> Genesis 3.7, from L.O.J.  I: 74 and endnote Adam 69.

7-God described Adam as "*he forgot, and We did not find in him any determination*" 20:115

8-The Devil was directed against Adam's descendants. God addressed the Devil to "Set *upon them with your calvary and your manpower.*" 17:64

9-Life was made a prison for himself and his progeny.

10-God threatened Adam before not to let the Devil "*drive you both from the Garden or you will both suffer.*" 20:117 Now Adam had to work by the sweat of his brow.* Gen 3:19

Eve received additional suffering for her role in seducing Adam and God said, "I shall make her bleed once a month, she shall carry her baby in discomfort and deliver in pain* and instead of the Gen 3:16 graceful woman I have created, she shall be a fallen one.[1]

Although Adam begged for forgiveness and said, "Are You banishing me from the Garden for one mistake?" no forgiveness was granted. Adam pleaded again with God saying he ate the fruit unintentionally. God said, "Whoever so disobeys Me will not stay in My trust." Adam then saw written on the Holy Throne, "There is no deity but God and Muhammad is His prophet." Adam said, "Lord I beg You in the name of my son Muhammad to forgive me." God asked Adam how he knew Muhammad was Adam's descendent, to which Adam replied, "I saw his name written with Your name on the Throne and realized he will be a prophet of high eminence." God replied, "I forgive your sin for the sake of Muhammad." As Adam was leaving the Garden he looked back, saw the serenity and its delights, and saw the tree of *Tūbā*.[2] He saw the branches of the holy Sidra tree, the shade of the Holy Throne, the light of the Mighty

---

[1]-In Taf-Bagh only the first two penalties are mentioned. In Ara-Tha, the author increased Eve's suffering to fifteen and included in them all the social inequities of women in the eleventh century C.E. such as not being a head of a state, or having any divorce rights.

[2]-Tuba is a tree in Paradise, it would take a bird seven hundred years to fly around it.

Presence, the beauty of the *Houris*[1] and the grandeur of its palaces. He cried and said farewell to everything in the Garden. All the trees but the Aloe mourned for him. It said, "I will not cry for those that disobey God." God told the Aloe tree, "I will glorify you but you will be burned. The tree asked God why it was to be glorified, yet burned. God said, " You glorified Me, and that is why you will be glorified but your heart did not burn in sorrow for Adam, who loves me. So you will be burned."[2]

When Adam reached the door of the Garden, he stepped outside and said, "In t*ɦe name o*f Go*ɖ* t*ɦe* Bene*f*icent, t*ɦe* Merci*f*ul"1:1. Hearing this, Gabriel granted him leave to stay for one hour, saying, "A mercy may come from the unseen." Gabriel appealed to God and said, "Adam called You Merciful, so have mercy on him," and God said, "Let him go, he will return with thousands of sinners descended from him to see my gratitude over them and realize how great My mercy is."

Gen 3:24      Adam and Eve left the Garden,* holding hands, feeling hungry, strange and isolated. When Gabriel told Adam to let go of Eve's hand, he did so and they lost each other. Adam descended to the Mount of Sarandib in India, the highest mountain on earth, while Eve descended to Jeddah in Arabia. After a long separation they met each other at the Mount of Arafat close to Mecca. Adam's footprint can still be seen in the rocks of Sarandib peak, where lightening, thunder and incessant rains keep the footprints clean and exposed. And dislodge rubies and diamonds that tumble down the mountain side where they can be collected.[3]

---

[1] - Houris are the beautiful maidens of Paradise.

[2] -The aloe-wood, 'Aguilaria agallochum,' is a fragrant wood that grows in northern India and China and reaches up to 120 feet in height. It gives a pleasant incense when burned and was used for embalming dead bodies.

[3] - Ara-Tha 31-31; Al-Wafa, Ibn al-Jawzi I:33.

### Adam's repentence

*Adam recieved words* [of inspiration] *from his Lord and he turned towards Him.* 2:37 These words are "*Our Lord, we have wronged our own souls, If you do not forgive us and bestow upon us your mercy, we will be losers.*" 7:23

### Adam on Earth

Because of Adam's enormous size,[1] even after his descent to earth on the mountain of Sarandib, his head remained high in the sky and he could hear the angels' hymn which he enjoyed. But the angels, seeing his head through the cloud, feared him and complained to the Almighty. God then curtailed his great height to sixty cubits, but because his head had continually come in contact with the clouds he had become bald, a trait which his descendants inherited. The leaves of the fig tree that Adam was wearing soon died and crumbled. Their remains were scattered all over India, and from them grew the incense-wood plants as well as other aromatic herbs. The deer who ate the fig leaves became musk deer, and the whales who partook became ambergris whales. The worms which ate from it became silkworms, and the bees became honey bees.[2]

Adam and Eve cried for two hundred years for the good life they had lost. They did not eat nor drink for forty years, and they did not sleep together for one hundred years. When God bestowed His mercy once again He taught Adam to say, "*There is no deity but You, glory and praise to You, I was unjust to myself* 21:87, forgive me as You are the Best Forgiver."

When the leaves of the fig tree dried and were spread over India, Adam and Eve were left nude. They complained to Gabriel,

---

[1]- A hadith by Al-Bukhari said " God created Adam 60 cubits tall." Adam's gigantic size was mentioned in Hebrew literature; Tehillim 139; Tanhuma Midrash B.III,37; from L.O.J. I: 59 and endnote Adam 22.

[2]- From Ara-Tha 31. Some Hebrew literature spok about thirty kinds of trees and herbs brought from Paradise by Adam to earth. Tehillim 104,445 2Alphabet of Ben Sira 21b.

who brought them a large sheep with thick fleece. He said to Adam, "Let Eve spin this wool and make your clothing from it." Eve was upset and questioned why she had to do this task. As compensation for her, God made Adam responsible for Eve's support. And when Adam thought this too much of a burden, Eve's inheritance was made half of Adam's. Eve spun the wool and made a dress and a scarf for herself and a shirt and pants for Adam.[1]

Adam complained to Gabriel about his unusual feeling and the Angel explained that this was hunger. Two red bulls from the Garden were given to Adam to use in cultivation, as well as blacksmith tools so that he might make tools with which to plow. The kiln's fire was to be lit with a spark from Hell, brought down by Gabriel, but it fell from Adam's hand seven times and went into the sea. After washing Hell's fire seven times, it had cooled enough to be used on earth. It spoke and said to Adam, "Adam, you will not be able to control me and I will take my revenge on your descendants in the hereafter." Gabriel said, "Adam, fire will not obey you, but I will imprison it so it can be used safely." He imprisoned it in stone and iron.[2]

Gabriel, after giving him the plowing implements, also gave him three grains of wheat and taught him how to till the earth and plant the wheat. The bulls cried for the good life they missed, and their tears ran into the earth from which the millet grew. They urinated, and from it grew chickpeas, and from their dung the lentils grew.

Gabriel taught Adam how to cultivate; to winnow the chaff from the grain, then grind the wheat between two stones, sift out the bran and knead the flour, make a fire to bake bread, and finally to eat what they had made.[3] After all of this toil Adam's eyes were filled with tears, "Do I have to work this hard for one loaf of bread?"

---

[1]- Ara-Tha 32.

[2]- When two pieces of iron or stone are knocked together, a spark comes from the im-prisoned fire.

[3]-There is a similar story about cultivating wheat in the book of Adam and Eve of S. C. Malan, ch. LXVI 9-10 and LXVII 1.

"Yes," answered Gabriel, "this is what God promised you when He said, [The Devil] *is an enemy to you and your wife. Do not let him drive you out of the Garden, or you will suffer.*" 20:117.

After his first meal Adam had an unpleasant feeling, and Gabriel explained that this was thirst. He brought him a pick and told him to dig, and Adam dug until he reached water which he drank, and at last felt good. Adam was very busy on earth making a living and complained to God, saying, "Lord, making a living takes all my time, and I have no time for worshiping and praising You." God sent him a rooster, the first fowl used by Adam, and it had the ability to hear the praise of angels. The rooster would crow when he heard the angels and, in turn, Adam would hear the rooster and he would praise God.[1]

### Adam Built the Ka'ba[2]

After Adam's descent from the mountain he complained to God, saying, "Lord, I was close to You in Your Garden, enjoying its benefits when You sent me down to mountain, but still I could hear the angels praising You, smell the scent of the Garden and would see the angels surrounding Your Throne. Then You reduced me to sixty cubits and I can no longer hear the angels nor smell the Garden." God said, "Your own sin has brought this upon you, but I have a sanctuary on earth under My Throne. Go and build a shrine for Me and walk around that shrine as you see My angels fly around My Throne. There I will answer your prayers and those of your descendants who will become My disciples." God sent the Angel Gabriel to show him the place of sanctuary, and together they walked to it. Every step Adam took measured fifty leagues, and every resting

---

[1]- Ara-Tha 32-35.
[2]- Muslim scholars and historians maintained that the Ka'ba was built by Abraham thePatriarch, but some scholars say that Abraham actually rebuilt it on the foundations of an old temple built by Adam. This is a literary interpretation of Q 3:96 "*The first house was built for public [worship] is the one in Mecca, blessing and guidance to all people.*"

place they stopped became a great city, while where they did not stop remained a wilderness. When they reached the place of Mecca they built the holy shrine of the *Ka'ba*. The angels helped Adam in the building. They dug until they reached the seventh layer of earth. The angels filled it with rock until it reached the earth's surface, and Gabriel brought from Heaven a large red ruby with four white corners and placed it in the monument. Adam built the *Ka'ba* from the stones of five mountains: the Mount of Sinai, the Mount of Ḥarra, the Mount of Olive (in Jerusalem), the Mount of Lebanon and the Mount of Judi.[1]

### The Death of Adam

Adam lived nine hundred and sixty years, (one thousand years less the forty years he gave to his descendant David). When he realized he was dying, he requested some grapes from the Garden and his sons went to bring him this last request. On the way they met a group of angels and when the angels heard what Adam's sons were looking for, they told them that they were too late. The angels then went to Adam, collected his soul, ceremoniously washed him, scented him, wrapped him in a shroud, and finally after praying at his funeral, buried him.[2] He was laid to rest at Sarandib, in India, the place where he descended to the earth. Eve died three days after Adam and was buried with him.

---

[1]- From Ara-Tha 31; also pub. by Taf-Bagh with different details 2:127. The Mount of Judi is where Noah's Ark landed. The Mount of Harra is where The Prophet Muhammad received his first revelation in one of its caves.

[2]- Rep. by *Ubay bin Ka'b*. Pub. by Qis-Kath I:17-18. This hadith was used to confirm the doctrine that Adam's garden was on earth and not in Heaven. A similar story came in the book of "Life of Adam and Eve," in which Adam became sick and asked Seth and Eve to go to Paradise and beg the Lord for oil from the tree of mercy to anoint Adam, but they were told that this oil would not be given before the Last Day. Vita 40-42; ApMos 13. The burial of Adam and the rules of the angels were also mentioned in the same book ApoMas 31-42.

## Adam's Sons, Abel and Cain (*Hābīl* & *Qābīl*)

The first child born to Adam was *Al-Hārith*,[1] followed by a series of twins: Cain and his sister *Iqlīmya*, then Abel and his twin sister *Labūda*, *Aswaf* and his twin sister, then Seth and his twin sister and so on until Eve delivered forty times. God announced to Adam that Cain was to marry Abel's twin sister and Abel should marry Cain's twin sister. Because Cain's twin sister was prettier than Abel's, Cain became angry and envious. Adam told his sons to bring both their offerings to the Lord and the one whose offerings are accepted will marry *Iqlīmya*. Abel was a shepherd and Cain was a tiller of the soil.* Cain brought the Lord a stalk of wheat from the best of his crop. Abel brought his largest and fattest ram. God considered Abel's gift by summoning fire from the sky and burning the ram. This, once again, made Cain both angry and envious.[2]* Cain said to Abel, "I shall kill you," and when Abel queried "Why?" Cain answered, "Because God considerd your offering and disregarded mine. He supported your argument and denied mine; people will now say that you are more devout than I." Abel said, "God only has regard for those who guard against evil; if you reach out your hand to slay me, I will not bring forth my hand to slay you. I fear God, the Lord of the

Gen 4:1

Gen 4:3-5

---

[1]- From a hadith pub. by *Imam Ahmad, At-Tirmidhi* and others, and traced to the Prophet, which said that Eve named her son *'Abdul Harith'* according to the suggestion of the Devil, so he will live because her previous children had all died. *Ibn Kathir* believed this hadith can be traced to a sahabi and not to the Prophet.

[2]- Rep. by *Ibn 'Abbas* & *Ibn Mas'ud*; Pub. by Tar-Kath I:92. In the book of "Adam and Eve" translated by Rev. S. C. Malan, and pub. in 1882 in England, Eve gave birth first to Cain and Luluwa, and the second time she delivered Abel and Aklemia. Ch. LXXIV & LXXV. Adam and Eve made a decision to marry every boy to his non twin sister but Cain did not like this arrangement. Ch. LXXVIII 3' 12. In the "Cave of Treasures," Eve gave birth to Lebuda and Qelima along with Cain & Abel and when the children had grown, Adam said to Eve: "Let Cain take Qelima as a wife since she was born with Abel, and let Abel take Lebuda, who was born with Cain." Then said Cain to his mother Eve, "I will take my own sister, and let Abel take his own" for Lebuda was very beautiful.

*World, I wish you to bear the sin committed against me and your own sin."* 5:27-29

Cain determined to slay his brother but did not know how, when the Devil *Iblīs* captured this opportunity and showed him how. He brought a bird and smashed its head with a stone, killing it. Cain used this same method and slew his brother as

Gen 4:8 he slept, killing him.\*When Cain killed his brother the earth trembled for seven days, then it absorbed his blood as it absorbed water. God called to Cain, "Where is your brother Abel?" Cain said he did not know, "Am I supposed to be his guardian?" God said, "Your

Gen 4:9-10 brother's blood is calling me from the dirt.\* Why did you kill him and where is his blood?" Since then, God prohibited the earth from absorbing blood,[1] Cain's act became the first homicide on earth. He felt sorry for what he had done but did not know what to do with his brother's body. With the fear that wild animals would devour Abel's body, Cain carried him in a sack, but the body began to stink and he was soon pursued by wild animals. God sent two crows to earth, and one was killed by the other. The remaining crow picked the dirt with his beak, dug a hole and put the carcass in it, and this showed Cain what to do with the body of his brother. Cain was watching and said, *"Woe is me! Do I lack the strength that I should be like this crow and cover the body of my dead brother?"* 5:31

Adam was making a pilgrimage to the *Ka'ba* at that time and upon his return, not finding Abel, he asked as to his whereabouts. Cain had no answer. Adam spent seven sleepless nights until he saw Abel in a dream crying, "O my father, o my father!" Adam awoke, then passed out until Gabriel came to console him for the death of his son. In his sorrow Adam said, "I disown Cain." God said, "I disown Cain." God showed Adam where Abel was buried, uncovered the body and saw his head, covered in blood. Adam cried, "O my son, o my sorrow!" And the angels cried for his sorrow. Adam cursed the earth when he found that Abel's blood had dried upon it.

---

[1]- Blood, unlike water, is not absorbed by the earth because it clots.

Adam traveled to all parts of the world, all the time carrying Abel's body before finally burying his son. After committing his crime, Cain ran into a valley at Yemen, east of Eden.* When Adam <sub>Gen 4:16</sub> disowned his son, God asked the earth to swallow him and it did swallow him up to his knees. Cain prayed to God saying, "My Lord, You are more merciful than any mercy giver. Do not abandon Your mercy because of my sin,"* and God asked earth to release him, <sub>Gen 4:13</sub> which it did. An angel then came to him and broke his arms and legs, put cuffs on his hands and pulled him around the earth seven times. In the winters, he was tortured on the snow-covered mountains and in the summers he was tortured on the mountains of fire. Later he was killed by one of his sons.[1]

When Abel was killed, the earth became full of dust. All earth's bounty was reduced in size. The taste of all fruits were changed and became flat. The sunshine and the moon's glow were both dimmed. The scent of flowers, the perfumes, all things that grew on earth, as well as the freshness of the water, were altered. Adam recited this poem:

> **The lands and its people have changed**
> **The face of the earth has become ugly full of dust**
> **Every taste and color have been altered**
> **A pretty face no longer has any charm**
> **My sorrow is great over my son Abel, slain lying inside his grave**

Eve heard him and answered:

> **There is no use in complaining**
> **Mourn does not replace your loved one who lies in his grave**

---

[1]- From Taf-Tab 5:27-31; also presented in most other tafsir books and in Ara-Tha. The argument about the sacrifice was quoted from *Ibn 'Abbas, Mujahid, Ibn 'Atiyya, Qutada, & As-Siddi*. The killing of Abel with a rock while he was asleep was quoted from *Ibn 'Abbas* & other Sahaba. The story about how the Devil taught Cain to kill was quoted from *Mujahid & Ibn Jarij*. Cain carried his killed brother on his back for a whole year in *Ibn 'Abbas' version*, and the torturing of Cain by fire & snow from *Mujahid's*.

No one will last forever.

When *Iblīs* heard this, he responded like every one else, with a poem:

Stop talking about the land and its inhabitants.

The Garden, because of me, became a prison to you.

You and your wife had the best life.

Your heart was away from the hardships on this earth.

But, because of me and my deception, you lost life immortal.

If not for the mercy of the Almighty, the only thing that will remain with you from the Garden is the wind.

# 4     Noah / *Nūḥ*

*Peace be upon Noaḥ throughout the Universe.*
       – Qur'an 37:79

## Introduction

This is a story of a flood which was so severe that it covered all the earth, and all mankind and animals alike perished, except for those that survived by seeking refuge on an ark, which was built by the hero of the story. After the flood, these people and animals re-inhabited the earth.

This story is the best known motif shared by many cultures and religions over the past few thousand years. The oldest record to reach us are the Babylonian tablets which were written about 1700 B.C.E. during the reign of the Babylonian king *Ammi Saduqa* who was on the throne from 1702-1682 B.C.E. The text was written by *Nur-Aya,* the priest, and Atrahasis is the name of the hero in this story.

Another Babylonian version of the story was found at the library of King *Ashurbanipal* in Nineveh, who died in 626 B.C.E. Here the story of the flood is part of the *Gilgamesh epic,* and the hero's name is *Utnapishtim.* The story was modified from the *Atrahasis* version to harmonize with the epic as a whole, to be a part of the constant *Gilgamesh* search for eternity.

We are positive that the Sumerians also had a flood story because in the list of Sumerian kings there is a distinction between the antediluvian kings, mythological figures living thousands of years, and those kings coming after the flood having a normal, human life span. We believe the Sumerian flood story is the most ancient. We do have a Sumerian tablets which describe the great flood, and the hero's name in that tablet is *Ziusudra*. But this story does not appear to be the original, and is most probably a translation from the Babylonian version.

These three versions are not the only ancient ones extant, and the premise of the flood changed constantly in names and details from one civilization to another. The story in the writing of *Berossus of Babel,* in 281 B.C.E., was aimed at introducing the Babylonian culture to the Greeks, and it incorporated new names and details.

It almost became an accepted fact that the Biblical version of the flood in Genesis was redacted from at least two different sources which are now called the "J" and "P" sources. These can be identified separatly because the "J" called God Yahweh while the "P" source called Him Elohim. The story of the Biblical Noah found in both versions showed a marked change from the Babylonian and Sumerian stories by replacing the multiple deities with that of one God. This change happened in response to monotheism, which had spread throughout the middle east.

The story of Noah must have been known in pre-Islamic Arabia as well as in other nations. It was mentioned in the poem of *Umayya bin Abiṣ-Ṣalṭ* whom I mentioned before:

**"God rewarded the honorable Noah in a true and generous way."**

Also, Noah was mentioned by the poet *Al-A 'shā* in his poem which praised a man named *Ayās*:

**"God, may He reward Ayás his best accolade,**
**As he rewarded Noah when he became old**
**And built the ark from the boards and doors which he gathered."**

Noah's sons were also mentioned in a poem by *Al-Afwah al-Awdī*.

# The Story of Noah

The Noah of Islam differs somewhat from the Noah of the Bible. The Qur'an repeats many times that Noah was a prophet sent by God to his people to preach and guide them towards the true religion of God. His message was, "*You will not worship any but God.*" Noah cautioned his people that if they refused his message "*I fear for you the punishment of a painful day.*"11:26 His message of salvation was, "*You should serve God, fear His threats and obey Him. [If you do these things] He will forgive some of your faults and grant you a delay to an appointed term. God's term when it comes is not postponed.*"71:3-4 [1]

God gave Noah his message when he was 480 years old.[2] He preached for 120 years; nevertheless, few people accepted the teachings. Noah complained to his Lord about his unsuccessful mission: "*My Lord, I have preached to my people both night and day, but my appeal has only made them flee further away from me. Each time I appealed to ask for Your forgiveness, they put their fingers in their ears, covered themselves with their garments , persistent in their ignorance, and remain puffed up with pride. I have called to them and spoke to them both in private and in public. I said, 'Ask for forgiveness from your Lord, He is the true forgiver. He forgives you, He sends down abundant rainfall to grows gardens for you, helps you to have wealth and sons, and makes the rivers flow.' *"71:5-12

---

[1]- Noah's preaching was mentioned in Josephus Antiquities 1:73, and in the Revelation of Paul 50.

[2]- Rep. by *Ibn 'Abbas*, pub. by Tar-Kath I:101 and Taf-Bagh 11:26.

Noah said, "*My Lord, they have defied me and followed someone whose wealth and children have added nothing but loss. They have hatched a great plot and said, 'Do not forsake your gods, do not leave Wadd nor Suwa' nor Yaghuth, nor Ya'uq nor Nisr.'* "71:21-23 But Noah's people objected to his preaching, which attracted only the poor. They said to him, "*You are mortal just like us, and those who followed you are the meanest of us. We do not see in you any excellence over us, we deem you and your followers liars.*"11:27

Noah refused to expel his poor followers, saying, "*Who will protect me from the wrath of God if I drive them away?*" He said, "*I do not claim to have the treasures of God, I do not know the unseen, nor do I say that I am an angel.*" But Noah's people refused to listen to him anymore, and challenged him, saying,"*You have argued with us for a long time. Make good on your threat if you are telling the truth.*" 11:30-32 "*And if you do not stop your preaching, you will be stoned to death.*" 26:116 His people actually beat Noah until they thought he was dead, wapped him in a piece of felt and left him in his house. The next day, to their surprise, he was preaching once again.

Noah said, "*My Lord, my people rejected my preaching, therefore judge justly between us and deliver my believers and myself.*"26:117-118 God revealed to Noah, "*None of the unbelievers will believe anymore, therefore do not grieve at what they do, make the ark before mine eyes and according to the revelation, do not speak to Me in concern of the unbelievers, they shall be drowned.*"11:36-37

Noah asked, "My Lord, what is an ark?"

"It is a house floating on water." God said.

"But Lord, where is the water?" asked Noah

"I can deliver what I will."

"But what about the wood?"

"Go and plant trees," God replied. Noah planted trees to be used in the building of the ark.[1]

For forty years, Noah stopped preaching. God made all the women of the unbelievers infertile, and there was not one child born

---

[1]- Rep. by *Zayd bin Aslam*, pub. by Taf-Bagh 11:38.

during this time.[1] After that Noah cut and dried the trees in the sun, and with the help of his sons, Shem, Ham, Japhet, and hired carpenters he built the ark. He made it 300 cubits in length, 50 cubits in width and 30 in height.[2] He built it with three floors and painted both the inside and the outside with tar, which came from a tar spring God had provided. He also used iron nails in its construction.

After Noah used all the wood he had in building the ark, he found he was four boards short in completing the task. God told Noah, "Go to the banks of the Nile, there you will find the tree you need." Noah asked Og, the giant, to bring him that tree. Og accepted the order with the condition that Noah would fill his stomach with food. Upon his return, Noah gave him three loaves of barley. Og laughed, saying: "Every day I eat twelve thousand loaves and that does not satisfy my appetite." Noah asked him to say, before his meal, *"In the name of God the merciful, the beneficent,"* 1:1 and Og was filled, even with the paltry share given to him. The unbelievers used to laugh at Noah, saying, "You became a carpenter after being a prophet."[3]

Noah used a dog to guard the ark at night, and he was the first man to use a guard dog.[4] Noah asked God, "My Lord, give me a sign to know it is coming, so I can be ready." God said, "The sign is that water in your oven will burst." And when this happened, Noah brought the animals to the ark and they, along with Noah's family, entered the ark. The storm began and was described in the Qur'an, *"We[5] opened the gates of the clouds with water pouring down, and we made water flowing forth to the land, and springs and the water gathered together."* 54:11-12

---

[1]- The idea is to not drown any children in the flood.

[2]- From Ara-Tha 48 and Taf-Bagh quoting *Ibn 'Abbas* who borrowed it from Gen. 6:15.

[3]- From Taf-Bagh 11:38; Ara-Tha 48.

[4]- From Hayat ul-Hayawan, Ad-Dumayri II 415.

[5]- The majestic "We" is commonly used in Qur'an when God refers to Himself.

Noah's son[1] refused to board the ark, and Noah saw him on the land running for shelter. Noah called to him and beckoned him to join the others on the ark, but he refused, saying, "I will take refuge in a mountain where I will be protected from the water." Noah answered, "There is no protection today from God's punishment, but He who has mercy." Then the waves separated them and he drowned. Q 11:43

All species of animal were accommodated on the ark. The meat eaters were stabled on the lower floor, livestock and the plant eaters on the middle floor, with the upper level reserved for Noah and the other people with him. These persons included Noah's three sons, their families and a few believers.[2] The last animal to enter the ark was the stubborn donkey. *Iblīs* the Devil was hanging on to the donkey's tail, making it difficult for the animal to proceed into the ark. Noah was losing his patience trying to coax the donkey on board and said, "Come inside, you devil!" *Iblīs* let go and both he and the donkey entered the ark. When Noah discovered the Devil on his ark he exclaimed, "Who gave you permission to enter?" "You did," said the Devil, "when you said 'Come inside, you devil.' "[3]

The goat had difficulty in boarding, so Noah gave a push to her backside, and he broke her tail. This is why the goats' shame is not covered, but because he rubbed the tail of the sheep their shame was covered. Noah and the other passengers were afraid of the lion, so God brought a fever upon him that left him weak and unable to cause any trouble.[4] The snake and the scorpion asked Noah to carry them, and he said, "You are a cause of misery, why should I let you board?" They said, "If you'll carry us, we'll pledge not to bite or sting any one mentioning your name."[5] When the animals' dung

---

[1]- Noah's son is innominate in the Qur'an but some mufassirun gave him the name of Canaan. In the Bible, Canaan is the grandson of Noah.

[2]- The number of the people on the ark differ according to the one reporting it. *Qutada* reported eight, while *Ibn Jarir* thought the number to be ten and *Muqatil* had the number at 78, from Taf-Bagh 11:40.

[3]- From Taf-Tab 11:38; Taf-Bagh & Taf-Khaz 11:40 quoting *Ibn 'Abbas*.

[4]- From Ara-Tha 49 quoting *Wahb* and *Zayd bin Aslam*; Qis-Kath I: 99.

[5]- From Ara-Tha 49; Taf-Khaz 11:40; also Taf-Qush and Hayat ul-Hayawan II 192.

accumulated on the ark and became a problem, God told Noah to pinch the elephant's tail. In doing so, both male and female pigs dropped from the elephant, and they began eating the excrement. The mice on board rapidly reproduced and caused damage to both the food supply as well as to the ropes of the ark. God told Noah to strike the lion between the eyes, and once done, male and female cats came out of his nose and kept the mice in control.[1] Noah ordered that no male should copulate with a female on the ark, but the dog jumped the bitch and Noah cursed them which was meant to cause them difficulty in completing the act.[2]

During the flood, God raised the Ka'ba from the earth for protection, and Gabriel hid the black stone at the mountain of *Abu Qubays*.[3] The ark sailed for ten days in *Rajab*–the second month of the Arabic calendar–and was on the water 150 days. It decked on the *Judi's Mount*. All mountains were pushing themselves up to receive the ark, but the Judi humbled itself, and God flooded every mountain but kept the Judi dry for the ark to dock.[4] The passengers stayed on the docked ark for a month, then they left the tenth day of *Muḥarram*, the "first month of next year."

Before allowing for disembarkation, Noah sent a crow to bring back a sign for land. The crow found a dead animal, ate it and never returned to the ark. but when Noah sent a pigeon, she returned with an olive branch in her beak and mud on her feet. For this Noah cursed the crow, and that is why it does not nest close to humans. Noah also blessed the pigeon and prayed that it shall have peace and shall nest with humans.[5]

Noah remembered his son who perished in the flood, and called upon his Lord and said, "My Lord, my son belonged to my own family, while Your promise is true at the end and You are the wisest

---

[1]- From Taf-Bagh & Taf-Khaz 11:31; also by Taf-Tab quoting *Yusuf bin Mahran* in a long story about Ham, son of Noah, who was raised from death by Jesus to tell the Apostles what happened on the ark. *Ibn Kathir* commented on this story by saying, "It is an odd story," Tar-Kath I:116.

[2]- From Ara-Tha 49 quoting *Al-Kalbi*.

[3]- From Taf-Bagh and almost every book of tafsir at 11:40.

[4]- From Ara-Tha 50 quoting *Mujahid*.

[5]- From Taf-Bagh 11:44.

Judge." God said, "Noah, he no longer belongs to your family, his behavior was dishonorable, do not ask Me about something of which you have no knowledge; I so caution you lest you become ignorant." Noah said, "My Lord, I take refuge with You from asking You something of which I know nothing about. If You do not forgive me and show me mercy I may become a loser." Then Noah received the command, "Noah, land in peace from Us, blessings will rest on you and some of the nations who may spring from you." 11:45-48

All the non-believers perished in the flood except for the giant Og. The water reached only to his knees. God saved him because he helped Noah finish building the ark. Og was the son of Ung, who was the daughter of Adam. He measured 23333 cubits in height, and when he stood up his head reached above the clouds. He drank water from the clouds, took whales from the ocean and fried them by holding them close to the sun. He lived to be 3000 years old until he was killed in the time of Moses.[1]

The flood occurred 2242 years after Adam's expulsion. Noah was 600 years old at the time of the flood, and lived for another 350 years.

---

[1]- From Taf-Bagh; originally the character of Og was borrowed from the Hebrew lite- ratur although there are many original Islamic stories based on that character. *Ibn Kathir* commented on these stories saying, "They mentioned that he was 3333 cubits in height, as well as other hallucinations which I will not quote, except that they are written in some tafsir and history books. These stories contradict common sense and the true traditions." Tar-Kath I:114. In Hebrew literature Og survived the flood by riding atop the ark. Pirke de Rabbi Eliezer 23; Targum Yerushalmi Deut. 2.11&3.10. From L.O.J. I, 160 and footnote 35.

## Comparative study

### The Gods

In the Babylonian version, the assembly of gods as a whole were involved in the planning and execution of the flood. They included Anu, their father. The warrior Ellil. Their counselor Ninurta. Their chamberlain Ennugi. Their canal controller. Shamash the god of storm. Ishtar the goddess of love and war; and the farsighted god Ea, who in spite of the oath of secrecy informed Utnapishtim of the planned flood. In the "J" biblical version the name of the one God is Yahweh but according to the "P" biblical version the name Yahweh was revealed to humanity at the time of Moses and because of that it is not used in stories before him. Instead, the name Elohim was used. The name of God in the Qur'anic version is Allah.

### The Cause of the Flood

In the Babylonian version, the gods decided to end life on earth because people multiplied and became too boisterous, and this affected the well-being of those gods. In the "J" version, the reason that Yahweh was angry with humans was because "the sons of God found the daughters of men fair and took wives for themselves, as many as they wished." The resulting progeny from these unions became a race of giants. In the "P" version, there is no such mention, but it is said that the Lord saw that the wickedness of man on earth was great, and all their hearts' inclination was toward evil. He regretted that He made man on earth and was grieved to His heart. The Lord said, "I will wipe from the earth man whom I have created, man and beast, crawling creatures and birds of the air as well." In the Qur'an the cause of the flood is that God wanted to punish the people, as they did not believe in the teaching of Noah.

### The Description of the Ark

In the Babylonian version Utnapishtim said that he built a ship with a surface measurement of one acre, with an elevation of ten poles shaped like a cube. He made it seven stories and divided the middle into nine parts. He supplied it with paddles, then poured three measures of bitumen in the kiln, and three measures of pitch inside. In the Biblical "P" version God said, "Make an ark of resin wood, make it tight with fibers and cover it with pitch both inside and out. The length should be 300 cubits and the width 50 cubits, and its height should be 30 cubits. Make an opening for the ark and finish it with a cubit from the top, and set a door on its side." The ark was not described in the Qur'an and tafsir books borrowed its description from biblical sources.

### What Noah Carried on the Ark

The Babylonian story said that Utnapishtim carried with him food, all his gold and silver, the seeds of every living thing, his relatives, all the craftsmen and all the animals and beasts. The Biblical "P" version states that he took every sort of living creature in twos, both a male and a female. The Biblical "J" version said that Noah took seven pairs of all clean animals and birds, while from the unclean he took only two, a male and a female. The Qur'anic version sides with the "P" version, taking only one pair of all animals.

### The Duration of the Flood

The Babylonian story mentioned that the storm lasted six days and six nights, and then the ark docked on the mountain of Nimush for six days. The Biblical "P" version mentions the flood caused by water breaking from the ocean below the earth and coming down from the firmament. The flood remained for 150 days and took 220 days to recede. In the Biblical "J" version the storm lasts forty days and recedes in three weeks. The Qur'an gives no duration of either the storm itself or the flood, but the mufassirun say Noah embarked on the ark the first day of the seventh month of the Arabic calendar and the ark stayed afloat for six months. It docked on the mountain of *Judi* on the tenth day of the first month of the following year. The ship remained there for one month, after which they were given permission to leave the ship.

### The Release of the Birds

In the Babylonian version, Utnapishtim released a dove which flew away and then returned. He then released a swallow which first flew but returned. Finally, a raven was released which flew away, never to return. In the Biblical "J" version, Noah released a dove three times, the first time to return, the second time returning with an olive branch in her beak and the third time flying away for good. The "P" version of the Bible has Noah releasing a crow that kept flying back and forth until earth became dry.

# 5     Job / *Ayyūb*

*And Job, cried out to his Lord, "Adversity has afflicted me."*
–Qur'an 21:83

## Introduction

The story of Job and his suffering was a well-known legend in ancient Mesopotamia. It centered around a man who endured much misery and many catastrophes inflicted on him by the Devil. But Job accepted the calamities without complaint until the misery became too much and he called upon God for help. God answered his pleas, reversed his suffering, and restored his health, his fortune and his family.

The story was probably used by religious leaders to teach how the power of God overcomes and destroys the power of the Devil, and that devotion to God can be helpful in times of need. The legend continued as an oral history until it was written in Hebrew by a wise man. The writer modified the story to accommodate his religious agenda by adding a philosophical discussion between Job and three friends, and between Job and God. Later, a fourth friend, "Elihu," was added and his sermon was introduced to the book. The purpose of the discussion was to point out that reasons for great suffering may never be made clear, nor is there any guarantee that living a virtuous or innocent life will allay any misfortune.

The legendary Job, however, was not a Jew, and the author of the Hebrew book did not attempt to make him one. Louis Ginzberg commented on this after reviewing all of the Hebrew writings, and said that the old writers considered him a contemporary of the biblical patriarchs, but not one of them. But later Hebrew writers would not let such a pious man not be a Jew, so he was made one.[1]

The Book of Job was written before the end of the second century B.C.E., before the other two known books about Job were made; 'Tragum of Job' and the 'Testament of Job.' But the book did not stop the continuation of the oral tradition spreading throughout Mesopotamia and at the time of Prophet Mohammed it was very much alive and different from the Hebrew book. These differences are reflected in the Qur'anic version of the story, and It may be that the oral tradition of Job stayed alive in Arabia because Job or *'Ayyūb'* was an Arab. Job raised camels, something the Jews have never done but something Arabs have always done. The names of his friends and their tribes sounded Arabic. Other scholars thought Job was an Edomite, from an Arab nation living in the Jordanian desert and famous for their wisdom. Sir J.W. Dawson in 'The Expositor' thinks that the language of the book of Job and its theology can be explained if we suppose that it is part of southern Arabian Minean literature. Unfortunately, the only part of the Arabic story that had not been corrupted is the end which was protected by the Qur'an, but the beginning was modified by *Wahb bin Munabbih*, and Job's discussion with his three friends was added to it from the Hebrew book after some modifications; but Elihu's sermon was rewritten completely by Wahb.

---

[1]- L.O.J. footnotes, Job 382.

# The Story of Job/ *Ayyūb*

Job was a man whom God put through severe tests, but his faith in the Lord did not waver. Job was a wealthy man of property, owning five hundred acres of land, livestock, including camels, cows, sheep, donkeys and horses and five hundred slaves with their wives and children. Job was blessed with a number of children and was a pious man, having pity on the poor, widows and orphans, and he was a generous host and helpful to those outside his city.

At the pinnacle of Job's success, God chose to take everything away, his livestock, land, slaves, and his own children. Further, his skin became covered with pus-filled sores, and he was rejected by his townspeople and banished to the town dump. His friends had always thought of Job as a pious man, but were convinced that he must have committed a grievous sin for God to put him through such torture.

In spite of all Job's travails, he never lost faith in God, and believed that his previous luxuries in life were gifts from the Lord, which could be taken away at any time. His wife was the only person who still believed in his pious heart and stood by him, bringing him food and water and selling her long braided hair[1] when she had nothing else to sell. Eventually she had to resort to asking for charity.

The Devil was hoping that Job's adversity would cause him to renounce his faith, and when it appeared that this was not going to happen, he thought the best way to achieve his goal was to influence Job through his wife. The Devil presented himself to Job's wife as a man and greeted her as she was asking for charity. He said, "Woman, where is your husband?" and she answered, "Rubbing his sores and the worms that crawl on his skin." The Devil reminded her of the luxury she once enjoyed and the prestigious life she once led. She cried loudly when she remembered how content she and Job had

---

[1]- In "Testament of Job," Sitis, Job's wife, sold her hair to the disguised Satan for threeloaves of bread. O.T.P. I:848.

been in their youth before their lives had become so utterly miserable. The Devil then brought her a lamb and said, "Ask Job to sacrifice this lamb for me, and he will be cured." She went to her husband, pleading, "Job, how long will Your Lord torture you, when will He show mercy? You have lost your possessions, your children, your friends, your clothes have become rags, your healthy body is full of sores and worms. Why do you not sacrifice this lamb and end this misery?"

Job scolded her, saying, "The enemy of God has been insinuating his evil ways on you and attempting to mislead you. And woe to you if you respond to him! What you long for–our wealth, our children and our health–who but God gave us these things, and who but God can take them away? For how many years did we have a happy and contented life?"

"For eighty years,"she answered

"And how long were we tested?" he wondered.

"For seven years," said his wife.

"So is it not fair that we endure the hardship for as long as the good period lasted?" queried Job, and he continued, "I swear to God, if He heals my affliction I will give you one hundred lashes for asking me to sacrifice to other than God. After what you have asked, I will not touch the food or drink that you bring to me. Get out of my sight!"[1]

After Job's outburst he realized that he had lost the only person who still had pity and passion for him, and the only person providing him with any sustenance. Job turned his heart to God, saying, *"Adversity has truly affected me and tortured me."* 38:41 God commanded him to *"Stamp your foot,"*38:42 and when he did, spring water burst forth and he was told to wash and drink from it. In doing so, his thirst was quenched and his sores were healed. He was healthier than he had ever been, and he stepped out of the spring and sat down on a hill in contemplation.

Job's wife left as she had been told to do, and vowed not to return. But when she thought of him, without anyone to provide him food or water, she realized she could not leave him to die of

---

[1]- Rep. by *Al-Hasan & Wahb*; pub. by Taf-Tab 21:83-84.

starvation. She went back to where she had last seen Job, living in the midst of garbage but could not locate him.  She began to weep and went searching for her husband.  Job saw her and asked, "Woman, what are you looking for?"

"I am looking for that unfortunate man who resides in the garbage dump" she responded. "What has happened to him?"

"Why are you looking for this man?" Job asked

"He is my husband."

"Would you know him if you saw him?" he asked

"Of course I would know my own husband.  He would look just like you if he was not sick."

"I am Job, you asked me to sacrifice to the Devil but I obeyed God and disobeyed the Devil, and God returned to me what I had lost." And his wife hugged him.  God sent him a rain made from golden locusts, and Job collected the gold.  God asked, "Have I not given you enough?"  Job answered that he had, but "who will turn away Your sustenance?"  After his recovery Job wanted to honor his vow and whip his wife one hundred lashes but with God's mercy he was told to gather one hundred twigs and strike his wife but once.  This allowed him to keep his vow and not hurt his wife.  God said, *"We found him to be a patient and attentive servant who is to be favored."*38:44  God returned to him his wealth, his livestock, and multiplied them, and gave him more children than what he had before.[1]

This ends the story of Job.  Only the end of the story is mentioned in the Qu'ran. The beginning of the story came from the Islamic story tellers later on. In their attempt to bring the whole story to their audience, they redact the beginning from the oral tradition, modified by their knowledge of the Hebrew book.

### How Job's Travails Started

The story began, as told by *Wahb bin Munabbih*, when the devil "Satan" realized how much praise God bestowed upon Job.*  Job 1:8

---

[1]- Ibid; This part of Job's story came from Qur'an, and from pre-Islamic and Islamic legends.

He was jealous and ascended to Heaven where he told God, "My God, I have thought about your servant Job. He is just a servant and he praises You, but in no way have You tested him. I guarantee that if You were to fill his life with strife and affliction, he will reject and
<sub>Job 1:9</sub> forget You." God gave Satan permission to do just that.*

With this introduction, Wahb had to explain how the Devil could, after his eviction from Heaven with Adam, have the ability to return and speak with God. Wahb explained it by saying, "Satan was not prohibited from any place in Heaven, and that is how he reached Adam when he caused his banishment. Satan continued to enter Heaven until Jesus had risen into Heaven, and it was then he was prohibited from the four upper levels but could still use the lower three. When God sent the Prophet Muhammad with his message, Satan was then denied all access to any of the seven Heavens."

And *Wahb* continued the story saying that when God granted Satan's request to antagonize Job, he came to earth, gathered the most powerful demons and asked them, "What kind of power and knowledge do you possess? I have been given authorization over Job's possessions and want them to vanish." One of the demons spoke and said, "I have the power to change myself into a tornado of fire. and can incinerate all that I pass through." Satan said, "Go after the camels and their herdsmen."

As the camels grazed in their pasture, a tornado of fire burst forth from the ground and, spurred on by hot winds, destoyed every camel and its keeper. Satan went to Job as a herdsman and found him standing in prayer. Satan said, "Do you know what your Lord, whom you have chosen to worship, has done to the camels and their keepers?"

"All the livestock belong to Him and they are only on loan to me" answered Job. "If He wants to take them away, that is His privilege. He can make me and all I possess disappear." Satan said, "Your Lord sent a fire which incinerated every-
<sub>Job 1:17</sub> thing in the pasture.* People are looking at your charred camels in wonder. Some think that if your God was able to, He would protect His servant. Others think He destroyed your herd and the loss will sadden your friends and make glad your enemies."

Job said, "Praise God who gave me everything and who can take everything from me. Naked I came from my mother's womb,

naked I will go to my grave and naked I will be resurrected before the
Lord. You should not be overjoyed with what you have borrowed,
nor be worried when He takes back what He has lent.* If He sees   Job 1:21
great potential in His servants, He will gather their souls with those
of the martyrs. Should He find wickedness He will delay their time
and clear them from torment as chaff is separated from the wheat."

Satan was humiliated and returned to his people and asked for
their help, as he had not dulled Job's heart. A powerful demon
announced that his resounding scream could kill anyone who hears it,
and Satan told him to inflict this scream upon a herd of sheep and its
shepherd.* When the demon did as instructed and delivered his   Job 1:16
terrible yell, all the sheep with the shepherd immediately died.

Satan went to Job as a shepherd and again found him standing
in prayer. He reiterated his plight but, once again, Job was not moved
to renounce his Lord, and again rebuked Satan's claims. The Devil
met with his people and once more asked for help as he could not
weaken Job's heart. Another demon told of his ability to transform
himself into a very hot and dry wind that parches everything it
touches. He wreaked havoc on the farmlands in the form of this hot
wind and destroyed everything in his wake. Satan went to Job as a
farmer and told him of the farm's devastation, but still Job's belief in
his Lord was strong. When Satan realized that Job lost all his
possessions but still praised God and accepted his fate with no ill
will, he became very upset and went to his customary place in Heaven
and said, "My Lord, Job believes that any material possessions he has
in this life have come from You. Would You give me control over
his children, because to lose his children, or see them suffer or in
torment, is a dreadful fate that no man's heart would endure."

God granted Satan permission, and he went directly to the
palace where Job's family resided. He shook the building until the
walls collapsed around the inhabitants who were mutilated by falling
stones and wood.* After turning the palace upside down, Satan went   Job 1:19
side down, Satan went to Job in the guise of the children's teacher,
his head covered in blood, and told Job of the catastrophe. He
described in gruesome detail how the children were bludgeoned by
the falling beams and rocks, their brains smashed and seeping from
their eye sockets and blood oozing from their nostrils and mouths.
He exclaimed to Job, "If you had seen how their stomachs were

ripped open, their insides spilling everywhere, if you saw this your heart would have broken from sorrow."

He continued with these grisly details until Job became emotional and began to cry. The Devil thought that Job had finally lost faith, so he went immediately to Heaven to report this to God. But Job quickly repented and asked for forgiveness, and his guardian angels took his repentance to God and reached Him before Satan. And once again the Devil was humiliated.

He now said to God, "My God, Job's loss of his estates and children were not difficult for him as he knew You could replace them, but if You allow me to test him through his own body, I guarantee he will deny You and all You represent." God again gave Satan permission to test Job, but warned, "You have permission to harm his body but you cannot touch his mind, his heart nor his tongue."* God allowed this to happen and make Job a symbol to all worshipers who must suffer through difficult times.

Job 2:4-6

Satan rapidly descended and found Job bowing to God in prayer. He came to him from underneath where he knelt and blew into his nostril. Job felt as if he was on fire, and on his skin appeared wart like sores which itched him terribly.* He scratched himself until he lost his nails, then used his rough clothing which quickly deteriorated. Job then scratched himself with stones and pieces of clay until the sore became ulcerated and began to ooze pus. People of his village removed him from their midst and put him under a small roof for shelter in the dump where he was rejected by everyone but his wife.[1]

Job 2:7

## Job and His Four Friends

This is not a part of the original Mesopotamian oral story, but was added to it by the writer of the Hebrew book. It stayed out of the Arabic Islamic story until *Wahb bin Munabbih* introduced it into the original story. This part describes a visit to Job by three of his friends during his sickness: Eliphaz the Temanite, Bildad the Shuhite and Zophar the Naamathite. They had with them a young man called

---

[1]- Ibid; This part of the story came from pre-Islamic legends about the demons and jinn, pri-Islamic and Islamic legends about Job, and from the Book of Job.

Elihu Rebukes. They had a philosophical discussion about why God tests his servants, and *Wahb* translated these talks into Arabic for the first time, and it is still the only Islamic source for these discussions. But *Wahb* also edited the talks so they would not antagonize Islamic teachings. *Wahb's* work was later adapted by Qur'an interpreters. This translation is not word for word, but rather it is a "whole idea to whole idea" translation. But this partial edition of the talks made the sentences contradict each other, and these can often be confusing. To separate the actual translation from the *Wahb* edition I put the translation in *Italics,* with the referral from "The Book of Job" after it.

**Job began the discussion,** *"My Lord, why did You create me? If You did not want me prosperous, why did You bring me into the world? I wish I had been aborted or died in my mother's womb before she knew me, and before I knew the world.* 3:11

What kind of sins have I committed which none before me has committed? What evil deeds have I committed to turn your generosity against me? Why did You not end my life and have me join my ancestors?

*Death would be better for me as with all the kings who thought they would live forever, protected by their swords and armies. Those kings now lie in their graves, along with mighty persons who collected and hoarded gold and treasures, built great cities and forts which existed hundreds of years, only to end as ruins inhabited by beasts and demons."* 3:13-15

**Eliphaz said,** *"Job, we are not able to make you understand our point of view, and when we speakto you you do not accept what we have to say, but it is difficult to say nothing with the affliction you are burdened with. We have seen many of your good deeds and believe you will be rewarded someday."* 4:1-4 Man gathers what he plants and will be honored for his good works.

God's Majesty can neither be comprehended nor His generosities be counted. *He brings rain from the sky to begin new life, raises the humble and strengthens the weak. The wisdom of the sage is nothing compared to His wisdom,* 5:10, 11, 13 and the knowledge of wise people is nothing compared to His knowledge.

*Whoever asks for help from the Almighty God and depends upon Him will be satisfied. God both breaks and heals."* 5:17-18

**Job responded**, "*I hang my head in shame and bite my tongue so not to speak.* 6:3  I know His punishment erased the glow off my face, and His might took away my strength, but I am His servant and whatever He wills my sentence to be I must accept.

*If my bones were made of iron, my body copper and my heart of stone still I could not tolerate what has happened to me.* 6:11-12  but He tested me and He will be my salvation.

You came to me hostile and angry before hearing any ominous talk, and crying, before anything evil had befallen you. *What if I asked you to give charity on my behalf, so God might save me, what if I asked you to sacrifice an animal on my behalf so God might accept it and be pleased with me?* 6:22-23

*When I am awake, I wish I were asleep and able to rest, but when I sleep I feel as if I am giving away my soul.* 7:4 & 13, 14  *My fingers are lost, I use both hands to hold the food and they reach my mouth only with severe effort. My palate has fallen off, my head is decayed with nothing left between my ears. You can see from one ear through to the other. My brain is dripping from my mouth, my hair fell out as if it was burned away by fire, my eyes have dropped on my cheeks, my tongue has swelled and I choke with everything I eat. My lips are bruised, the upper lip covers my nose and the lower lip covers my chin, my guts have been torn and the food I eat is left undigested.* 19:20-22 & 30:17-30  *My legs have lost their power and they feel like two sheep skins filled with water, and they cannot hold me.* 7:5

I have lost all my money and I beg for help. *People whom I used to feed are now feeding me, but they never let me forget their charity and do their best to disgrace me.* 30:1  My sons and daughters have been killed and not one is left to help me endure this torment, but the real agony is not in this life, because there will come a time to rest in peace. Blessed be those who will have the ultimate rest in never-ending life, and happy are those will be happy there and miserable are those who will be miserable there."

**Bildad said**, "*How can you say that with your own tongue? Do you say that He the Just can be unjust, or that the Mighty can become weak?* 8:2-3  *Cry for your sins and beg Your Lord to have mercy on you and forgive your mistakes. If you are innocent, He credits your suffering in the hereafter.* 8:4-6

If your heart has become hard, what we say will not help you nor affect you. *Papyrus does not grow in the wilderness, and reeds do not flourish where there is no water.* 8:11 *And those who depend on the weak cannot expect to be protected.* 8:14

Those who denied justice cannot be expected to be treated justly."

**Job said**, *"What you say is the truth. Man cannot fight with his Lord and I cannot complain even if I had the power to do so.* 9:2-3 *He is the one who created the sky and He alone positioned it and He alone can destroy it.* 9:8 *He is the one who created the earth and had the mountains rise from the plains and He is the one who can shake the mountains from their foundations and turn them upside down.* 9:5-6

What can I say to Him who created the Mighty Throne with one word and put all creation–the heavens and earth–within it? He spoke to the oceans and they understood and obeyed His commands. He understands whales, birds and every creature. He speaks to the dead and His words revive them, He talks to stones and they understand and obey His commands."

**Eliphaz said**, "Your words are direful Job, and they give me a feeling of foreboding when you claimed your suffering was not caused by your sin. With your words and your attitude you have put yourself in a precarious position.

*Your sins are many and your accounts* [of good deeds] *are small. You embezzled monies from the legitimate owners, dressed yourself when others went with nothing to wear, and enjoyed your food while some went hungry. You locked your door from the poor and kept your food and help from the needy.* 22:5-9

You hid your wrongdoings from everyone while exposing only what you wanted the world to see. And you believed that God would only have you account for your seen deeds. But how would He, who is cognizant of what is hidden beneath the earth and covered by the shroud of darkness, not know what you have concealed?"

**Job replied**, *"Whatever I say will be of no benefit, and my silence does not grant me an excuse.* 16:6 My deceit has fallen upon me, and I have displeased my Lord with my sin, and my enemies now gloat over my grief, and in doing so I have left myself open for criticism. *God, You forced me down a path of trials and tribulation, and I have become a target for temptation.* 7:20 You sent me one affliction after the other with no respite.

*Have I not opened my home to outsiders and been a supporter of the poor and a guardian to widows and orphans? For every stranger I saw, my home was his home and for every poor man I was his family. For every orphan I saw I became another father for him, and at all times I was the humble servant.* 29:12-16 & 31:16-22

I did not speak of my good deeds because the credit goes to my Lord and not to me. If I have done wrong, my penalty is in His hands; the disaster which has befallen me could not be tolerated by a mountain. How can I be expected to endure?"

**Eliphaz said**, "Do you argue with God about His decisions, do you wish to dispute your sinful ways, or be declared innocent though you are not? God created heavens and earth in truth and justice, and sensed what He created. Do you think He does not know what secrets you have kept? He knows your deeds and has punished you for that. God positioned the angels around His Throne and everywhere in His Heavens. *God was veiled in light so His servants were unable to see or reach Him.* 22:12-14 The most powerful are very humble before Him, yet you wish to dispute Him though you cannot see or even hear Him.

*In you we recognize His justice; whoever wishes to deceive God will be brought down and the humble will be raised.*" 22:15-20

**Job responded**, "If He finishes my life, none will argue about His decisions, nothing but His mercy reverses His anger. Nothing helps His servants save begging for mercy. *My Lord, face me with Your mercy and let me know what is my sin and why You turned Your generous face away from me.* 10:2 *Why are You treating me as if I was Your enemy when You used to honor me?* 13:24

Nothing escapes Your notice; You know how many raindrops fall, how many leaves are on the trees and how many grains of sand lay on the earth. My skin is like a rotting dress falling from my body. Grant me relief and escape from my misery with Your power which resurrects the dead.

*Do not allow me to die without enlightening me as to my transgressions.* 7:20

*Do not spoil Your own hands' work, even if You have no need for me.* 10:3

In Your decisions there is nothing unjust, and in Your wrath there is nothing done in haste. Only the weak fall to injustice, and the insecure fall in haste.

*Do not mention my sins and mistakes, but rather think how You created me from mud into a lump of tissue; then you made my bones, covered them with flesh and skin, strengthened them with tendons and made arteries to support my body. You raised me as a child and gave me sustenance as an adult.* 10:6, 8, 9, 12

You kept Your promise and executed Your commands. *If I sinned, point it out to me and if I do not please you, continue to torture me. You are aware of my deeds, but if I ask for forgiveness You do not forgive me. When I do good deeds, I do not boast of those good deeds, but when I fall You do not help me up.* 10:14-15 Though You know my weaknesses and hear my supplication.

*Why did You create me? Why let me come from my mother's womb? it would have been better had I never been born.* 10:18-19 Neither my world nor my body can withstand Your wrath and Your torture. Deliver me from this anguish and let me be healthy before I end in the confines of the grave, under the darkness of the earth and the grief of death."  10:21-22

**Zophar said**, "*No one can prevent you from speaking and maintaining your innocence. But do you think that your claims of being blameless will benefit you, knowing that God is omnipotent?* 11:1-6

You say you are sure that God will forgive you, but there is much you are unsure of. *Do you know how high is the sky, how thick is the air, how wide is the earth and how deep is the sea? And do you have any way to measure those things? As you are aware, God created all of those things and knows all the answers.* 11:7-9

*And if you had stopped this kind of talk and asked for forgiveness He may have sent you His mercy.* 11:13 *But you did not regret your sins and prayed only in times of need while continuing to sin like water, which can not keep itself from flowing into a pond.* 11:16

God answers the prayers of those who deny their desires and become supplicants before Him and grants those deserving His mercy, *But rejects the prayers of the insincere and the wrongdoer.* 11:20

**Job said**, *"You are a proud people.* 12:2 *Men used to honor me and none would deny me my rights. I used to subdue those who seek to subdue me today.* 12:4

You (Zophar) question me about the unseen knowledge of God which I am not conscious of. Man does not advise his brother when he is receiving torment but he cries with him. If you are serious about your questions, I will tell you I do not have the answers to your queries.

*Ask the birds in the sky and see if they have any answers, ask the beasts of the earth, ask the predators of the wild. Ask the whales of the ocean and perhaps they can describe those things you question. You know God created the earth in His wisdom and arranged it with His kindness.* 12:7-9

*Humans know only what their ears hear, what their mouths taste, what their noses smell and what their eyes see but the knowledge you seek is known only by God who is the Creator. To Him and Him alone belong such Wisdom, such Might, the Greatness and Kindness, the Majesty and the Power. If He has made any mistake, who is going to correct Him? If He misunderstands, who will ask for a clarification? If He looks at the oceans and deems it necessary, they will become dry from fear or swallow the land with His permission.* 12:7-15

Kings are humbled at His reign and men of knowledge surrender to His wisdom. *The false claimer loses all claims of power at His sovereignty.* 12:16

He remembers those who are forgotten and ignores the well-known. This is the limit of my knowledge. His creation is more mighty than my mind, and His might is greater than anything known to me."

**Bildad said,** *"The hypocrite is punished by what he has kept secret while the uncovered, cheating work which he depended on for reward will not help him. His name and memory will vanish from the earth and no one will mention him. He will have no property nor children to inherit. He leaves nothing to be remembered for and those who did know him will forget him.* 18:5-19 The poets will not mention him."

**Job answered,** *"If I am a dishonorable man my dishonesty will turn against me,* 19:4 but if I am an innocent man I have no support. No one will cry with me and my silence will not grant me an excuse.

My hope is gone as are my dreams. *My friends have rejected me, and when I summoned my slave he refused to obey.* 19:4-5 Disasters have fallen on me and you are rejecting me, which is the most difficult thing to bear. Have you not heard what has happened to me? Are you not impressed by my horrendous ailments which plague my body? If I was a slave arguing with my master I would have more hope that judgement would be in my favor, but My Lord is the Mighty One. He sits exalted in His Heavens while abandoning me here without a thought. He does not accept my excuse, nor allows me an audience so I may argue my cause. He hears me but I do not hear Him, He sees me but I cannot see Him, and if He appeared before me, my body will be destroyed, and my soul will desert me.

*If He takes away my awe and I am permitted to speak, then I will know why I am being tortured.* 9:34-35 & 13:21-22

**(Elihu)** a young man who had believed in Job said, "You, as the elders, have every right to speak, you have more experience than I and you see and understand what I do not. But you have omitted a crucial part of Job's dilemma, and he has favored you more than you admit. He has allowed you to question his rights to his very existence, and allowed you to invade his privacy, but have you questioned just who this man is that you have accused and put to shame? Are you unaware that Job is a prophet of God and God's favorite from the humans He has created? He chose him for His revelations and trusted him with His message. You have no real knowledge that Job is guilty of any wrongdoing, nor that God has deprived him of any honor, nor that he has, at any time, manipulated the truth. If the misery he is now in has made you think less of him, you should know that God tests His prophets, holy men, martyrs and other good men, and that the torment He wreaks is not a sign of His displeasure. Job is not to be disgraced, but honored. However, even if Job was not an upstanding man, you, as his friends, should not blame him nor take pleasure in his misery, but rather have pity on him, cry with him, offer him solace and ask God for mercy. If you do not know this, you have no wisdom."

Then he addressed Job, saying, "You used to avoid these kinds of arguments and humbled your heart by remembering the

Majesty of God and the certainty of death. When God's obedient servants remember His greatness and His awe-inspiring presence, their tongues become paralyzed, and their minds cannot concentrate, all because they cherish God and exalt Him, as well as fear Him. In everyday life their  good deeds bring them closer to God, and although they consider themselves sinners and neglectful, in reality they are innocent. They are never satisfied by only a few good deeds, and they deem no great deed an excess. They never point out their good  works to God and are always humble, submissive and willing to confess.

**Job said**, "God plants wisdom and pity in the heart of both young and old, and once it grows in their hearts God manifests it in their tongues. Wisdom is not exclusive to old age. If God made His servant wise in his youth, that does not reduce his sagacity." After that, Job was covered by a dense cloud, so thick his friends thought he had disappeared. And he heard God speaking.[1]

**God said**, "Here I am, close to you though I have never really been away. Present your argument and explain your innocence. Stand before Me with dignity and might, for only someone with strength can argue with me. *Someone who can put the reins in the mouth of a lion,* 38:3 Someone who can put the kid in the mouth of the phoenix, and the bridle in the mouth of the dragon?

*Who can measure one unit of light.* 38:19 Who can weigh one carat of wind, gather and contain sunshine and make yesterday tomorrow? You were led by your ego as you could not exist on your strength alone. You should realize where your ego was taking you. Did you think you could debate with Me using your own argument, or did you think you could surpass Me with your weakness? Or quarrel with Me over your mistakes?

*Where were you the day I created earth from its foundation? Do you know by which standard I measured My work? Were you*

---

[1]-This part of the story which includes the discussion between Job & his friends is a modi-fied  translation from the Book of Job by *Wahb bin Munabbih* who, as we see, ignored a few chapters: '13, 14, 15, 16, 17,' most probably because they are too far from Islamic theology, and he wanted to keep the audience's interest and not get them overwhelmed. Elihu's talk here  is different from his talk in the Hebrew book.

*with Me as I surveyed its boundaries?  Do you measure the angle of its curvature or do you know on what I did place it?*  38:4-6  *Does earth carry water at your command, or water cover the earth as a blanket by your wisdom?*  38:8

Where were you the day I raised the sky, with no supports to hold it from above, nor columns to support it from below? *Does your wisdom require that the stars should shine and turn in the night sky, or that night and day should differ?*  38:12
*Where were you the day I filled the oceans and made the rivers run? Is it your power which forces the waves to stop at the shore, or is it your power that opens the wombs  at their term?*  38:8-11

Where were you when I flooded the earth with water and raised the lofty mountains? Do you have enough strength to hold these mountains?  Do you know how many specks of dirt are contained in these mountains? Do you know where the rain came from? *Was it begotten by a father or delivered by a mother?*  38:28 Does your wisdom number the rain drops and distribute the sustenance?  *Does your power entice the clouds to sprinkle with rain?*  38:9

Do you know what makes the sound of thunder, or from where the lightning emanates? Do you see the depth of the ocean, or do you know what lies above the air? Do you keep the souls of the dead?

*Do you know where the storehouse is which has the snow and the hail?*  38:22
Do  you know where the day hides at night, or where the night hides during the day?  What constitutes the path of light, or what language the trees speak, where the wind is kept, and how is it kept locked in? Do you know who gave humans their minds, or shaped their senses? Angels submit to His reign and mighty people submit to His might, and His wisdom is distributed to both humans and animals.

*Who gave the lion his sustenance?*  38:39  *Who taught the birds to work for their food and gave them sympathy for their chicks?*  38:41 *Who released the wild animals from serving humans, and allowed them to abide in the wilderness, untamed and unafraid of kings?*  39:5-8

Is it by your wisdom these animals know to feed their cubs from their own stomachs and favor only them? Or does your wisdom allow the skyhawk to see prey in the far-off distance?

*Where were you when I created the behemoth? They live under the lotus plants at the end of the land.* 40:22 *Their teeth are like pine trees, their heads are as large as a mountain, and the tendons in their legs are like piles of iron.* 40:17 *Their skin is as hard as rock.* 41:24 *Their bones are like copper pillars.* 40:18 Did you fill their skin with flesh, or their skull with a brain? Did you share in their creation with your own hands? Are you strong enough to block their path and turn them back?[1]

*Where were you when I created the leviathan, whose sustenance comes from the sea but who lives in the sky? Its eyes are flames of fire.* 41:18 *Its nostrils blow smoke.* 41:20 *Its ears are like a rainbow with flames spinning from them like a tornado of dust, from its mouth spews forth burning rocks.* 41:14 *Its teeth resonate with the sound of thunder.* 41:19 *The reflection in its eyes is like flashes of lightning. Armies may pass by, while he is relaxed and has no worry of them. Their arrows will not pierce his body.* 41:13 *Falling boulders cause no harm, it counts iron as straw and copper as thread.* 41:27 It can fly through the air and destroy everything in its path, for he is the king of beasts. *Do you have the power to catch him in a snare, or put reins in its mouth?* 41:5-7

Do you know its age, how long it will live, what it will destroy and how would you endure its wrath, or would it obey your commands ?[2]

**Job said,** "I abused my misery, and wish the earth would open and swallow me for having displeased my Lord. I know everything has been created by You, in Your wisdom, and there is nothing You cannot do, nor is there anything that is hidden from You. Who will think they can conceal something from You when You know the temptation in their heart? My torture taught me what I did not know before. I am more afraid of You now than ever before. I used to hear of Your wrath, now I can see it . I said what I said

---

[1]- *Behemoth* is most often identified as a hippopotamus, but here, and to a lesser degree in Hebrew text, he is glorified to be a legend. Islamic scholars put it as is without any interpretation. The phrase 'they lives under the lotus plants' came from the Greek text and was not included in Taf-Tab, but was included in Ara-Tha.

[2]-*Leviathan* is a legendary animal, the dragon of the sea, which breaths fire. In Arabic text it was translated as '*At-Tannin,*' which means the dragon.

hoping to excuse myself and kept silent to have mercy on me–but it will not happen again. I kept my mouth closed and bit my tongue so as to keep silent in my attempt to be humble. My mistakes silenced me. Forgive me and I will not displease You again."

**God answered** Job, "My plan for you has been executed. I forgive you for what you have said and grant mercy upon you. Your family will be returned to you and your fortune will be doubled as a lesson to the people who suffer and  to console the people who endure."

# 6    Abraham / *Ibrāhīm*

*Abraham was so lenient, worried, concerned.*
                                      – Qur'an 11:75

## Introduction

Although there has been no written record ever discovered, such as an engraved stone or a clay tablet with the patriarch Abraham's name inscribed on it, stories of this legendary man proliferate throughout the area encompassing Mesopotamia, Babylon, Syria and Egypt.  Both the Muslim and Hebrew peoples venerated Abraham, and in their writings they have preserved his stories, proffering testimony about Abraham's existence in history.  The stories and legends of Abraham began in the first millennium B.C.E. as oral stories, among what I have termed 'Abrahamic nations,' multiple nations living in northern Arabia and Syria.  It is very possible that some of his teachings and stories were written after his death, but the oldest existing record is in the Book of Genesis. Biblical scholars tried many different ways to connect the story of Abraham and his descendants to the historical records of Mesopotamia, Anatolia, Media or any other country, but their attempt was unsuccessful, and as result, we have many different dates for the Abrahamic period, and the date which can be calculated from the Hebrew Bible chronicles, "2090-2083 B.C.E.", is very problematic.

In northern Arabia, Abraham became one of the pre-Islamic personalities whose picture was kept in the Ka'ba, before Prophet Muhammad took over Mecca and removed all vestiges of its former function as a pantheon.  In describing the picture's removal, *Ibn Hishām* explained that the picture showed the patriarch performing *'Istiqsam,'* a Ka'ba priestly duty in which the priest chooses one arrow from a bunch and reads the directive written on it as instruction from

God for those who seek direction in their lives. Arab historians tell us about people before Islam who rejected the paganism of the Arabs and followed *Hanif* faith which was said to be the faith of Abraham. All of the followers were monotheistic and believed in life after death, and some such as *Waraqa bin Nawfal* combined the Hanif faith with Christianity. Most simply proclaimed themselves as Hanifs as did *Zayd bin 'Amr bin Nafīl, 'Ubayd-Allah bin Jaḥsh, 'Uthmān bin al-Ḥuwayrith, Umayya bin Abiṣ- Ṣalṭ* and others. Arab historians also mention that the pre-Islamic Arabs had two rituals which originated with Abraham: circumcision and the glorification of the Ka'ba, which was built by Abraham and his son *Ismā'īl* (Ishmael). The Jews of Medina, who themselves glorified Abraham, rejected any oral story which did not parallel what was contained in their books and which attempted to make Abraham one of their own. This attitude extended to the time of Islam, but the Prophet Muhammad did not accept their tenets, as is clearly evidenced in the Qur'an: *"Abraham was not a Jew nor a Christian, but a Hanif, and surrendered himself to God."* 3:67 *"O People of the Book, why do you argue about Abraham, when both the Torah and the Gospel came after his time?"* 3:65

The stories of Abraham presented in this chapter are mainly those of an Arab Islamic nature. Some of these stories–with some modification–are shared with the Jews, while some are original and have no Hebrew parallel. As the years progressed, stories of Abraham were exchanged between Muslims and Jews, as they were both avid collectors of any lore pertaining to this revered man.

While Islamic literature abounds with references to Abraham, there is a dearth of information on his son *Ismā'īl*, though his birth, marriage, the building of the Ka'ba and the story of the sacrifice are well documented. He was a priest and the custodian of the Ka'ba, but little is known of his life in the priesthood. Many tribes in northern Arabia, who are famous for memorizing their genealogy, claim to be direct descendants of *Ismā'īl*. The historians who preserved their genealogy did not reach back to *Ismā'īl* in any ancestral record. Even when it came to the Prophet Muhammad and his tribe *"Quraysh,"* the genealogy goes back to the Patriarch *'Adnān*, a total of twenty-one ancestors. It has been reported that the Prophet said that any attempt to go beyond *'Adnān* was speculative, but this did not deter those who sought to extend his genealogy to reach *Ismā'īl* by adding seven and up to forty ancestors, using corrupted Syriac names.

Some critics raised questions about the *Ismā'īl*-Arab connection: Is the building of the Ka'ba by Abraham and *Ismā'īl* an Islamic story or pre-Islamic legend? And similarly, is the story of the sacrifice pertaining to *Ismā'īl*, Islamic or pre-Islamic? As to the first point of contention, the critics maintain that the Ka'ba is but one of many holy buildings in Arabia, housing idols or a stone, as the examples of the Ka'ba of Narjan and the Temple of *Dawmat ul-Jandal* attest to, so the glorification of the Ka'ba and its association with Abraham came about after the advent of Islam. But the fact remains that the poet *Zayd bin 'Amr bin Nafīl*, a pre-Islamic poet, mentions the connection with Abraham in his famous line:

**"I seek refuge with what Abraham sought**
**when he stood up and faced the Ka'ba."** Aghani 3:117.

A stone which sits beside the Ka'ba now and is known by the name of 'the step of Abraham,' or *Maqām Ibrāhīm* was known by that name befor Islam.  As to the story of the sacrifice, Luis Ginzberg, in his book 'The Legends of the Jews,' cites competition as the motive that inspired Muslims to concoct the sacrifice of *Ismā'īl* to glorify the Ka'ba in Mecca, which parallels the story of Isaac and the sacrifice at the Temple of Jerusalem. The Muslims, however, never used this story to glorify the Ka'ba. For them it was enough that it was built by Abraham the Patriarch and his son *Ismā'īl*, while others insisted its history was even more renown, having been built by Adam. We also find support in the Arabic Islamic belief in the pre-Islamic writings of the "Mandaeans," who believed that the Ka'ba was built by Abraham, and  is the house of Jupiter, the highest of the planets.[1]

Regarding *Isma'il* versus Isaac, it is doubtful that these two differing points of view could have been spontaneously conceived, had there been unanimous agreement about the name at the time of the Prophet or before.  Islam inherited this long-standing and ongoing controversy between the biblical supporters and the supporters of the

---

[1]-From Sidra rabba.

Arab view. *Ibn 'Abbās* reported that he saw the horns of sacrificed rams hanging in the Ka'ba where they remained until they were burned in the time of *Ibn az-Zubayr*. Though the horns may not have been the horns of the sacrifice story, they do give credence to the fact that this story is of pre-Islamic origin.

# The Story of Abraham

King *Nimrod* of Babylon was one of the most powerful kings in the history of the world, and one of the few kings who conquered and then reigned over all of civilization. He proclaimed himself a god, and was worshiped by his subjects whose lives he controlled. But this self-appointed divinity was destined to face God's appointed prophet in the person of Abraham, the Friend of God.[1]

Before the birth of Abraham, Nimrod had a dream in which he saw a star so bright it outshone the sun and the moon. This dream concerned him, and he summoned the magicians and priests from the temples and asked for an interpretation. They said, "A man will be born this year and he will be the cause of the demise of you and your family, as well as the end of your reign." To prevent this disaster, Nimrod sent all the men away from the city to his camp and barred all women from entering the camp. After some time Nimrod found he needed to conduct some business in the city, but he could not leave the camp. He sent *Āzar* (Terah), a trustworthy man, to handle the business, which he did. *Āzar* also decided to visit his wife, and once he saw her he could not stop himself and slept with her. Thus, Abraham was conceived.[2]

When *Āzar*'s wife became pregnant with Abraham, the temple priest informed Nimrod, "The mother of the child we told you about became pregnant tonight." Nimrod ordered that every child born that year will be killed.[3] When Abraham's mother went into labor she

---

[1]-Abraham in Chr.20:7 was described as God's friend. In the Qur'an, 4:125, he is 'Khalil Allah' with the same meaning. This title is exclusively applied to Abraham.

[2]- From Taf-Bagh & Taf-Khaz 6:76; rep. by *As-Siddi & Ibn Ishaq*.

[3]- Rep. by *Ibn Abbas*. There are many different stories about the time Abraham stayed hidden in the cave, from a few weeks to seven or thirteen or seventeen years. I adopted here the version of *Ibn Ishaq*, which was published by Taf-Tab and Taf-Bagh 6:76. In <u>Hebrew literature</u> the same disagreement exists. The

went to a nearby cave to deliver Abraham, She wrapped him in a
cloth, closed the entrance to the cave, and went back to the city. She
checked on him daily and found him alive, sucking his thumb. She
looked at his fingers and found that one finger gave water, another
milk, the third finger gave honey, the fourth date syrup, and from the
fifth came butter. *Āzar* questioned her about her pregnancy, and she
told him she had given birth, but the baby died.

  When Abraham was born, Nimrod felt that his throne was
weakened, and he heard a voice saying, "To those that  will not
believe in Abraham, God will cause  much suffering." Nimrod asked
*Āzar* if he had heard the voice and *Āzar* replied that he had. Nimrod
asked *Āzar*, "Who is this Abraham?" and *Āzar* replied, "I do not
know." Nimrod had another dream wherein he saw a man rise from
*Āzar*'s chest. A light was extending between heaven and earth, and
he heard a voice saying, *"The truth has come and a falsehood has
vanished,"* 17:81 and he saw his idols falling from their stands. He
awoke and was extremely frightened.

### Abraham Recognizes his Lord

  Abraham grew up in the cave unbeknown by his father. When
he became a young man he asked his mother, "Who is my lord?" and
she answered, "I am." He asked, "Who is your lord?" and she
replied, "Your father." He asked, "Who is my father's lord?" and was
told, "King Nimrod." When he questioned who Nimrod's lord was,
he was told to be quiet. At last Abraham's  mother told *Āzar* that he
had a son, and they went to the cave to see him. Abraham asked *Āzar*
who King Nimrod's lord was, and was struck in the face by *Āzar* and
again told not to ask such questions. Abraham asked his parents to
take him out of  the cave and they agreed,  so for the first time
Abraham saw camels, horses and sheep. He asked his father what
these creatures were, and did they not have a lord that had created
them?[1] He then looked up at Jupiter, rising above the horizon, and

---

time of hiding  varies from three years to thirteen years in Pirke de Rabbi Eliezer,
from L.O.J.  I, 189 and endnote Abraham 16.
  [1]- From Taf-Bagh & Taf-Khaz 6:76. Islamic scholars maintained that
Abraham recognized His Lord at an age old enough to be able to debate with his
people about his belief. In the Hebrew literature, Abraham recognized His Lord

said, "This is my lord." But when it had set and disappeared from view, he exclaimed, "I do not respect the one who appears, then disappears." When he saw the moon, he said, "This is my lord," but was disappointed once again when the moon faded from sight. Abraham said, "If my lord had not guided me, I should be of the erring people." The sun appeared and he was sure that this must be his lord. But once again the sun rose and set and he said, "O my people, I am rejecting what you are worshiping. I have turned my face to Him who originated both heaven and earth—who has no companion."6:76-79

## Abraham Argues with his Father and his People

Āzar was in the business of making idols, and he brought his son into the trade. Abraham was to sell the idols his father made, but instead of praising his merchandise he used to shout, "Who would like to buy an idol which neither helps nor harms?" and of course nobody would buy from him. At the end of the day he took the idols to the river and sunk their heads in, saying, "Drink from this river," making fun of the idols and the people who worshiped them.

His people heard of this and argued with him. He said, "Do you doubt me respecting God, who has guided me ?"6:80 and they replied, "Be careful of what you are doing; these idols might make you sick or insane." Abraham announced that he had no fear of the idols. He then told his father, "What are these idols which you are devoted to and worship?"21:52 His father explained that they were worshiped by their ancestors and he was following a tradition. Abraham admonished his father, "You and your ancestors are wrong and in great error."21:54 "Your Lord is the Creator of heavens and earth."21:56

---

after he left the hiding place, in early childhood. There are many different versions of this legend in the Apocalypse of Abraham; Bemadber Rabbah; 'Aseret ha-Dibrot; Ma'aseh Abraham; Yashar. But some Hebrew literature maintains that it occurred at the age of 48. Maimondes,Yad,'Abodoh Zorah. From L.O.J. I, 189-193 and endnote Abraham 16.

### The First Hymn

After this argument, Abraham said, praising God, "*The Lord of the universe created me, He guides me and is the one who feeds me and gives me something to drink. Whenever I fall ill He heals me, He is the One who will cause me to die, then bring me back to life again. The One Who I expect will forgive me my mistakes on the Day for Repayment. My Lord, bestow discretion on me and acquaint me with honorable men. Grant me a truthful reputation among later men. Grant me inheritance in the Garden of Bliss. Forgive my father even though he may be considered lost. Do not disgrace me on the day they are raised up again, the day when neither wealth nor children will benefit anyone exept for someone who comes to God with a sound heart.*"26: 77-89

### Abraham Praying for his Father

*Āzar* told Abraham that unless he stopped preaching he would cast him out, then he asked him to leave. Abraham answered by saying, "*Peace be upon you, I'll seek forgiveness for you from my Lord, He has been so Gracious toward me.*"19:47 Abraham did plead for forgiveness on his father's behalf, but when it became clear to him that his father was God's enemy, he declared his innocence of him. Q 9:114

### Abraham and the Idols

Abraham's people held an annual feast. The day began by their visiting the idols and offering them food. They then enjoyed their feast, ending the day by returning to the idols, first bowing to them and then eating the food they had left. The night before the feast, Abraham was asked to accompany them, but he looked at the stars and said, "*I am sick.* "37:89 He went to the idol house on the feast day and found it was a great hall full of idols, with the proffered food placed in front of each idol. Abraham looked at them and said: "Why do you not eat?" They did not answer and he continued, "Do you not know how to speak?" And he took an axe to the idols until they were smashed into small pieces. He left the grand idol, made of solid gold with eyes of rubies, and placed the axe in its hands. Abraham destroyed seventy-two idols, some made of gold, of silver, of lead, iron, wood or stone.

When the people returned to the great hall and found what had happened, they angrily questioned who had done this to their idols. Someone described Abraham as the perpetrator, and heard that he wanted to make a mockery of the idols. Abraham was brought in front of everyone and questioned. He said, "I *am sure the grand idol did this. Why do you not ask them*[1]?"[21:63] They thought about what he had said and understood how foolish it was to worship something without even the power of speech. But their common sense was silenced and they asked, "How do you expect us to ask them when you know they do not speak?" Abraham reasoned with them saying, "How can you worship away from God when you do not benefit from their worship, and if you neglect them, no harm will come to you?" This response silenced them until they found themselves able to pronounce sentence on Abraham. He was to be burned to death.[2]

## The Burning Fire

After Abraham was securely incarcerated, people were encouraged to bring firewood. If they had recovered from a sickness or reached a goal, this would be a vow of good faith. They collected the wood for forty days. The fire was set and the resultant smoke darkened the city. The sound from the crackling fire was heard for miles, and birds, attempting to fly above it, were burned to death. But no one knew how to get close enough to throw Abraham on the fire. *Iblis* appeared and introduced the catapult, which Abraham was strapped to. Heavens and earth, the angels, all the creatures except the humans and jinn cried aloud, "Lord of Abraham, this is your friend, thrown in the fire, the only one to worship You, give us permission to save him!" God said, "He is My friend and I have no other; I am his Lord and he has no other. If he asks any one of you

---

[1]- This was one of the three times in his life that Abraham lied, the first being his exclamation ,"I *am sick*," and the third when he claimed Sarah was his sister. Hadith pub. by *Al-Bukhari* # 3385 and *Imam Ahmad*.

[2]- Rep. *by Mujahid , Qutada, As-Siddi & Ibn Ishaq*; pub. by Ara-Tha; Taf-Bagh & Taf-Khaz 21:57-67. In Hebrew literature the imprisonment of Abraham was mentioned in the Talmud and Pirke de Rabbi Eliezer 25.

for help, you may help him." The Angel of water told Abraham that, if asked, he could extinguish the fire. The Angel of wind told him he could blow out the fire . Abraham answered, "I do not need you; God is sufficient for me and the most excellent of protectors." Abraham was then thrown onto the fire. Gabriel received him and said, "Do you have any requests, Abraham?"

"Not from you," Abraham replied.

"Why do you not ask Your Lord?"

"It satisfies me to know that He is aware of my plight."

All the animals tried to extinguish the fire except the lizard which was blowing into the flames. God said, "O *fire, be a comfort and peace to Abraham.*"21:69 The fire lost its power to burn, and all the fires in the world on that day were extinguished. The angels put him down on earth, and Gabriel presented him with a silk garment from Paradise. As he helped him dress, Gabriel told him what God had said: "Did you not know that fire will not harm those I love?" And a spring from the earth burst beside him where roses and narcissus bloom.

Nimrod was able to see Abraham from his high tower, sitting in a garden, in the company of angels, surrounded by a fire. He called to him saying, "Abraham, He is a Mighty Lord Who is able to protect you from this fire. Are you not afraid that if you walk through it will harm you?" "No," said Abraham, and Nimrod encouraged him to walk through the fire. When Abraham did walk safely through the fire Nimrod said, "I will sacrifice four thousand cows to your Lord." Abraham said, "He will not accept your sacrifice unless you leave your religion and accept mine." Nimrod said he could not do that, but would still make the sacrifice, and following that Nimrod no longer troubled Abraham.[2]

---

[1]- Rep. by *Ibn Ishaq*. In Hebrew literature the burning mentioned in Ma'seh Abraham which was copied from the Qur'an including a translation of the verse 29:59 and the verse 6:103. The story is also mentioned in Pesahim 118a; Berashit Rabbah 44.13; Tanhuma B II, 100, from L.O.J. I, 198-201 and endnote Abraham 32, 33 & 34.

[2]- Rep. by *Ibn Ishaq*; Ibn *'Abbas; Ka'b; Ad-Dahhak; As-Siddi; Qutada* and others. Pub. by Taf-Tab, Taf-Bagh & Taf-Khaz 21:68; Tar-Kath I:154

## The Debate

Later on, Abraham had a debate with Nimrod. Abraham was describing the power and the might of God, and Nimrod discussed his own might. Abraham said, *"My Lord brings life and takes it away."* Nimrod said, *"I do that too."* And to prove his point he brought two prisoners and ordered one to be killed and the other to be released. Abraham thought that this kind of argument would lead nowhere so he said, *"God raises the sun in the east, can you raise it from the west?"*2:258 When Nimrod heard this, he had no answer.

## Abraham Moving Away

When Abraham realized that his people would not accept his teaching, he said *"I am going away to meet my Lord, He will guide me,"* 37:99 and left his home town with his wife, Sarah, and his nephew, Lot, first going to Haran, then moving to Ar-Raha where Lot went to Jordan; while Abraham went to the Syrian desert (the Holy Land). Sometime during this period, Abraham and his wife went to Egypt. The Pharaoh of Egypt, *Sinān bin 'Alwān*, saw Sarah, a very pretty woman, and wanted her for himself. He asked Abraham, "What is this woman to you?" Abraham said, "She is my sister."[1] The Muslim scholars said he meant that she is his sister in belief. He said that because he was afraid the king would take her and kill him if he knew she was his wife. So the king took Sarah to his palace, but when he attempted to touch her, he found that his arm was paralyzed. That scared the pharaoh, and he demanded an explanation from Sarah. She said, "I am a married woman, and Abraham is my husband." He asked her to pray for him to return the strength back to his arm. Sarah did so, and she was released and given a female slave named Hagar.* After that, Abraham and his Gen 12:10-20 family went back to the Holy Land.

## Hagar and her Son in the Hot Desert

When they returned to the Syrian desert, Sarah gave Hagar to Abraham and said, "I did not bear you a child myself, but I hope Hagar can give you one." Hagar did become pregnant and delivered

---

[1]- This is one of Abraham's three lies, Sah-Bukh # 3385; Sah-Mus # 1609.

a boy, who Abraham called *Ismā ʻīl*. But Sarah became very jealous
of Hagar, and begged Abraham to send her away.  God revealed to
Abraham that he should take *Ismā ʻīl* and his mother  to the  Arabian
Gen 21:9-13  desert,  and Gabriel would show him the way.* Gabriel took them to
Mecca, which was  in the desert and where the shrine built by Adam
had once stood. The Amalik Tribe, the first inhabitants in the area,
lived in the surrounding mountains.

Abraham helped Hagar to build a hay hut, then left them and
proceeded to walk back toward Syria.  Hagar, realizing she had no
one, and was without food or
water, followed Abraham and beseeched him, saying, "To whom are
you leaving us?"

"To God," he answered.

"Did God ask you to do this?"

"Yes," answered Abraham.

"That is what I need to know."[1]

Hagar went back to her son.  Abraham walked a few steps,
turned and looked back.  There stood his son, and the mother of his
son. There was no shade, no shelter and no water.  He felt his heart
torn apart in sympathy for them.

### The Second Hymn
Abraham said, "My lord, Make this countryside safe and keep me and
my sons away from worshiping Idols. My Lord, they have led so many
men astray! Anyone who follows me belongs to me, just as anyone who
disobeys me will still find You are Forgiving Merciful.

Our Lord, I have settled my son in a dry valley unsuitable for
agriculture near Your sacred house. Our Lord, make the hearts of
Your people yearn towards them, and provide them with fruits that
they may be grateful.

Our Lord, You know Whatever we hide and whatever we
display; nothing on earth nor in the sky is hidden from God, praise be

---

[1]- Pub by Taf-Khaz 2:125; Anwar at-Tanzil 2:125; Tar-Mak 5456.

to God Who has bestowed Ismā'īl and Isaac[1] on me in my old age.

My Lord is so Alert to anyone's appeal!

My Lord, Make me keep up prayer and have my offspring do so too.

Our Lord, accept my appeal.

Our lord, forgive me, both my parents and believers on the Day when the Reckoning will be set up." 14:35-41

## The Ordeal of Hagar

Abraham went back to the Syrian desert. Hagar soon used the few dates and water she had. They both became extremely thirsty, her breast milk stopped and *Ismā'īl* passed out. Hagar could not bear the sight of her son in his condition and said to herself, "I cannot stay and watch him die." She went to the *Safa* hill, climbed to its peak and prayed to her Lord for help. She went down and walked toward the *Marwa* hill. From this vantage point she could see her son and found he was still the way she had left him. She walked between the two hills seven times, which was the origin of the traditional walk during the pilgrimage.

After her seventh revolution, she heard a voice and followed it to her son where Gabriel appeared to her. He kicked the earth with his heel, and from that spot water burst forth.* Hagar was worried about losing the water and Gen 21:19 surrounded it with dirt to make a pond. She took a drink and immediately her breast dripped with milk, and she nursed *Ismā'īl*. Had Hagar not captured the water with dirt, it would have become running spring water, but as she did so, the water became the famous well of *Zamzam*, known to every Muslim who visits the blessed land of Mecca. The Angel told Hagar, "Do not worry, this water will not run out, your son will grow up here, his father will visit him from Syria and they will build a shrine. The shrine will be visited from all around the world, responding to the call of God. They will walk around the shrine, and the water will be enjoyed by its visitors." and Hagar felt good and praised God.

---

[1]- Mentioning Isaac here creates a discrepancy between the Qur'anic verse and the timing of the hymn. Most mufassirun time it later on after the birth of Isaac.

When two young men from the the the tribe of *Jirhum* came down from the hills looking for a lost camel, they were amazed to see birds coming to the valley. They were unaware that there was water in the valley, and followed the route of these birds until they reached the mount of *Abu Qubays*. From there they were able to see the water and the hut, and Hagar talked to them and told her story. They knew she did not lie, as no one had been able to find water before in that area. They went back to their families and told them about their discovery. The families soon joined Hagar and together made a new settlement. *Ismā'īl* played with their children, and Hagar was happy to have them as neighbors.[1]

### Abraham promised by God to have another son "Isaac" and a grandson "Jacob"

This promise happened when Abraham received a visit from the angels, on their way to destroy 'the people of Lot.' This was a surprise announcement because Abraham's wife was an old lady in her menopause. But that was what happened, and Sarah gave Abraham his second son, Isaac.[2]

### The Sacrifice

Abraham visited Hagar and *Ismā'īl* once a month, riding on the '*Burāq*', an animal smaller than a horse but larger than a donkey, with a human face and with an enormous stride, each one capable of reaching the horizon.[3] He would leave early in the morning to reach Mecca by noon, and return to Syria before nightfall. When *Ismā'īl* was thirteen years old, Abraham had a dream. In that dream he heard Gen 22:2 a voice telling him: "God is asking you to sacrifice your son."* This dream was repeated for three consecutive nights, and Abraham realized that this dream was a divine order. Abraham told his son to bring him a knife and a robe, and they would collect firewood. When they left, the Devil presented himself as a man to Hagar and asked

---

[1]- Rep. by *Ibn 'Abbas*, pub by Al-Iktifa; Tar-Kath 1:149-156; Tar-Mak 149-156; Sah-Bukh # 3364 & 3365.

[2]- See the next chapter 'TheVisiting Angels.'

[3]-The Prophet Muhammad used the Buraq to travel from Mecca to Jerusalem, and from there he ascended to Heaven in his *Mi'raj*.

her, "Do you know where Abraham has taken your son?"

"They have gone to collect some wood."

"No, I swear to God he has taken him to sacrifice him," the Devil replied. but Hagar was not convinced.

"No, he has mercy on him, loves him and would not do what you claim." Hagar responded, but the Devil explained that God asked Abraham to commit this act.

"If the Lord has asked him to do this, he has done the right thing by obeying."    The Devil, after giving up on Hagar, went to *Ismā'īl* [1] and found him walking behind his father.

"Young man, do you know where your father is taking you?"

"We are collecting firewood for the family."

"That is not true, he is going to slay you," said the Devil. When *Ismā'īl* questioned why this was to happen, the Devil replied, "He claims the Lord has told him to do it."

"He should do what the Lord has asked for," *Ismā'īl* responded

When the Devil failed to unite Hagar and *Ismā'īl* against Abraham, he spoke to Abraham,

"Where are you going, old man?"

"I am going between these two hills for something I have to do."

"I think the Devil has talked to you in a dream and asked you to slay your son." Abraham realized that this man was the Devil. He said, "Get away from me, you enemy of God." Abraham threw seven stones at the Devil until he left. He attempted to once again accost Abraham, who threw another seven stones . And once again he appeared before Abraham, and for a third time he threw seven stones

---

[1]- There are disagreements between Islamic scholars about which of Abraham's sons was supposed to be sacrificed. The group which maintained he was *Ismā'īl* included *Abdullah bin 'Umar, Sa'id bin al-Musayyib, Al-Sha'bi, Al-Hasan al-Basri, Mujahid, Ar-Rabi' bin Anas, Muhammad bin Ka'b al-Qadi & al-Kalbi*, and they claimed the place of his sacrifice was at Mecca. *'Umar, 'Ali and Ibn Mas'ud*, from the sahaba, along with *Ka'b, Sa'id bin Jubayr, Qutada, Masruq, 'Akrama, 'Ata, Muqatel, Az-Zahri* and *As-Siddi* maintained that Isaac was the sacrifice and that it happened in Jerusalem, which is in agreement with the book of Genesis.

at the Devil . This is the origin of the ritual "stoning of the Devil," which the pilgrims enact at three different places on the pilgrimage.[1]

When Abraham reached the sacrificial area, he told his son about his dream. *Ismā 'īl said, "My father, do what you have been commanded, with God's help you will find me a patient son."*37:102 Abraham had his son lie on the ground on his side. His son said, "Father, tie me firmly so I do not shake, keep your clothes away so as not to be stained with my blood, which will disturb my mother, sharpen your knife and pass it over my throat quickly; this may make it easier and it is very hard to die. When you go home, give my mother my greeting, and please give her my dress, which may be of comfort to her." Abraham did as his son had requested, kissed him, Gen 22:9 tied his arms and legs tightly, and they both cried.* The gates of Heaven opened; the angels were watching and also cried. Abraham put the knife to his son's neck, but it would not cut. He sharpened the knife and tried twice, but it would not cut.

Then Abraham heard a voice saying, *"You have shown the truth of the vision, this was a manifest trial."*37:105-106 Abraham saw Gabriel holding a big ram. Gabriel said, "With this ram your son will Gen 22:13-14 be ransomed, sacrifice him instead."* Gabriel, *Ismā 'īl*, Abraham and the ram shouted, "God is great!." Abraham took the ram to Mina, where it was sacrificed. This was the origin of the tradition of 'ram sacrifice,' which was and is still done by Muslims on the first day of *'Eid al Aḍhā*. It is also done by pilgrims as part of the pilgrimage ritual.[2]

### How do You Raise the Dead?

Abraham asked God, *"My Lord, show me how You raise the*

---

[1]- Rep. by *Ka'b, Ibn Ishaq, & Ibn 'Abbas.* Pub. by Taf-Bagh & Khaz 37:103

[2]- Rep. by *As-Siddi, Ka'b, Ibn Ishaq, Ibn 'Abbas* & in the poem of the pre-Islamic poet *Umayya bin Abis-Salt.* Pub in Al-Iktifa; Anwar ut-Tanzil; Taf-Bagh & Khaz 37:102-106; Tar-Kath I:157-160. In Hebrew literature Satan appeared to Abraham to deter him from sacrificing his son. When he failed he appeared first to Isaac and then to Sarah. Berashit Rabbah 56.4; Tanhuma B. I, 114; Yashar Wa-Yera 44b-45a (XXIII 25-34). From L.O.J. I, 276-278 and footnote Abraham 234.

dead." God asked him, *"Are you not a believer?"* *"Yes, I am,"* answered Abraham, *" but that will bring serenity into my heart."* God asked him to kill four birds and cut them into small pieces. He was then to spread the remains on many different hills. Abraham was then to call to them and watch as they once came together as four live and flying birds. Q 2:260

**Abraham, the Imam**

God put Abraham to many tests: the burning fire, the sacrifice of his son, the threat on his wife by the king of Egypt, and he passed them all. So God told Abraham *"I am appointing you Imam* [religious leader] *for all people."* Abraham asked if it were possible to give some of his descendants the same honor. God granted his request, but He warned Abraham that His covenant would not include the unjust people. Q 2:124

Abraham was praised in the Qur'an as he *"formed a community that was devoted to God since he was righteous, worshiped only God and grateful for His favors. He chose and guided him on Straight path. God gave him contentment in this world, and he will be among the honorable in the Hereafter."* 16:120-122

***Ismāʿīl* and His Two Wives**

When *Ismāʿīl* became a man he married a woman from the Amalik tribe. Abraham came to visit while *Ismāʿīl* was shepherding his sheep, and stopped at *Ismāʿīl*'s tent. "Peace be upon you, people of this house," said Abraham, but his wife did not return his greeting. When Abraham asked if she had a place for a guest, she told him she did not. Abraham asked her, "How is your food, your water and your sheep?" She said, "We have no food, the water is bad as you can see, and the sheep are so emaciated that they have hardly any milk."

"Where is the lord of this house?"

"He has left to tend to his business."

"When he returns give him my greeting and tell him to change the threshold of his house." And Abraham went back to his home. When *Ismāʿīl* came back he enquired of his wife whether they had any visitors. She described the visitor and told him what he had said.

*Ismā'īl* then divorced his wife in response to his father's request, and remarried, this time to a woman from the *Jirhum,* a Yemenite tribe that had recently settled in the Valley of Mecca. Her name was *Rayla bint Mudād.* When Abraham came to visit and said, "Peace be upon the people of this house," Rayla returned his greeting and welcomed him. Abraham asked, "How is your food, your water and your sheep?" She answered, "Well, thanks be to God, plenty of milk, meat and delicious, fresh water."

"Do you have grain?"

"We have grain – God willing, we are in His blessings."

"God bless you," replied Abraham.

*Rayla* asked Abraham to dismount from his horse and come to eat and drink, but he apologized that he could not leave his horse. She said, "You look as if you are full of dust; can I wash your hair for you?"

"Yes," he answered," you may do that for me if you like."

*Rayla* brought a stone from the tent and placed it beside the horse for Abraham to put his leg on, and he was able to tilt his head toward her. She washed first one side of his head and then moved the stone and washed the other side. His foot left a mark on that soft stone. That was the *Maqām* stone which is now kept near the Ka'ba shrine in Mecca. Abraham told her to tell *Ismā'īl* to "keep the threshold of his home." She did tell *Ismā'īl* of the visitor and about the message he had left. *Ismā'īl* was very happy upon hearing Abraham's words, and asked *Rayla* if she knew the identity of the guest. She told him she did not, and he explained to her that the visitor was "The Friend of God, my father, Abraham, and when he said to keep the threshold of the house he meant to keep you the mistress of this house. You were precious to me, but now you are more precious than ever." *Rayla* cried, saying, "I wish I had known he was your father, so I could have honored him more than what I did."[1]

---

[1]- Rep. by *As-Siddi* and *Ibn Jubayr* quoting *Ibn Abbas.* Pub. by Ara-Tha; Taf-Bagh & taf-Khaz 2:125. In Hebrew literature, the name of Ishmael's two wives are Aisha and Fatima. These are actualy the names of the wife and the daughter of the prophet Muhammad and this showed the Islamic effect in some of the Hebrew literature. These names are found in Pirke De Rabbi Eliezar and

## Building the Ka'ba Shrine

When Abraham was one hundred years old and *Ismā 'īl* was thirty, God instructed them to build the House of God. Abraham asked, "Where shall I build it?" God revealed to him, "follow the sakina,"[1] a wind which looks like a snake with two heads. Abraham followed the sakina from Syria to Mecca. There it made a big circle in the air and a voice emanated from it, saying, "Build the House of God exactly in the shadow of the sakina." The area the sakina revealed was around a red hill in the center of the Valley of Mecca. Abraham and *Ismā 'īl* dug to the foundation of the house which had been constructed by Adam. They built the house of God on top of that same foundation, with Abraham using the stones which *Ismā 'īl* had brought. The House of God , the Ka'ba, was built with stones from five mountains: the mounts of Olive, Lebanon, Judi, Sinai, and the Mount of Hara in Arabia. The original dimensions of the shrine were 30 by 23 cubits and 9 cubits in height. They built it without a roof, made a small low door without a gate, and dug a well beside the Ka'ba to be used for storage of the gifts that people would bring. During the building, Abraham needed a stone of a certain size to complete the edifice. Gabriel descended with the original 'Black Stone' which was raised to Heaven during Noah's Flood, and Abraham placed the stone in its proper place. It is still part of the Ka'ba building and may be the only original stone from Abraham's construction.

## The Third Hymn

After finishing from building the Ka'ba, Abraham said, "Our Lord, accept this from us! Indeed you are the Alert, the Aware!

Our Lord, leave us peacefully committed to you, and make our offspring into a nation which is at peace with you. Show us our ceremonies and turn toward us us, You are so Relenting, the Merciful.

---

TargumYerushalmi Gen. 21.21.

[1]- *Sakina* in Arabic means serenity, and that is the meaning of the Qur'anic verse, "God brought sakina into your heart." In this story, sakina takes another meaning which is very close to the Hebrew 'Shakina.'

*Our Lord, send a messenger in among them, from among*
*themselves who will recite Your verses to them and teach them the*
*Book and wisdom, and will purify them, for you are the Powerful, the*
*Wise"* 2:127-129

## Announcing the Hajj

After Abraham finished the building with the Black Stone in
it and the Maqam Stone on one side, God asked him to announce that
the House of God was ready for its visitors. Abraham asked, "How
will my voice reach all the people?" God instructed Abraham to
speak, and assured him the proclamation would be heard. Abraham
stood on the Maqam stone and it rose up higher than any mountain,
and Abraham called his people, "O People of God–I call upon you to
visit the revered House of God." And he received responses from all
parts of the world and from under the seven seas. After that, God
asked Abraham to identify the borders of the sanctuary which he did
with Gabriel's help. Then Abraham and *Ismā'īl* completed the first
pilgrimage performing the rituals as taught to them by Gabriel.
Abraham then returned to holy land.[1]

---

[1]- From Anwar ut-Tanzil; Al-Iktifa; Taf-Bagh & Taf-Khaz 2:127; Tar-
Kath I:163-166; Tar-Mak 59-66. The legend that the Ka'ba was first built by
Adam, then destroyed and rebuilt by Abraham, is an early Islamic legend fortified
by the literary interpretation of the Qur'an passage *"the first house raised for people*
*is the one in Mecca, blessing and guidance to all people."* On the other hand the
legend that Abraham built the Ka'ba is an old pre-Islamic one. The stone of
'Maqam' which existed before Islam and was kept beside the Ka'ba, had been
called 'Maqam of Abraham.' We also know that pre-Islamic Christian Arabs gave
respect to the Ka'ba and even swore upon it, although it was, at that time, a temple
of idols. The picture of the patriarch Abraham was displayed inside the Ka'ba, and
Arab historians witnessed Prophet Muhammad erasing the pictures inside, saving
only that of the Virgin Mary with her son. The pilgrimage ritual, which included
walking around the Ka'ba, running between the Safa and Marwa hills, staying
overnight on the Mount of Arafat, stoning the Devil in three different places and
sacrificing a sheep are all pre-Islamic. Moslems believe that these rituals were
passed down from the time of Abraham, and this tradition continues to this day.
The sanctuary is an area around the Ka'ba which encompasses a few miles. On its
border, the pilgrims shower and change into their *ahram* clothes; two pieces of
seamless cloth, one to cover the waist, the other to cover the shoulder. The Black
Stone, the only stone known to belong to the original Ka'ba building, is part of the

## Abraham sees the Creations on Earth and in the Heavens

God raised Abraham to a high place and opened to him all the Heavens, and there Abraham saw all of God's creations, including his place in it, as well as earth and all that happened on it. During this total and universal vision, Abraham saw a man commit adultery, and he said, "Let him perish." Immediately the man perished. He saw another adulterous situation and again asked for his death, and the man perished. When he observed the third adulterous situation and wanted him to perish, God intervened and said, "Abraham, wait, do not be hasty; you are blessed with an answered prayer, but do not pray against any of My servants. The sinner may repent and I will forgive him, or I might bring from him pious descendants. If he insists on a sinful life, I can punish him later."[1]

## Abraham's Last Testament

In his last testament, Abraham Told his sons, "*My sons, God has selected your religion for you, do not die unless you are Muslims.*" 2:132

*Who would shrink from joining Abraham's sect except someone who fools himself? .... When God told him "Commit yourself to live in peace"; he said "I have already committed myself peacefully to the Lord of the Universe!*" 2:130-131

## The Death of Abraham

Abraham asked God not to collect his soul unless he requested it. So when Abraham's time arrived, God sent the Angel of Death in the shape of a very old man to him. Abraham welcomed the old man and offered him food, but he was so feeble and unable to eat properly

---

western wall. The pilgrims, when walking around the Ka'ba, are supposed to kiss it if they are able to reach it. Traditionally it is believed to have been brought down from Heaven by the Angel Gabriel. It had been cracked into many pieces during the fire of the Ka'ba at the time of Ibn az-Zubayr, and these were put back together using silver to bind them.

[1]- Pub. by Taf-Tab, Taf-Bagh & Taf-Khaz at 6:75 and they referred it to *Salman*. This story is reported in details in the "Testament of Abraham" in both A & B recension. R. Rubinkiewicz, who translated the book into English, believed it was written circa 100 C.E.

that the food and saliva ran all over his face, beard and chest. When
Abraham questioned the old man, he was told that it was old age that
brought about this condition. Abraham asked how old he was, and
the old man replied that he was two years older than Abraham. Then
Abraham said, "God, take me to You before I have to go through
that." And the old man, the Angel of Death, granted the request.[1]

### Mecca's Community from the Time of *Ismā'īl* to Quraysh

*Ismā'īl* was the custodian of the Ka'ba until his death and was
buried at *Al- Hajar*, beside the Ka'ba, where his mother Hagar was
buried. *Ismā'īl*'s son *Nābit* then became the custodian, but after his
passing, the stewardship transferred to his grandfather *Mudād* of the
*Jirhum tribe*. This Yemenite tribe had custody for several generations
until they were displaced by the *Khuzā'a tribe*. That tribe, with the
help of the Ishmaelit tribe *Kināna*, became the masters of Mecca and
crowned one of their own, *'Amr bin Subay,* as king. But his control
was challenged by the Ishmaeite tribe of *Quraysh,* who then took
contol of Mecca.    Their leader, *Qusay bin Kilāb*, became the
unchallenged king of Mecca. Prophet Muhammad, peace be upon
him, is the fifth generation descendant of *Qusay*.[2]

### The End of Nimrod

After the miraculous rescue of Abraham from the burning fire,
Nimrod, the King of the Babylonians, was very disappointed that he
lost the fight with Abraham's God, and he decided to kill Him. To
reach the God of Abraham who resided in heaven, Nimrod built a
tower 500 cubits in height, but that still was not high enough for that
purpose,[3] so he brought four eagle chicks and raised them feeding
them meat and wine until they reached adulthood. He then made a

---

[1]- Pub. by Ara-Tha, quoted from "those knowledgeable in history &
stories."

[2]- Tar-Mak 80-110.

[3]- The building of the Tower of Babel was mentioned in Gen. 11:4, but
its connection with Nimrod is a conclusion that can be deduced from Gen. 10:6-10.
This connection was expressed clearly by Josephus Antiquities 1:113-114 and
Pseudo-Philo Biblical Antiquities 4:7,6:13 and also by Jerome, Hebrew Questions
in Genesis 10:8.

wooden box with two openings, one at the top and one at the bottom, and fastened the eagles to the four corners of the box. He put a piece of meat on a stick above each eagle and released the eagles with Nimrod and a companion as passengers. The eagles, in their effort to reach the meat, flew higher and higher continuously for two days. When Nimrod gazed down upon the earth from the lower opening, it was dark and unrecognizable. He opened the upper opening and shot an arrow into the sky; the arrow went up and was returned to him spotted with blood. He said, "I took care of the God in heaven." After that he reversed the position of the meat, and the eagles returned to earth.[1]

But when he was back on earth, Abraham told Nimrod that God had said, "Choose an army consisting of whatever you would like and I will fight you," and he said, "Let Him fight me with mosquitoes." Nimrod raised a large army to protect himself, and God sent an army of mosquitoes to attack both Nimrod and his army. The mosquitoes were so thick they filled the air and covered the sky. They ate their armor, their hair, their skin, flesh and bones. Nimrod escaped to his tower, but God sent a single mosquito and it flew around Nimrod for seven days, and he was unable to kill it. Then it bit his lip and entered his nose. His physicians tried to remove it using all their skill and tricks, but they failed. The mosquito kept eating parts of his brain for many months, and during that time the only thing he could do to alleviate his misery and quiet the mosquito was hit his head with a hammer. In the end, he hit his head so hard his skull was cracked and he died.[2]

---

[1]- Taf-Bagh 14:46.
[2]- Pub. by Ara-Tha 85; Tar-Kath I:149.

# 7    Lot and the Visiting Angels

And to Lot We gave discretion and Knowledge.
—Qur'an 21:74

Lot was Abraham's nephew, who along with Abraham, Abraham's father Terah, and Sara left the land of Babylon for Palestine. Lot was a believer in Abraham's faith, while Terah (*Āzar*) retained the old beliefs, and it was when they reached Harran that he died. Abraham and Lot moved on to Syria, then Egypt, then back to Syria. Abraham settled in Palestine while Lot went into the Jordan valley and settled in Sodom.\*The people of Sodom were non-   Gen 13:12 believers and sinners, and though Lot preached to them his sermons were all in vain.\* "The people of Sodom rejected the emissary that   Gen 13:13 was sent. Lot said to them, 'Will you not do your duty? I am a trustworthy messenger sent to you, so heed God and obey me. I do not ask any payment from you, my payment only concerns the Lord of the worlds.' "26:160-164.

And Lot continued, "You indulge in sexual misconduct the likes of which the world has not seen before. You even accost men and intercept [them on] the highway, you commit such a horrible acts in your club. "29: 28-29

The Sodomites would sit along the highway laughing at or stoning any passerby. Lot preached to them, warned against their continued wrongdoings, told them to worship God or suffer His wrath, and told them to repent. But they resented his interference and said, "If you do not stop your incessant preaching, you will become an exile. "26:167 They also reprimanded him, saying, "Bring us God's torment if you are so truthful. "29:29

Lot eventually gave up on the Sodomites, saying, "My Lord,

*support me against such degenerate folk."* 29:30   God answered Lot's prayer and sent the angels Gabriel, Michael and Israfil to destroy the Sodomite cities. They were also to see Abraham and deliver the good news that Sarah would give him a child. The angels came to Abraham in the shape of handsome young men and Abraham, a very generous man, was happy to greet them and enjoyed havng guests at his table. In their honor he served a roasted calf, but when they did not indulge in the meal he grew mistrustful and somewhat fearful of them. They allayed his worry, saying, "Fear not Abraham, we have Gen 18:1-8  been sent here to rid the world of the Sodomites."*

Abraham's wife Sarah was told of her impending good fortune, that she would give birth to Isaac, and from Isaac will come Jacob.    Sarah laughed at this, she was ninety years old and her husband one hundred and twenty. She said, *"Alas for me! Shall I bear a child while I am an old woman and my husband is an old man? That would indeed be a wonderful thing."* The Angel answered, *"Do you marvel at God's command? God is mercy and His blessings are* Gen 18:10-14  *on all of you in this house."** 11:69-73 Sarah asked Gabriel for a sign as proof of his prediction, so Gabriel took a dry stick in his hand and turned it between his fingers, when it suddenly became a green branch with leaves.

Abraham was excited by his good news, but argued with the angels over the fate of the Sodomites. He queried, "Will you destroy the town if you find four hundred believers?" and they said they would not. He asked if they would destroy the city with three hundred believers."No," they answered. "Two hundred?" "No," said the angels. Nor would they with forty believers. Abraham then asked if fourteen believers would be enough to save the city from Gen 18:22-33  destruction. "Yes," answered the angels.* Abraham specifically asked if fourteen people would be spared, as he believed that to be the number of Lot's family, and Lot's wife was included as one of the believers.

The angels reached Sodom at midday and met Lot's daughter *Raytha* carrying water to her home. They inquired of the young girl whether she knew of a place where they might spend the night. She told them to stay where they were, while she went to her father and said, "There are three handsome young men at the city gate. If you do not reach them first, the Sodomites might reach them, and do them some harm." *Raytha* knew that the Sodomites had prohibited Lot from hosting any male visitors, and the travellers should instead be directed to those who had issued the edict. Although Lot felt the day held a feeling of foreboding and was uneasy in helping the men, he did bring them surreptitiously to his home.

Lot's wife was an evil woman and told the Sodomites about the young men and how attractive they were, which brought the Sodomites hurrying to Lot's door. Lot said, *"My people, these are my daughters\*and they are pure, you should marry them and heed God.* Gen 19:7-9 *Do not shame me through my guests. Is there not a normal man among you?"* They replied, *"You know we have no rights to your daughters, and you know what we want."* 11:78-79 *"Did we not prevent you from having male guests?"* 15:70 Lot felt helpless and said, *"If only I had some power over you or could find solace or safety with someone to guide me."* 11:80 At that moment the guests revealed themselves and said, *"Lot, we are Your Lord's messengers and they will not overtake you. Take your family, travel late at night and let not anyone of you look back."*11:81

The Sodomites were not to be deterred. They kept knocking on Lot's door until it was opened and the Sodomites entered. God gave Gabriel permission to torture the intruders and now, in his true shape, spread his wings, struck, and blinded the Sodomites.\* Gen 19:10 They screamed for help accusing Lot and his company of sorcery, then they retreated, while threatening to return in the morning. Lot, realizing who the guests were, asked them to destroy the Sodomites immediately. But the angels said, *"Their time will be in the morning."* 11:81

As the dawn was drawing near, Lot with his wife and daughters left the town,\* while Gabriel swooped down on the four towns Gen 19:14 of the Sodomites and gathered them in his wings. The inhabitants of the first heaven heard their roosters crow and their dogs bark as they were snatched up in Gabriel's wings. Gabriel then dropped them as God pelted them with stones—as hard as baked clay—layer after layer, descendin up on them until no one was left alive.\* Gen 19:24-25 Lot's wife turned to wittness the carnage, saying, "Oh, my people," and was at once struck with a stone and killed.\* Gen 19:26

A solitary Sodomite was temporarily spared as he was in the sanctuary of Mecca. The stone sent to kill him followed but the angels of Mecca stopped it and orderer it to leave the refuge. The stone waited, poised in the air for forty days outside the sanctuary, and when the man completed his business and stepped outside, he was struck down and killed by the stone.[1]

---

[1]- The story of the visiting angels had been published in every tafsir book at 11:69-83.

# 8  Joseph / *Yūsuf*

*There were signs for inquirers in Joseph and his brothers.*
—Qur'an 12:7

## Introduction

There is no indication that, outside of those persons who were interested in biblical study, the story of Joseph was known in pre-Islamic Arabia. Perhaps that is why this story came in the Qur'an in one piece. In sura twelve, of the one hundred eleven verses in this sura, ninety-nine of them pertain to Joseph, and it is the longest sura devoted to one personage. Joseph is also mentioned in suras six and forty, and in both instances he is mentioned only briefly.

In the Qur'an, 12:3, the story of Joseph is described as a superlative narrative, and has become an extremely important part of the Islamic tradition, having been rewritten by Islamic authors and in particular by Persian writers in Farsi. Details such as the dinner party hosted by *Zulaykha* for her skeptical friends and the story of the talking wolf were copied in many Hebrew books, including the famous <u>Sifr Ha Yashar</u>. Joseph became a symbol for beauty in a pure and non-sexual form which was and is still used by poets, i.e., *Ahmad Shawqī*, who describes a beautiful woman:

> I swear by the beauty of Joseph and his sura that you are the only one who exemplifies such beauty.
> Everyone of those women who cut their hands wished to be raised to behold you.

In Islamic literature, Joseph is famous for his unusual beauty. In Arabic, beauty is a character of perfection and can be applied to both the male and female genders. In the hadith of the Prophet, peace be upon him, he said, "God allocated two

thirds of all beauty to Joseph and divided the other third among his
servants."[1]  He was light-skinned, with a handsome face, big eyes,
muscular legs and arms, a flat abdomen, a curved nose, with a dark
mole on his cheek, and a light-colored mole between his eyes.  His
eye lashes were as beautiful as the feathers of an eagle; when he
smiled a beam of light emanated from his teeth, and when he spoke
light flashed from his throat.  No one had adequate words to describe
Joseph.[2]

---

[1]-This hadith was reported by *Ka'b*. Wahb reported it in a different
way: "Joseph was blessed with nine out of ten of what God had created as beauty,
while the remainder was to be divided among the rest of the world."  From Ara-Tha
95, Taf-Tab and most tafsir books.

[2]-This description was reported by *Ka'b* who said that Joseph inherited
his beauty fromhis grandfather Isaac, who inherited it from his mother Sarah and
she was blessed with the beauty of Eve. From Ara-Tha 95.

# The Story of Joseph

Joseph was the favorite son of Jacob, son of Isaac, the son of Abraham the Patriarch. Jacob was a man of God and a bedouin who lived in the Syrian desert in the time of antiquity and fathered twelve sons from four wives. God gave Jacob a tree which grew in his courtyard and every time a boy was born to Jacob, God added a branch to the tree, and in time the tree grew thick with foliage. When each son married, Jacob would cut the branch and give it to that son. But when Joseph, the eleventh son, was born, the tree did not grow the special branch. When Joseph had grown into a young man, Jacob asked God to give him instead a branch from Paradise, and Gabriel brought a branch of a green emerald and gave it to Joseph.[1]

### Joseph's Dreams

When Joseph was seven years old, he had a dream that his branch had been planted in the ground, and that it flourished with all manner of fruits. His brothers brought their branches and planted them around his; not only did their branches not grow but a strong wind came and uprooted the brothers' branches and pitched them into the sea. Joseph awoke and was very alarmed by the dream. He told his father and his brothers, but the brothers were not amused and believed that the dream meant Joseph was trying to claim superiority over them, as the master holds authority over his slaves.*[2]      Gen 37:5-8

At twelve years old Joseph was upset by yet another dream. He saw the gates of Heaven open, and from them a strong light was emitted, lighting up the stars and the mountains. The seas became heavy with high waves and the whales praised God in many tongues. Joseph saw himself in sartorial splendor, in a dress of brilliant light,

---

[1]- Ara-Tha 96, from what he called "those knowledgeable of the Prophet's life stories and the stories of old times."

[2]- Ara-Tha 97.

and from its glow saw all of the earth's treasures thrust toward his hands. He saw eleven stars, the sun and moon shouted down from Gen 37:9-12 the heavens and bowed to him.* Joseph told his father about the dream and his father warned him not to mention it to his brothers for fear of their reaction. But Joseph's stepmother did relate the dream to the brothers, and it did cause ill will against Joseph. They said, "the Gen 37:9-11 son of Rachel wants to enslave us so he will be our master."*[1]

## The Conspiracy

Joseph's half-brothers would discuss Joseph and his relationship with their father. They said, "*Joseph and his full brother* Gen 37:2 [Benjamin] *are dearer to our father than we are.*\* *We are united together* in this matter, and our father is clearly mistaken. *Let us kill Joseph or throw him into exile, so our father's attention will be directed toward us, we will then repent and become pious persons.*"12:8-9 Judah, who was the wisest among them said, "*Do not kill Joseph, toss* Gen 37:18-22 *him into the bottom of a well so some traveler may find him.*"12:10\* They realized that Jacob did not trust them with Joseph and rarely let him out of his sight, but Reuben, the eldest, had a plan. He had the brothers play with Joseph, making sure everyone was amusing and entertaining so that Joseph would want to join them when they went to tend their sheep in the grasslands. Joseph did enjoy playing with his brothers, and he asked them to entreat their father for his permission to accompany them. They went in unison to their father and said, "*Our father, do you not trust us with Joseph? We are sincere about him, send him along tomorrow. He can play, we will all enjoy life and he will be looked after.*"12:11-12 Jacob answered that he was worried about allowing Joseph to go with his brothers, as they were careless and they might lose him to a hungry wolf. The brothers allayed their father's feelings, saying, "*How could we allow a wolf to eat him when we are together, and should that happen, we would be the losers?*"12:14 After hearing this, Jacob was appeased and decided to trust them, and when Joseph told him how much he wanted to go, Jacob relented and gave his permission. Jacob's fear of the wolf

---

[1] -Ara-Tha 97

came to him in a dream in which he saw Joseph on a mountain top being attacked by ten wolves, with an eleventh wolf protecting him. A cave then opened in the mountain and Joseph entered, and did not emerge for three days.[1]

On the day of Joseph's departure, Jacob walked with his children, giving them instructions for Joseph's care. He brought the basket which had been used by Abraham to bring food for Isaac, and filled it with food for Joseph. He told his sons, "I ask you, in the name of God, to feed Joseph when he is hungry, provide water when he is thirsty, and do not exhaust him." They assured him that Joseph would be in good hands, saying, "He is our brother and one of us, and we recognize your special love toward him." Jacob hugged and kissed Joseph and said, "I leave you in the trust of God, the Lord of all people."[2]

As soon as the sons were out of Jacob's sight, they showed Joseph their true feelings by hitting him repeatedly and treating him as an enemy. He begged for help from each of them by name, but no relief came. His food was taken from him and given to the dogs, and inspite of his great thirst and pleadings for water before killing him, they refused. The angels in Heaven cried in sympathy for him. Judah objected to the killing and reminded them of their promise to Jacob. They decided to put Joseph in the bottom of a well dug by Shem, son of Noah. The well was isolated and in a desolate area, deep and dark and impossible for Joseph's egress, and full of salt water. They tied a rope around Joseph and attempted to lower him into the well, but he clung to its rim. They then removed his shirt and tied his hands around his neck. He begged them to leave his shirt on as it would be his death shroud, and to leave his hands untied to protect himself from insects. The brothers responded, saying, "Why do you not ask the sun, moon and eleven stars to dress you and keep you company?" and with that they cut the rope and threw him into the well. *[3]          Gen 37:24

---

[1]-Ara-Tha 98, rep. by *Ibn 'Umar*.

[2]-Rep. by *Ibn 'Umar & As-Siddi*. Pub. by Taf-Tab 12:12; Ara-Tha 99.

[3]-Rep. by *Ibn Mas'ud, Ibn 'Abbas* and other sahaba, also reported by *Al-Hasan*, pub. by Ara-Tha 99; Taf-Tab, Taf-Bagh & Taf-Khaz 12:15.

### Joseph in the Well

God provided a soft rock for Joseph to land on. His brothers called to him, curious if he had survived the fall and Joseph thought they had mercy upon him and answered, but this only caused them to consider stoning him before Judah intervened and prevented it. God illuminated the well and changed the salt water to fresh water. An angel was sent to Joseph, who untied his hands, dressed him and brought a cushion from Paradise to rest on. Joseph did not want the angel to leave, because he was lonely. The angel taught him to pray, "O Lord, You listen to those who call for Your help, and answer them, and relieve their suffering. You see where I am and know my condition. Nothing about me is hidden from You." When Joseph said that prayer, God sent him seventy angels who kept him company for three days in the well.

On the fourth day Gabriel came, and when Joseph asked if he could escape, Gabriel told him to pray. "My Lord, You are present at every gathering and witness every whispering. You are close to your seekers and the companion of lonely people, the Victorious never defeated, Knower of the unseen, Immortal and Resurrector of the dead. There is no deity but You. I am asking You, Creator of heavens and earth, the Owner of all creations, Almighty and Generous to bless Muhammad and his descendants and to rescue me from this situation."[1]

After throwing Joseph in the well the brothers slaughtered a sheep, used its blood to dirty Joseph's shirt, and then barbequed and ate the sheep. In the evening they went back to Jacob who was waiting by the side of the road. When they were close enough to be heard, they began wailing, weeping and tearing at their clothes. They told him, "*Father, we were trying to outrun each other and left Joseph with our belongings. A wolf appeared, attacked and then ate him. You may not believe us but we are telling the truth.*"12:17 Joseph wept and asked to see Joseph's shirt. When he was shown the shirt with the dried spots of blood he said, "I have not before seen such a tidy wolf, one who can kill and devour a person without so much as a tear or a cut anywhere in the material." He passed out and when he awoke

---

[1]-Ara-Tha 100; Taf-Khaz 12:15.

he wept, took the shirt and smelled it, kissed it and put it to his face.*[1]  Gen 37:31-35
    Jacob told his sons to bring him the wolf that had eaten his
son. They went to the desert with their ropes and sticks and caught
a wolf. When they brought him to Jacob with his legs bound, Jacob
asked that he be untied. Jacob told the wolf, "Come close to me."
The wolf walked toward Jacob and stopped directly in front of him.
Jacob said, "You ate my son, the love of my heart, you gave me great
sorrow and pain." The wolf answered, saying, "I swear that I did
not eat your son, Prophet of God, we are prohibited from eating the
flesh or blood of the prophets of God. I am a stranger from Egypt,
having come here to visit my relatives in the Land of Canaan."[2]
Jacob told his sons, "*Your egos have made [evil] things attractive to
you, but I must remain stoic, God is the one whom I seek help
from.*"12:18

## The Enslavement

    After three days in the well Joseph recited the prayer which
was given to him by Gabriel. On the fourth day a group of travelers
from Midian on their way to Egypt lost their way and found
themselves close to the well. *Mālik bin Da'r*, an Arab, was sent to
fetch water, and when he pulled the bucket up from the well he found
Joseph hanging on and exclaimed, "*What a godsend, this is a
youth.*"12:19 *Mālik* and his companions kept this find a secret from the
rest of the group, for they wanted to sell him as a slave and did not
want the rest of the caravan to share his price.
    Judah went to the well and, seeing that Joseph was gone,
began to search. He located him and returned to his brothers who in
turn went to *Mālik* and said, "This is our slave who has run away
from us." Joseph said nothing, afraid of their actions. *Mālik* listened
to their claim and agreed to buy Joseph from his brothers. They
accepted his offer and *Mālik* paid only a trifling amount, only a few

---

[1]-Ara-Tha 101.

[2]-Ara-Tha 101.The story of the talking wolf was borrowed by the Hebrew
Sefr Ha Yashar, Wa Yesheb.85a-85b (XLIII 41-46).

coins, and acted quite indifferently toward him, so Joseph was sold

Gen 37:28-29 for twenty coins."*[1]

The cause of Joseph's enslavement can be traced back to Abraham. When Abraham left Egypt he was riding a horse on a journey to the Land of Canaan. He was followed for five miles by the ascetics of Egypt, walking behind him to honor him. Abraham stayed on his horse and did not deign to dismount and walk with them. God said to him, "You would not humble yourself before my ascetics, and as a punishment one of your descendants will be sold into slavery."[2]

*Mālik* and his company took Joseph with them on their journey to Egypt. On their way they passed his mother's grave, and upon seeing it Joseph jumped from his camel and ran to the grave. He cried and said, "My mother Rachel, wake up from your death and raise your head from under the ground, and see your son Joseph and how much he has suffered. If you see my humiliation and frustration, you will have pity on me. Mother, I wish you had seen them when my shirt was taken from me, I was tied to a rope and thrown on my face. Stones were tossed at me, no one had mercy on me and I was sold as a slave." Joseph heard a voice behind him saying, "For the sake of God, have patience."

*Mālik* looked back and, not seeing Joseph on his camel, stopped the caravan and said, "My slave has run back to his people." When they had retrieved him, *Mālik* slapped him and forced him back onto his camel.[3] When the caravan reached Egypt, Joseph was ordered to bathe and was afterward clothed in a proper dress and offered for sale. Joseph was bought by the Royal Treasurer of Egypt,

Gen 39:1 Potiphar,* in the reign of *Ar-Rayyan bin al-Walīd*, the pharaoh of

---

[1]- There is disagreement about the sale price of Joseph, and I have reported here from *Ibn Mas'ud;* but *Mujahid* put Joseph price as 22 coins, and *'Akrama* as 40. In the Bible it is twenty pieces of silver. Pub by Ara-Tha 102 and Taf-Tab. The Bible is not clear about who bought Joseph, they are the Ishmaelites in Gen 37:28 or the Midianites in Gen 37:36, Hebrew writings later on solved this problem by saying that the Ishmaelites, who bought him first, sold him to the Midianites who took him to Egypt.

[2]- Ara-Tha 102, Taf-Bagh 12:86.

[3]- Rep. by *Ka'b*, pub. by Ara-Tha 103.

Egypt. He was purchased for twenty dinars, a pair of shoes and two white dresses.[1]

## Joseph and Zulaykha

Joseph was taken to Potiphar's home where he told his wife, *"Let his stay here be dignified, perhaps he will be of benefit to us or we may adopt him as our son."** 12:21 The Qur'an does not mention the wife's name, but some Moslem scholars have her Zulaykha, and some call her Ra'il.[2] Gen 39:3-4

Once she saw Joseph with all of his charm she fell in love, but he did not reciprocate,* and as she attempted to seduce him, she sang his praises. One day she said to him: "You have nice hair." Gen 39:7

"It will be the first thing to fall from me after death." Joseph answered.

"You have beautiful eyes."

"They are the first thing to liquefy after death."

"I love your face," Zulaykha continued.

"The dust will eat it."

"The gardens are in flames and you should extinguish them."

"If I did that I may burn myself," responded Joseph.

"The garden needs to be watered."

"The owner of the garden should be the person to water it."[3]

Zulaykha tried to entice him to satisfy her desires, but Joseph said, "Why should I respond and lose my place in Heaven?"

"Come with me under the covers and do not worry, we will be covered and protected."

"Nothing will protect me from God lest I disobey him."

Zulaykha was not to be deterred and continued, "Joseph, put your head on my breast and make me feel happy."

Joseph told her that only his master had this right. But Zulaykha said, "I will poison your master with mercury and keep him

---

[1]-Rep. by *Ibn 'Abbas*, pub. by Ara-Tha 103.

[2]- Potiphar's wife has no name in the Hebrew writings except for Yasher who used the Islamic name 'Zulieka'.

[3]- Rep. by *As-Siddi* and *Ibn Ishaq*, pub. by Ara-Tha 104 and Taf-Bagh 12:24. Similar discussion can be found in Yasher (XLIV 17-25).

in his bed, no one will know he is gone and you will have all of his possessions."

Joseph said, "The punishment will come on the day of judgment."

"I have a lot of pearls and rubies. It is all yours, spend it to make Your Lord in heaven satisfied."[1]

She was a beautiful young woman and he a young man with a strong sexual desire. He resisted all temptation until he found himself alone with her and felt he could resist no longer. He would have fallen had he not seen the manifest evidence of the Lord.[2] He saw, in a vision, his father Jacob who said, "Joseph, how can you behave this way while your name is on the list of prophets?"[3] But what ultimately brought Joseph to his senses was when he saw Zulaykha covering the idol in her room. She told him that she was embarrassed and ashamed to let the idol see her and Joseph together. Joseph told her, "You feel shame from an idol who neither hears, nor

---

[1]-Rep. by *Ibn 'Abbas* and pub. by Ara-Tha 105; Taf-Bagh 12:24.

[2]- Rep. by *Mujahid, Sa'id bin Jubair,* and *Ibn 'Abbas. Ibn 'Abbas* reported that Joseph untied his belt and he placed himself between her legs in a suggestive position. Pub. by Ara-Tha 105, Taf-Tab, and most tafsir books at 12:24.

[3]-Thereare different stories about the incident which prevented Joseph from proceeding with his sexual exploits. *Ibn 'Abbas* said that he saw a hand coming between them and written on it were the words *"Over you stand noble guardians that know and write all what you do."* 82:10-12 Joseph was afraid and ran from her but returned after his fear subsided and tried again. Once again the hand appeared with the words *"Heed the day when you will be brought back to God"* 2:281 engraved on it. He ran again and on his third attempt the hand appeared with the inscription *"Do not commit adultery."*17:32 He left but returned a fourth time, but God interfered this time and told Gabriel to save his servant Joseph before he commits a sin. Gabriel hit Joseph in the chest and immediately Joseph's desire left him through his fingers. Another story was reported by *Al-Hasan. Mujahid, 'Akrama* and *Al-Dahhak* all said that the roof split and Joseph saw Jacob who bit his finger, and Joseph then felt ashamed and stopped his unseemly actions. Another story is that he heard a voice saying, " Don't be like a bird who becomes fatherless after committing adultery." The story which said that Zulaykha covered an idol so he could not see the action was adapted by 'Jami' in his 'Yousef wa Zulaykha' book. Pub. by Ara-Tha 105; Taf-Tab, Taf-Bagh & Taf-Khaz 12:24; also in most books of Islamic narratives and tafsir.

speaks, nor understands. Should I not be ashamed from whom all has been created?" Joseph then ran to the door, with Zulaykha pursuing him. He was running away from sin while she was running to catch Joseph and satisfy her desire. She caught hold of his shirt and tore it from his body. When they opened the door, they found his master standing there. Zulaykha was worried about what Joseph might say so she spoke up and said, *"What is the penalty for someone who has tried to seduce your wife?"*12:25 Her husband answered that the penalty is jail or torture, and Joseph said, *"But she tried to seduce me."*12:26

A cousin of Zulaykha was outside the door with Potiphar. He said, *"If his shirt is ripped from the front, she has told the truth, if it is ripped from behind, she has lied and Joseph has told the truth.*[1]*"* 12:26-27 When Zulaykha's husband saw that the shirt was indeed ripped from behind, he realized what had happened and said to her, *"This is one of your wicked female tricks, you are in serious trouble and should ask forgiveness."*12:28 He asked Joseph not to mention this incident to anyone.*                                                                                         Gen 39:11-19

But the story of the failed seduction became the town gossip. The women of the town would say, "The official's wife wants to seduce her house boy, she is madly in love with him and has gone completely astray." When Zulaykha heard of what was being said about her, she invited these ladies to a dinner party. At the dinner she served citron, melon, bananas and pomegranate, and provided a knife for every guest. She asked Joseph to make an appearance. When he entered the room and the women saw him, they gasped at his beauty. They were transfixed by the sight and cut their hands, thinking they

---

[1]- Rep. by *As-Siddi, Ibn Jubayr & Ad-Dahhak.* They said that Zulaykha's cousin was a baby but God made him speak. He is one of four babies who spoke in the crib. Pub by Ara-Tha 106, Taf-Tab 12:25. The Bible mentioned that during the argument, Potiphar's wife caught hold of Joseph's garment, saying, "Lie with me," and Joseph ran away from her, leaving the garment in her hand. Gen 39:1. In the Hebrew text, Yashar (XLIV 54-75), Zuleika held only a piece of his garment. Yashar also mentioned that the baby who talked miraculously was Zuleika's son who described what he had seen. But the one who judged Joseph innocent from the site of the tear was a true priest judge.

were cutting the fruit. They said, *"God forbid, this is no human being, this is an angel[1] "*12:31

Zulaykha said, "This is the man I tried to seduce, can you blame me? If he does not do my bidding, I can have him jailed, and he may forget his pride, but so far he has not succumbed to my charms." The women told Joseph that he should listen to his body but Joseph did not surrender to the ladies' suggestion. As for the threat of jailing him, he said, *"My Lord, jail is more preferable to me than what they are inviting me to do.[2] Unless you ward off their advances, I will fall for them."*12:33

Zulaykha told her husband, "This Hebrew slave has caused a scandal by telling everyone that I have been trying to seduce him and he should be jailed to stop this gossip." And so Joseph was imprisoned. God made the jail a place for Joseph to purify and rid himself of the sin of temptation.[3]*

<sub>Gen 39:20</sub>

## Joseph in Jail

In jail, Joseph found himself with two inmates–the pharaoh's butler and baker –who had been charged with conspiracy to murder the pharaoh. While the butler did not go through with the plan to poison the pharaoh's drink, the baker did put poison in the food. When the pharaoh discovered the plot, he asked the butler to taste the drink, which he did with no ill effects. The baker refused to taste the food and it was given to an animal which died. However, both men were sent to prison.

In jail Joseph became well known for his ability to interpret dreams, and both the butler and baker asked for understanding of their

[1]- Rep. by *Ibn Abbas, Ibn Jubayr, Qutada, As-Siddi, Ibn Ishaq and Wahb.* Pub. by Ara-Tha 107, *Wahb* also reported that seven women out of the forty who attended the party died from their strong emotional feelings after seeing Joseph. In Hebrew 'Yashar' we also read about the ladies who cut their hands with the dinner knives when they saw Joseph. Yashar 87a-87b (XLIV 27-35) and Tanhuma Wa-Yesheb 5.

[2]- The same words are found in the Hebrew 'Yashar Wa- yesheb, 10b. (XLIV 78).

[3]- Pub. In Ara-Tha 108 quoting *As-Siddi.*

dreams. In his dream the butler saw himself in a vineyard, and on a vine there were three grapes which he squeezed and put the juice in the king's cup, and the king drank it.*  In the baker's dream he saw Gen 40:9-10 himself walking with three baskets on his head and with birds pecking at the food in those baskets.*  Joseph saw only doom in the Gen 40:16-17 dreams and did not want to tell them of his interpretation, but he did take advantage of their attention to enlighten them to the real religion of God.

He said, "I *have left the beliefs of those who do not believe in Him and who disbelieve in the hereafter, and I have followed the beliefs of my forefathers, Abraham, Isaac and Jacob. We do not associate any other deities with God, this is part of God's bounty toward us and toward mankind. Are multiple lords better than one God, the Almighty? Instead of serving Him, you are serving only 'names', which you and your forefathers have created. Discretion belongs only to God. He has ordered you to serve Him alone and that is the real belief even if you do not realize it.* "*12:37-40

But Joseph's cellmates were not to be deterred, and they insisted to hear the interpretation of their dreams, so Joseph said, "*My two jailmates, one of you will pour wine for his lord, while the other will be crucified and birds will eat from his head, your cases have been decided.*" He then turned to the butler and said, "*You should mention me to your lord.*"*12:41-42*                          Gen 40:12-15

Gabriel came to Joseph in his jail cell and said, "God sends His peace to you and asks, 'Are you not ashamed that you requested help from mortals, instead of God's help?'" Joseph asked Gabriel if God had accepted him, and when Gabriel answered that He had, Joseph said, "That is all I ask."

What Joseph predicted did occur, and the butler was released from jail. But the Devil made him forget Joseph's request to be mentioned to his master for seven years,*  and Joseph remained in jail Gen 40:22

during that time.[1]  One night the king of Egypt had an amazing and frightening dream.  He saw seven thin cows eating seven fat cows Gen 41:1-7 and seven green stalks with seven dried black stalks of wheat.*  He awoke very upset and summoned his council, which was made up of priests, magicians, and seers.  He told them about his dream and asked for an interpretation, and they remarked that this was a nonsensical Gen 41: 8 dream not subject to any coherent interpretation.*

At that time, the butler remembered Joseph and asked to be sent to the jail for an interpretation.  He met with Joseph and told him of the king's dream, and  Joseph told him, *"You will farm as usual for seven years. Anything that you harvest should be kept in its husk, except for a small amount which you will consume. There will then be seven years of drought which will eat up any of the crops you have* Gen 41:25-36 *saved. A good year will follow with enough rain for a good harvest*.* "*
12:47-49

When the butler returned to the king and told him what had been learned, the king wanted to know more, and an officer was sent to bring Joseph to the king.  But Joseph would not leave the jail until he had been judged innocent of the charges against him. The king brought together the women who had cut their hands while gazing at Joseph and demanded they give an account of the story of Joseph. They answered, saying, "God forbid, we have no knowledge of any evil concerning him."  And Zulaykha said, *"Now the truth will prevail,* I tried to seduce him, but he denied me. He *always speaks the truth. I have not betrayed him during his absence. God does not guide the plotting of traitors, I do not claim to be innocent myself, my soul is prone to commit evil unless my Lord with His mercy guards against* it. *"*12:51-53

### Joseph and the King

Joseph, now thirty years old, left the jail, had a bath and wore a new set of clothes to see the king. The king spoke seventy languages

---

[1]- From Ara-Tha 110 and Taf-Bagh 12:42. Joseph's extended im-prisonment was a penal- ty because he put his trust in a mortal instead of God when he asked the butler to intervene on his behalf.  As reported by *Al-Hasan, Wahb, Malik bin Dinar*, and *Ka'b*.

and every time he questioned Joseph in a different one, Joseph responded in the same language.[1] The king was impressed with Joseph's knowledge and quizzed him further. He challenged him to describe the king's dream in detail, and Joseph said, "You saw in your dream seven fat, brown cows coming out of the Nile, their breasts full of milk. Suddenly you saw the water recede until only mud was left, and from that mud came seven sick cows, very thin with hollow stomachs, no breasts, no hooves but with teeth and paws like wild dogs. They savagely attacked the healthy cows, ripping their skin and flesh and crushing their bones and skulls. You then saw seven green stalks and seven black and dried stalks on the same plant. While questioning how this could occur from one root, a wind began to blow intertwining the green and dry stalks, and a fire started which destroyed them all,[2] you then woke very disturbed by the dream"*     Gen 41:17-24

The king was very impressed both with Joseph and his interpretation and asked him, "What do you think? You are always truthful," Joseph told him to take advantage of the coming years and plant wheat everywhere, build storehouses and pyramids to store the additional crops. "Ask the people of Egypt to save one fifth of their food to be collected, and during the lean years people from all over will come to buy wheat. You will then collect more treasures than you have ever collected before."* The king asked, "Where can I find such a trustworthy man to organize this policy?" Joseph assured the king that he himself could successfully complete this task, and Joseph was appointed. The king crowned Joseph with his own crown, gave him his own sword and ring and had a golden chair made for him, encrusted with rubies and pearls and covered in silk brocade.*[3]     Gen 41:41-44

---

[1]-From Taf-Bagh 12:54, The Hebrew Yashar (XLIX 17) also mentioned the king's surprise when he found Joseph answering him in all of the seventy languages spoken by the king.

[2]- From Ara-Tha 111; Taf-Bagh & Taf-Khaz 12:54 quoting *Ibn 'Abbas*. In Hebrew Texts, the king tells Joseph his dream and he omitted certain details to test Joseph but Joseph related everything in the dream including those hidden points. Tanhuma Mikkez 3. From L.O.J. II, 70 and endnote 174.

[3]- Ara-Tha 112.

**Joseph the First Officer**

      The king gave Joseph the responsibility and authority to govern all of Egypt and he became Potiphar's replacement when Potiphar soon died. With the king's blessing, Joseph and Zulaykha were married.[1] When Joseph and Zulaykha first slept together, he asked her, "Is this not better than what you had planned?" She replied, "Do not blame me. I am a beautiful and desirable woman as you can see, who has had all manner of material possessions, but my husband did not sleep with me. God made you irresistible to me, and I could not contain my emotions." Joseph did find her to be a virgin and she gave him two sons. Joseph was a just man and was well loved in all of Egypt.[2]

      After a good and prosperous seven years, a period of depression began, and the Egyptians soon consumed everything they had saved from the good years. Joseph sold them food in return for gold and silver until he was in possession of all such precious metal. During the second year, he sold them food in exchange for their jewels until he owned all of the jewels in Egypt. The third lean year he took possession of their sheep and cows. The fourth year gave him their slaves. The fifth year they lost possession of their children who became slaves, and by the end of the seventh year, the people themselves sold themselves in to slavery to Joseph. Joseph then told the king, "As God is my witness, and you are my witness, I have freed every Egyptian from slavery and gave them back their lands, their

Gen 47:13-25 slaves and their children."*

      During the lean years, Joseph kept himself hungry and was asked, "You are hungry yet you control all the stores of food, why do you not eat?" Joseph answered, "I am worried that I might forget the hungry if I am satiated."[3]

**Joseph and his Brothers**

Gen 41:56-57        People came from all over to get grain,*but Joseph's policy

---

[1]- Taf-Tab & Taf-Bagh 12:56, In <u>Hebrew</u> text, Joseph married Potiphar's daughter 'Asenath.' Berashit Rabbah 85.1.

[2]- Taf-Bagh quoting *Ibn 'Abbas*

[3]- From Ara-Tha 113; Taf-Bagh & Taf-Khaz 12:57, This story was borrowed by the <u>Hebrew</u> <u>Midrash</u> '<u>Ben ha-Melek</u>, 12.

was to not give anyone more than what a camel[1] could carry, no matter who the man was. The drought affected not only Egypt but the lands of Canaan and Syria as well. Jacob felt the effect of the shortages and sent his sons, except for Benjamin, Joseph's full brother, to Egypt to collect some grain.* When they arrived and met Joseph, they did not recognize him, although Joseph knew them. Joseph asked them, "Who are you and what is your story?" They answered, "We are Syrian shepherds, and have had a very difficult time, and have come to get some wheat." He asked them how he was to know if they were not spies. They told him, "We are not spies, we are all brothers with one father, now an old man. He is a prophet of God, and his name is Jacob." Gen 42:1-4

When Joseph asked how many brothers there were, they explained that originally they had been twelve, with one perishing in the wilderness and one remaining behind with their father. "But how do I know you are telling the truth? You are unknown in this land." Joseph told them to return to their home and bring back the remaining brother, and to leave one of them in Egypt as a guarantee of their their return. It was decided that Simon would remain.*Joseph instructed his soldiers to return the silver which had been paid to him. It was put back in to the brothers' baggage, which was done unbeknownst to them. Upon their return home they told Jacob what had happened and said, "Father, we were denied our rations, so allow us to return with Benjamin to Egypt and collect our wheat." And they promised to look after Benjamin. But Jacob asked why he should trust them, as they had failed to protect Joseph all those years before. When they opened their baggage and found that their silver had been returned they said, *"Father, what more do we desire than this? Our silver has been returned to us, we will supply our family with wheat and will look after our brother. With him we will be entitled to an extra share of a camel's load."* 12:65 Gen 42:6-23

Gen 42:25-38

Jacob would not relent until they pledged before him and before God that they would keep Benjamin safe and return him unhurt, except in the case of an ambush. They took such a pledge and

---

[1]- In Gen. 42:26, it is the donkey which carries people and trade, not camels.

Gen 43:1-14 said, *"God is our witness for what we have said.\*"* 12:66 Jacob told his sons that they "Should enter the city in Egypt not by a single gate but by separate ones."[1] Ibn Abbas said that "They were tall and handsome," and because of the attention this may cause, Jacob was worried that they might be affected by the evil eye. He said, *"It will not help you in any way that goes against God. Discretion rests only with Him, on Him I rely as do all persons of virtue."*[2] 12:67

### The Second Trip to Egypt

The brothers entered the city as their father had requested, and presented themselves before Joseph. Joseph told them to enjoy his hospitality and asked them to stay in a guest house, but he kept Benjamin in his private home. He told Benjamin that they were brothers and not to feel distressed about anything that had happened. Benjamin wanted to stay in Egypt, but Joseph knew he would have to be charged with a crime in order to be kept there. The brothers were furnished with supplies and with them a goblet was secretly placed in a saddlebag. Shortly after they left, officers were sent to stop them, accusing the travelers of being thieves. The brothers asked the officers what they were looking for, and they were told that one of the king's goblets was missing. Anyone returning it would receive a camel's load of wheat. The brothers argued with the officers, "By God, you ought to know that we have not come to cause any trouble in this land, we are not thieves." The officers retorted, *"What should be the penalty if you are found to be liars?"* The brothers answered, *"If the goblet is found on one of our camels, the rider of that camel will himself be the penalty, that is the way we penalize thieves* by making them slaves to whom they steal from."Q 12:74-75 The officers began their search one saddlebag at a time until the goblet was discovered in Benjamin's bag, the last to be searched, and it was announced that Gen 44:1-13 Benjamin would become a slave.\* God's help was needed to contrive

---

[1]- In the <u>Hebrew</u> <u>Midrash</u> <u>Berashit</u> <u>Rabbah</u> 91.6; <u>Tanhuma</u> B.I, 193-194, Jacob asked his sons not to enter the city together from one gate, so no evil eye would be cast upon them. L.O.J. II, 80 and endnote Joseph 201.

[2]- Pub. In Taf-Tab; Taf-Bagh & Taf-Khaz 12:67 quoting *Ibn 'Abbas.*

this plot, as Joseph would never have taken his brother according to the Egyptian code.[1] When the goblet was retrieved from Benjamin's bag, his brothers looked down in shame. They chastised him, saying, "How could you bring shame on us in this way, you, the son of Rachel? We are suffering from your wrongdoing. Why did you take the goblet?" Benjamin answered them, "The sons of Rachel still suffer from you. You took my brother into the wilderness and killed him. The one who put the goblet in my bag is the same one who returned the silver to you." One brother said, " *If he has been caught stealing, a brother of his has stolen previously.*" Joseph said to them, "*You are in an unusual predicament, God is aware of what you describe.*"12:77 But Joseph kept his secret to himself and did not reveal it. The brother's comments referred to a time when Joseph stole an idol belonging to his maternal grandfather. He broke the idol and threw it into the street.[2]

The goblet and the brothers were brought in front of Joseph. He knocked on the goblet with his fingers and put it close to his ear. He said, "This goblet is telling me that you were once twelve men, but you sold one of your brothers. Benjamin bowed to Joseph and said, "Sir, ask your goblet about my brother, is he alive?" Joseph knocked on the goblet again, listened and said, "He is alive and you will see him." Benjamin said, "Please, sir, let the goblet tell you who stole it and placed it in my bag." "The goblet is angry," said Joseph. Reuben complained, "If you do not allow us to return home with our brothers, I will yell and scream, causing so much emotion that every pregnant woman in Egypt will miscarry." Reuben was furious and his hair was standing on end, and could be seen through his clothes. A characteristic of Jacob's descendants is that their anger dissipates with a touch of another Jacobite. To end Reuben's anger, Joseph instructed his son to touch him, once this was done, Reuben's anger

---

[1]- Pub. in Ara-Tha 117; Taf-Bagh & Taf-Khaz 12:67 quoting *Ka'b* and *Qutada*.

[2]- Rep. by *Ibn Jubayr* and *Qutada*. Other imams had different stories. *Ibn Jarij* said that he stole a golden idol from his maternal uncle according to his mother's instruction and broke it in pieces. *Mujahid* said he stole an egg from his home to gave it to a beggar. *Ibn 'Uyayna* said it was a hen he took from his home and gave to the beggar. Ara-Tha 117; Taf-Tab, Taf-Bagh & Taf-Khaz 12:77.

was gone. Realizing what had happened, Reuben said, "There is someone in this house who is a descendant of Jacob."[1] "But who is Jacob?" questioned Joseph. Reuben, angered once again, said, " Jacob is Israel of God, son of Isaac the sacrifice of God, son of Abraham the Friend of God." Joseph said he was keeping Benjamin, but the others could go. They begged and pleaded with Joseph to keep anyone but Benjamin, to no avail. Joseph explained that he would not keep anyone but the one in whose possession the stolen object was found. When they lost all hope of influencing him, the brothers held counsel. Reuben, the eldest, said, *"Do you not realize that our father had us take a pledge before God? We have been remiss before in dealing with Joseph, and I will never leave this land without* Gen 44:16-17 *our father's permission or on God's instruction.\* "* 12:80

### Jacob's Sorrow

The brothers returned to their father without Benjamin or Reuben and said, *"Father, your son has stolen the king's cup. We testify only about that which we saw. We are not guardians of the unseen. If you do not believe us, ask the townsfolk from whence we came or ask the caravan with which we returned. We are telling you the truth."* Jacob said, *"I think you have fooled yourselves this time, patience is a virtue, perhaps God will bring them all back to me. He is the Aware and the Wise."* He turned away from them and said, *"How upset I am over Joseph."* His sons were angered and said, *"By God, you keep remembering Joseph to the point that you will lose your mind over it or die."* 12:81-85   Over the years Jacob had become so distraught over Joseph that his eyes had clouded over from crying. Someone asked him how he had lost his vision and Jacob said, "From my sorrow over Joseph." When he was asked what had caused his back to curve, Jacob said, "From my sorrow for his brother." God asked Jacob, "Are you complaining to me? To My Might and Majesty I will not resolve any trouble for you unless you ask Me

---

[1] - Read about the argument between Joseph and Judah and the legendry strength of Jacob's sons in <u>Hebrew Yashar Wa-Yiggash</u>, 107a-108a (LIV 31-37).

directly." Jacob said, *"I complain to You about my sorrow and sadness."* 12:86 God told Jacob: "Even if he is dead, I will raise him for you to see." Jacob then told his sons to go back to Egypt and search for their brothers. *"Do not despair of finding God's comfort; only the disbelievers despair of His comfort.* [1] " 12:87

The Angel of Death came to visit Jacob and said, "Peace be upon you." Jacob was afraid when he saw the apparition, but he returned the greeting and asked, "Who are you, and how did you enter this place after I locked myself in to complain to God about my sorrow and sadness?" The Angel answered, "Prophet of God, I am the one who orphans children, widows husbands and wives, and separates families and friends." Jacob said, "You must be the Angel of Death." And the Angel confirmed Jacob's thoughts. Jacob questioned the Angel of Death, "Tell me, for the sake of God, do you collect the souls of men eaten by wild animals?" "Yes, I do," said the angel. "Are the souls collected en masse or one at a time?" The Angel told Jacob that they were collected one at a time. Jacob asked, "Did you collect the soul of Joseph?" And when the Angel said he had not collected Joseph's soul, Jacob felt better and asked the Angel for what purpose he had come. The Angel answered, "I came only to greet you, God will not take your soul until He brings you and Joseph together. God gave me permission to visit you with this good news, answer your questions, and to explain why you have been tested by the loss of your son, and the loss of your vision." Jacob asked the Angel to continue. "Do you remember the young female slave you bought one day long ago? She was separated from her parents, and it is for this reason that you were separated from your son. At another time you slaughtered a sheep and cooked it. Tamin, a servant of God, ventured by after a week of fasting and could smell your food, but you did not share it with him." Afterwards Jacob set free every slave he owned, and requested that every day two sheep should be killed and distributed to the needy.[2]

---

[1]- From Ara-Tha 119; Taf-Bagh & Taf-Khaz 12:86
[2]- Ara-Tha 119-120; Taf-Bagh & Taf-Khaz 12:86, no source had been mentioned.

## The Third Trip

On their third trip to Egypt,[1] when Jacob's sons met Joseph, they said, *"Sir, we and the rest of our family have gone through a very difficult time. We have come here with only meager merchandise; please fill our load for us and grant us charity. God rewards the charitable."* 12:88 The brothers brought wool, leather, butter and oil to exchange for the wheat. They also carried a letter from their father which read, in part, "From Jacob Israel of God, son of Isaac the sacrifice of God, son of Abraham the Friend of God, to the High Officer of Egypt who has brought justice and honesty in great measure; We are a family who has been sorely tested. My grandfather was tested by King Nimrod, who bound his arms and legs and threw him into a fire but God intervened and spared him any harm. My own father's arms and legs were tied and a knife was put to his neck when God substituted a ram in his place and my father was saved.[2] As for myself, my favorite son was taken by a wolf when he went to the wilderness with his brothers, and all I have left of him is his bloodied shirt. I lost my vision weeping over his loss, and his brother who was much company for me was left in Egypt, accused of stealing property of the king. He sits now in your jail. We are a family that does not steal and would not begat a thief. Release my son back to me or I will ask God to curse you and your descendants for seven generations."[3]

After reading this, Joseph could not help but to cry. He said to the brothers, *"Do you understand what you did to Joseph and his brother? Were you acting out of ignorance?"* 12:89 And at that time, Joseph took off his crown and the brothers all recognized the prominent birthmark on his forehead. They realized who this person really was. "You are Joseph, are you not?" they asked. He answered,

---

[1]- In the Islamic story of Joseph, only on the third journey to Egypt did Joseph uncover himself to his brothers. In the Bible this happened on the second journey.

[2]- Here the teller of the story maintained that Isaac was the intended sacrifice. For the other opinion that *Ismā'īl* was the sacrifice, see 'Abraham.'

[3]- From Taf-Bagh & Taf-Khaz 12:6; Ara-Tha 121. In Hebrew Yashar Mikkez 103a-104a (LII 29-41) Jacob sent a long letter to the 'Ruler of Egypt' with a similar opening.

*"I am Joseph and this is my brother. God has compensated us as He does with anyone who does his duty and perseveres. God does not lose track of the wages for those who have acted kindly. Today we will not exchange any blame. God may forgive you, He is the most Merciful."* Gen 45:1-8 12:90-92 Joseph then asked about his father, and they told him Jacob had lost his sight. Joseph told them to *"take this shirt and pass it over our father's face, and his sight will return."*12:93

This shirt was woven in Paradise. It was the same shirt that Gabriel brought to Abraham when he was thrown into the fire, and it was given to Isaac who was wearing it when he was about to be sacrificed. Jacob inherited it from Isaac and gave it to Joseph, who kept it as am amulet and wore it around his neck. When Joseph was held captive in the well, Gabriel took it from his neck and dressed him in it. Joseph told his brothers to go home and return with all the family together.[1]

The west wind requested permission from the Lord to bring Jacob the scent of Joseph. Jacob said to his family, *"Though you may think me not of sound mind, I do smell the scent of Joseph."* They replied, *"By God, you are confused."*12:94-95 The shirt was carried by Judah, who walked barefoot and bareheaded and did not rest until he reached his father in the land of Canaan. When the shirt was placed over Jacob's face, his sight was restored. The brothers said, *"Our father, seek forgiveness for us for our offenses. We have been mistaken."* Jacob told them, *"I will seek forgiveness for you from my Lord. He is the Forgiving, the Merciful."*12:97-98

### Jacob and His Sons Move to Egypt

Joseph sent a messenger with two hundred camels and clothes to the land of Canaan, and asked him to return with all of his family.* Gen 45:17-23 Joseph told the great king about his family coming   On their approach to the gates of the city, they were met by the king, Joseph, four thousand of his guards, and the people of Egypt who welcomed Jacob and his family. Jacob, walking with Judah's support, saw the

---

[1]- Rep. by *Ad-Dahhak*, pub. by Ara-Tha 122; Taf-Bagh & Taf-Khaz 12:93.

crowd and pointed toward a man, "Judah, is this the pharaoh?" "No," said Judah, "this is your son." When Joseph and Jacob reached each other, Joseph began to speak but God intervened and allowed Jacob to begin the salutation, "Greetings to you, the reliever of sadness." Joseph took his father and stepmother aside and said, *"Enter Egypt safely, God wishes it."*12:99 He helped them up on the platform and they knelt before him. Joseph said, *"My father, this is an interpretation of an earlier vision, and my God has made it come true. How kind He was to me when He let me out of jail and brought you in from wandering in the desert, after Satan made trouble among my brothers. My Lord is gracious in whatever way He wishes, He is the Aware and the Wise. My Lord, You have given me control and taught me how to interpret events, originator of heaven and earth. You are my Patron in this world and in the hereafter. Gather me in as a believer and unite me with honorable men."*12:100-101

### Death of Jacob and Joseph

Jacob lived comfortably in Egypt for another twenty years. Before his death he gathered all his descendants around and asked, *"Who will you worship after me?"* They replied, *"We will worship your God, God of your fathers, Abraham, Ismā'īl and Isaac."* Jacob said, *"My sons, God has chosen this religion for you, die with this faith\*."*2:133 He was buried in the Holy Land beside his father Isaac and his grandfather Abraham, according to his request. Joseph also requested to be buried there and when he died he was buried in a marble sarcophagus, and there it remained until Moses had it buried in the Holy Land.\*

Gen 49:28

Gen 50:26

# 9     Moses / *Mūsā*

*Who sent down the Book which Moses came with,*
*as light and guidance for mankind.*

– Qur'an 6:91

## Introduction

There exists a common understanding among the world's three major religions of revelation–Islam, Christianity and Judaism–regarding the man called Moses. He was both a man of God and a political leader who led the Israelite tribes away from the slavery of Egypt and offered them the Bedouin life in the Sinai. There he preached to them on the importance of worshiping one God, and prepared them for their next move to the cities of Canaan. Although the Islamic story of Moses is similar to the one found in the Bible, it retains its own spirit and theological background, and certain phases are unique to the Islamic narrative. The major difference is how Muslims connect Moses to themselves and to other religions; in Islam, Moses is one of the five major prophets: Noah, Abraham, Moses, Jesus and Muhammad, all having the same message to give to humanity, and all belonging to not one, but to every nation which believes in God. Understanding this reasoning, it should come as no surprise that, in Islam, Moses is, in actuality, a Muslim.

In one the many Islamic stories about Moses, *Al-Tha'labi* talks about the divine audience between Moses and God on the Mount of Sinai. God asks Moses to keep the love of Muhammad in his heart until he dies, and when Moses questions who Muhammad is, God answers, "He is the one whose name has been on My Throne two thousand years before I created heaven and earth. He is My prophet, the chosen and the best of all My creations, he is the one I favor above all other humans and the angels I have created."

In the great vision of the Prophet Muhammad's ascension into the Heavens, he reached "a distance of two bows in length," from the Divinity, and it was there he received the obligation to pray fifty times a day, a duty that included both himself and his nation. On his way down, Muhammad was stopped in the Sixth Heaven by Moses who, upon hearing of the obligation that had been conferred, advised Muhammad to return and mitigate His decision. Moses explained that his experience with the Israelites had made him doubt the ability of Muslims to fulfill or accept such a heavy obligation, which prompted Muhammad to return many times to the Lord, each time appealing for leniency until God relented and reduced the duty to five prayers a day. As a religious leader Moses can be claimed by all believers–Jews, Christians and Moslems–and there is no proof, including that of the Old Testament, that the religion of Moses had been accepted on a large scale by any group of people before the exile to Babylonia.

The story of Moses in the Old Testament appears in the Books of Exodus and Numbers, which was redacted from three sources, "J, E, and P." The biblical chronology dates the exodus from Egypt in the fifteenth century B.C.E. but most scholars prefer to date it at the thirteenth century, under the reign of Ramses II. This however, is all speculative, and Moses' story as a whole is a religious story, and the attempts to partially illuminate the story by the light of history have so far been unsuccessful.

The stories of Moses are found in more than ten suras in the Qur'an, and some, such as 'Moses and The Magicians,' are told more than once, but other biblical stories and details are omitted. Early mufassirun filled these gaps either directly from biblical and rabbinical sources from those who could read Hebrew, or indirectly by asking scholars of the Bible, and rabbis. This began as one-way communication between Jews and Muslims, but gradually developed into a two-way exchange which is evidenced by the many Hebrew books written in Spain during the Arab period, which reflect Moses in an Islamic light.

# The Story of Moses

The pharaoh who hired Joseph died while Joseph was still in his office and his reign was followed by *Qābūs bin Muṣ'ab*. It was during this period that Joseph died. After Pharaoh *Qābūs* came his brother, the powerful *'Abdul-'Abbās bin al-Walīd*, the pharaoh during the time of Moses. With the death of Joseph, the Israelites of Egypt multiplied and lost most of the teachings of Joseph, Jacob and Abraham.

Pharaoh *'Abdul-'Abbās* tortured and enslaved the Israelites, but chose to marry one of them, a girl named *Āsiya bint Muzāḥim*. He was an extremely fit individual who never spit, sneezed, coughed, never had any stomach problems and, it is said, was never sick. He ate and drank as anyone, but might not relieve himself for forty days. Because of these unique characteristics he proclaimed himself divine, and his people worshiped him.[1]

### The Birth of Moses
The pharaoh of Egypt had a dream in which he saw fire coming from Jerusalem and into Egypt, destroying the homes and lives of the Egyptian people, though the Israelites were not harmed. The pharaoh summoned the priests, magicians, seers and dream interpreters and asked for their explanation of his dream. They told him about a child that would be born to an Israelite mother who would become more powerful than the pharaoh, taking the pharaoh's kingdom, expelling his people, and changing their religion. The pharaoh took their words to heart and ordered that every male baby born to an Israelite mother be killed, and informed the midwives of his intention.* This policy, however, worried the Egyptians, who Exd 1:15-16

---

[1]-The Arab historians believed that Egypt at the time of Moses was under an Arab dynasty and they gave the Pharaohs Arabic names; this may be true for some of the Hexose kings. From Ara-Tha 84 & 167.

feared losing their slave supply and complained to the pharaoh, saying that if this policy continued the Egyptians themselves would be doing jobs fit only for slaves. As a compromise, the pharaoh agreed to killing the Israelite babies every other year. Moses was conceived and born in a year that meant death to Israelite male newborns, while Aaron was born during a year of amnesty and did not have to be hidden.[1]

When the labor pains began Moses' mother[2] sent for the midwife, who was also her friend. Friend or not, the midwife had intended to inform the pharaoh's guards of the delivery, but upon seeing the baby Moses, the midwife's body shuddered and she was overcome with love for him. She told Moses' mother to keep the baby, as he brought out such a special feeling in her, unlike that of any other birth, and that the pharaoh would not be informed of the birth. When the midwife left, she was noticed by a guard who became suspicious and went to search the house. Moses' mother, not realizing what she was doing, and her sanity having deserted her with the appearance of the guard, covered Moses and put him in a hot clay oven. The guard searched but to no avail, and left with the explanation that the midwife's presence was a social call, and not of a professional nature. Moses' aunt then came, and the two sisters looked for Moses until his cries gave him away, and they found him, safe, by the grace of God, hidden in the still lit tandoori oven.[3]

God told Moses' mother, "Nurse him, if you should fear for him, cast him into the river and do not fear nor be sad. I will
Exd 2:2 return him to you, and appoint him as a *missionary*."* 28:7 Moses was nursed for three months, but the pharaoh's guards were persistent in their search for Israelite babies, and his mother thought it best to release him to the river as God had instructed her. An Egyptian carpenter sold her a wooden box and enquired as to what purpose she intended to use it. As she did not want to lie, she told

---

[1]- Rep. by *Ibn 'Abbas, Ibn Mas'ud, As-Siddi* and many sahaba. Pub. in Ara-Tha 148;Taf-Bagh & Taf-Khaz 2:49; Taf-Tab 20:40; Tar-Kath 1:239, and other tafsir books.

[2]- Ara-Tha and Taf-Qur gave the name of 'Lukha' to Moses' mother. Exodus called her 'Jochebed'.

[3]- Rep. by Ibn 'Abbas, pub. by Ara-Tha 149; Qis-Kis 215.

him that she planned to hide her son in it. She took the box, and the carpenter went to the authorities to apprise them of what he had learned. But when he tried to speak, he found that God had locked his tongue. He attempted sign language but the guards took no notice, except to beat him and throw him out. Once back in his shop, he regained his speech and returned to the guards. But God had this time deprived him of both the powers of speech and vision, and the officers, having lost all patience, once again beat him and threw him into the street. The carpenter then vowed that if his senses were restored he would never disclose Moses' existence, and God, knowing his sincerity, returned the carpenter's ability to see and speak. And Moses was put into the box and set afloat on the river.[1]*    Exd 2:3

### Moses raised by Pharaoh

The pharaoh of Egypt had one child, a daughter, and she was very precious to him. But she had a skin disease which caused white patches and which had confounded every physician brought in by the pharaoh. It was finally decided that the cure would be found by rubbing her skin with the saliva of a person who would emerge from the river on a certain date at sunrise.

As the pharaoh and his family sat on the banks of the Nile, the box with Moses inside drifted down the river, becoming stuck in the weeds in plain view of the pharaoh. He instructed his officers to retrieve the box, which they did, but they were unable to open it. Asiya, the wife of the pharaoh, was the only one to see a light emanating from the box, and opened it. To her surprise, she found a baby inside, with a light sparkling between his eyes, sucking his thumb, and God gave her a great love for Moses,* and the pharaoh,    Exd 2:5-6 himself felt much sympathy for the infant. Asiya the Pharaoh's daughter, rubbed his saliva on the white patches of her skin, which disappeared immediately.[2]

---

[1]- Pub. By Taf-Bagh 28:7, Ara-Tha 159; Qis-Kis 216.

[2]- Hebrew sources called the pharaoh's daughter 'Bithiah' but Yashar called her 'Therutis'. She was afflicted with leprosy which caused white spots on her skin, but once she touched Moses' box she was cured. From L.O.J. II, 266 and endnote Moses 48.

The pharaoh was warned that this child might be the one in his dream, and he should be thrown back into the water. But Asiya pleaded with the pharaoh to keep him, and the pharaoh granted her request and she named him Moses. [1]

After casting Moses into the river, his mother asked his sister Mariam to follow Moses from a distance, and to let no one

Exd 2:4  notice what she was up to.*Moses refused every wet nurse that Asiya offered, which concerned her, as he might die from lack of milk. A servant was sent to the market in hopes of finding a suitable wet nurse, and Mariam went to the servant and said, "*Shall I lead you to a family who will look after him and take good care of him?*" 28:12  It was agreed that Moses be taken to his mother where she was able to satisfy his thirst. Asiya was pleased that an adequate nurse had been found, and asked that she come and stay with the pharaoh and his family. But Moses' mother apologized and told Asiya that she could not leave her own home, but would gladly keep the baby with her.

Exd 2:7-9  Asiya allowed this, and after a three day separation Moses* "*was reunited with his mother so he might comfort her, and she would not be sad, and so she would know that God's promise is true.*" 28:13

Moses grew and was raised by his parents. When he began to walk, Asiyah expressed a desire to see him, and arrangements were made. She told her friends of the impending visit, and they all sent gifts to Moses, which were presented to him on his way from his mother's house to the pharaoh's palace. Asiya was happy to see Moses, and happy to see he was being raised properly. She honored him with a gift and asked that he be presented to the pharaoh. Moses

---

[1]- In Exodus 2:5-6 the woman who found and adopted Moses was the pharaoh's daughter and not his wife, but in 3 Sibylline Oracles 253 and Josephus Antiquities II, 10:5, they addressed her as "the queen". In Exodus 2, she called him Moses because she said, "I drew him out of the water." The Hebrew writers later explained that the name Moses in Hebrew means the drawer, but that doesn't explain why the pharaoh's daughter would have given him a Hebrew name. But *Muqatil* said that the name Moshe is a Coptic 'old Egyptian' name from ' Mu,' which means water and 'she' which means tree.

[2]- Rep. by *Ibn 'Abbas, Mujahid, 'Akrama, Sa'id bin Jubayr, Abu 'Ubaydah, Al-Hasan, Qutada* and *Ad-Dahhak*. Published by Ara-Tha 151, and Tar-Kath I:239.

sat on the pharaoh's lap and plucked some hairs from his beard, which displeased the pharaoh a great deal. He said, "This child is my enemy," and made plans to have Moses killed. Asiya heard of his order and pleaded with him, "You gave me this child's life, why now do you want to take it away?" When she was told what Moses had done she admonished the pharaoh, "He is just a child and does not yet know what he is doing, he does not know the difference between a piece of burning charcoal and a ruby." The pharaoh decided to put him to just such a test and arranged for a hot charcoal and a ruby to be placed before Moses, on two separate plates. Moses extended his hand to reach for the ruby but the Angel Gabriel moved his hand to take the burning charcoal instead. He held it then put it in his mouth which burned him and left him with a speech impediment for the rest of his life. The pharaoh pardoned Moses who stayed in the palace and was honored and respected, God made him loved by everyone.[1]

### Moses Kills an Egyptian Man

When Moses was a young man he rode with the pharaoh in parades, wore the same dress as that of the pharaoh, and was called "Moses, son of the pharaoh." The pharaoh went riding on a day when Moses was away, and when Moses returned and found the pharaoh gone, he rode after him. Moses reached the city of Memphis at midday when the city was deserted, the shops were closed, and no one was on the streets. But he did come upon two men, an Egyptian and an Israelite, who were fighting each other. The Egyptian, called Phaton, was a baker to the pharaoh, and was forcing the Israelite to carry firewood for the ovens. Moses heard the cries for help and told the Egyptian to leave the Israelite alone. But Phaton said, "I am taking him for the pharaoh's work." Moses became angry and punched the Egyptian, who, much to Moses' surprise, dropped dead. Moses said, *"This is some of Satan's work, My Lord, I have wronged my own soul, forgive me,"* and God forgave him. Moses said, *"My Lord, since you have shown me such favor, I shall never be involved*

---

[1]- Rep. by *Ibn 'Abbas* and pub. by Ara-Tha 151-152; Taf-Tab 20:27; Tar-Kath I:249; Qis-Kis 218. The story of the burning of Moses' tongue was also mentioned in Exodus Rabbah 1:26.

Exd 2:11-12 *with criminals again.*"28:15-17* God revealed to Moses, "With My might and My Glory, if this soul you killed had confessed, in a blink of an eye, that I am the Creator and Sustainer, I would punish you for what you have done. But there was no confession."[1]

The following morning, Moses was fearful and on the alert when he came upon the same Israelite in a fight with yet another Egyptian, who again screamed for help. Moses was still in torment for what had occurred the day before, but could not resist a cry for help. He raised his arm to hit the Egyptian, but said to the Israelite, "You are the troublemaker." The Israelite thought that Moses was going to hit him and said, "*Moses, do you want to kill me just as you killed another yesterday? You want to be a powerful and violent man in this land and not a peacemaker.*"28:19 This stopped the fight and the Egyptian went to the authorities and told them what he had heard.

Exd 2:13-15 The pharaoh sent his guards after Moses.* But Moses had been warned by an Egyptian believer, Ezekiel, who ran through the city to reach him and said, "*Moses, the councilmen are deliberating about whether or not you are to be executed, take my sound advice and leave now.*"28:20

**Moses in Median**

Moses did not know where to go until an angel appeared on horseback, and Moses followed him to Median where he arrived eight days later. He was attracted to a well where the shepherds brought their flocks for watering. Moses noticed two women nearby holding their flock back, and when Moses questioned them, they explained that they could not draw any water until the herdsmen had finished. They went on to say that their father, the great holy man, *Shu'ayb*, now an old man, could no longer look after his flock. Moses helped the two girls, Lia and Zephura, water their flock, and then went to rest

---

[1]- Rep. by *Ibn 'Abbas, Sa'id bin Jubayr, 'Akrama, Qutada* and *As-Siddi.* Pub. by Ara-Tha152-153, and other books of tafsir. In Exodus, Moses made sure he was alone with the Egyptian and then killed him. The following day the two men fighting were both Hebrew, and when Moses asked the aggressor why he was striking a fellow Hebrew, he answered by saying, "Who made you a prince and a judge over us? Are you intending to kill me as you killed the Egyptian?"

under the shade of a tree. He prayed, "*My Lord, I am poor enough to accept anything you may grant me.*"[1]

Moses had not eaten for several days and would have been happy with even half a date. Not long after his prayer, Zephura returned and said to Moses, "*My father invites you to our home, in order that he may reward you with some payment as you have watered our flock.*"28:24-25 As Moses followed Zephura, he could not help but notice her dress, which had been taken by the wind and pressed tightly against her buttocks. Not wishing to bring any sexual desires upon himself, Moses told Zephura, "You walk behind me and guide me to your father's home. If I stray in the wrong direction, throw a stone to direct me towards the proper path. We, the children of Jacob, do not follow behind women."

When Moses reached Shu'ayb's home he told the holy man his entire story and Shu'ayb reassured him, "*Do not fear, you have escaped from the wrongdoers.*" Zephura told her father, "*Hire him, the best man to hire is someone strong and trustworthy.*" Shu'ayb told Moses he wanted to marry him to one of his daughters, "*Provided you hire yourself out to me for eight seasons. If you complete ten, then it is your own affair, I do not want to be hard on you, you will find me, with God's help, an honorable man.*" Moses answered , "*This is up to you and to me, whichever term I may serve, there will be no injustice done to me. God is the trustee for anything we say*.*"28:25-28 Exd 2:16-21

After nine years of working, Shu'ayb told Moses, "I will give you every white lamb which will be born next year," and to Shu'ayb's surprise every one of the sheep carried two pregnancies and delivered

---

[1]- This holy man has no name in the Qur'an, but in another sura the Qur'an talked about the people of Median and their prophet *Shu'ayb*. Some Qur'an interpreters came to the conclusion that these two people are the same. That is what *Al-Hasan* and *Malik bin Anas* maintained. However, others gave this holy man the biblical name of Jethrone, and this is the teaching of *Ibn 'Abbas* and Abu *'Ubayda bin 'Abdullah*. In another version of this story the well was covered with a huge rock and the two girls were waiting for the shepherds to come and remove it so they might water their sheep. Moses removed the rock by himself, which usually required ten people.

two white lambs the following year.  Shu'ayb realized that this was
a sign from God and gave Moses the promised lambs.[1]

**Moses' Staff**

Moses completed his appointed term and ,Shu'ayb granted
permission for him to leave with his pregnant wife and his sheep.
Shu'ayb told Moses, "Take from that room a staff from the many I
possess.  It will protect you and your flock from wild beasts."  When
Moses entered the room a staff jumped into his hand, but when
Shu'ayb saw him with it he said, "No, not that one, choose another."
Shu'ayb was the keeper of the staffs of the prophets, and that
particular staff was to be kept for the next prophet who was unknown
to Shu'ayb.  Moses made many attempts to take another staff but to
no avail, the same staff kept attaching itself to Moses' hand.  When
he appeared before Shu'ayb with the staff and explained that he could
not choose another, Shu'ayb realized that the staff was intended for
Moses.  Originally, the staff was brought out of the Garden by Adam
who took it from a tree.  On earth, the staff passed from generation to
generation until it reached Shu'ayb.  Moses' staff had two branches
at the lower end, which allowed him to do many amazing things.  In
the dark, the branches would illuminate a path, and Moses could see
to the full extent of his vision.  If he needed water, the staff could be
lowered into a well, its branches serving as a pail so that Moses could
extract fresh water.  When Moses required sustenance he would strike
the earth with his staff, and it would change into whatever fruit tree
Moses desired.  Should he meet an enemy, two fire breathing dragons
would spring from its branches and slay the offenders.  The staff
could dispatch rocks and thorns, clearing paths and opening roads for
Moses, as well as parting rivers so he might cross on dry land.  It
provided honey from one branch and milk from the other.  Moses
used it for transportation. It gave direction and warned him away from
danger.The staff was also used for more mundane purposes. Moses
would hang his clothes and supplies from it, push away wild beasts,
insects and snakes, and use it as a tool to shake down leaves for his

[1]- Rep. by *Anas bin Malik*.  Pub. by Taf-Tab 28:22-28; Tar-Kath I:246,
Ara-Tha 154-155; Qis-Kis 222.

sheep to eat. The staff also sprayed Moses with perfume when he
wished to refresh himself.[1]

## Moses' Audience with God

Moses and his wife walked from the land of Median through
the desert, and though unfamiliar with the roads they kept walking
until they found themselves on the right slope of the Sinai Mount.* Exd 3:1
During a very cold winter's night in a menacing thunderstorm, his
wife went into labor. Moses was unable to start a fire, but glimpsed
a flash of light on the mountain slope. He left his wife and went
toward the light, thinking it might be a fire and he could return with
an ember. Moses reached the mountain slope and saw a great light
extending from the sky to a burning bush, a bush that was becoming
greener despite the fire glowing from inside.* Moses was fearful, Exd 3:2
but his need for fire overcame his trepidation, and he walked toward
it and heard someone call to him from the tree in the blessed hollow
on the right bank of the wadi. "Moses, I am God, Lord of the worlds."
28:30 Moses saw no one, but was overcome by awe. His heart was
racing and his muscles so weak he could not stand. God sent an angel
to support him, and when he regained his strength he heard the call,
"Moses, remove your shoes, you are in a holy wadi."* 20:12 He took Exd 3:5
off his shoes and again heard the voice call and question him, "Moses,
what do you hold in your right hand?" And Moses answered, "This
is my staff, I lean on it, use it to beat down fodder for my sheep; it has
many uses."

"Throw it down, Moses." As Moses did so, it became a snake
which began to twitch, and seeing this, Moses took flight.

"Moses, come closer and do not be afraid, you will be safe. Pick
it up and we will return it as it was." Moses was wearing a thick,
wool coat, and he pulled down the sleeves to cover his hands. But he

---

[1]- Pub. by Ara-Tha 155-157, most probably from Hebrew sources.

[2]- The mufassirun disagreed over the reason for Moses removing his
shoes. *Ibn Mas'ud* maintained that his shoes were made of donkey skin and unclean,
while *Mujahid* and *'Akrama* said, "He removed them to touch the soles of his feet
with the blessed land." *Sa'id bin Jubayr* said it is a sign of being humble. from Taf-
Tab 20:12.

was told to uncover them and to use his bare, unprotected hands, fight back his fears and retrieve the snake.  As he grasped it, it once again

Exd 4:2-4  became his staff.*  The voice told him, "*Slip your hand under your shirt front, it will come out white without being harmed.*"20:17-22 Moses slipped his hand in and out and it shone with white light, in and out

Exd 4:6-7  again, and it was returned to its natural state.[1]*

"*These are two signs* [to show] *to the pharaoh and his councillors, they have acted as very immoral folk.*"  Moses said, "*My Lord, I killed a person from among them, and fear they may execute me.  My brother Aaron is more convincing with his tongue, send him along with me to back me up and vouch for me.  I fear they will talk me out of it.*"  God said, "*I am hearing and seeing what you see and hear.  We shall strengthen your arm by means of your brother, and grant both of you authority so they will not overtake either of you.  Because of Our Signs, you will both win out, as well as anyone who*

Exd 4:10-12  *follows you.*"28:32-35*

The audience with God was over, and when Moses was told by an angel that his wife delivered a boy, Moses' heart became occupied with his newborn son and wanted to circumcise him.[2]  The Angel took the baby from his mother and Moses picked two stones, rubbed them together until one attained a very sharp edge, and used it to circumcise his son.  The Angel took some of his saliva and put it on the wound which healed it immediately.  The baby was then returned to the mother, who did not know the whereabouts of Moses at this time.  A few days passed and a shepherd recognized Moses' wife and took her and her son to Median where they stayed with

---

[1]- Taf-Bagh 27:7-12; Taf-Khaz 20:9-36.  In Exodus 4:6, when Moses withdrew his hand from his chest, his hand was leprous, as if covered with snow. The Hebrew writers maintain that his temporary affliction with leprosy was a chastisement for his hasty words, but the Qur'an stresses the idea that his hand was discolored and white but with no illness.

[2]- The story of this circumcision is completely different in Exodus. Moses' son was born in Median but was not circumcised. On the return to Egypt the Lord met Moses and  tried to kill him, but Zipporah took a flint and cut off her son's foreskin and touched Moses feet with it, and saved his life.

*Shu'ayb.*[1] When news reached them that Moses had crossed the sea, his wife and baby were sent to join him.[2]

## Moses Meets the Pharaoh

After Moses was assigned to carry the massage of God, he went directly to Egypt, with God guiding and supporting him along the way. He traversed the roads alone, carrying neither food nor arms, only his woolen hat and cloak and, of course, his staff. God alerted Aaron, in Egypt, with the good news of not only Moses' arrival, but also with the instruction that Aaron was to be Moses' right-hand man and co-messenger to the pharaoh. Moses reached his parents' home at night and his mother, who invited him to dinner, did not recognize him until he introduced himself to Aaron, who embraced him at the dinner table. God revealed to the brothers, "Go to the pharaoh, he has been arrogant. Speak a soft word to him so that he may be reminded and perhaps even afraid." They both said, "O Lord, we both fear lest he crack down on us or act arrogant." God reassured them, "I am with you both, I hear and see for you. Go to him and say: 'We are both messengers of Your Lord, send the children of Israel away with us and do not torment them.'" 20:43-47*    Exd 4:15-16

The pharaoh lived in a heavily fortified city surrounded by seventy walls, and between the walls were farms and rivers, and for every wall he appointed seventy thousand soldiers. There was also a forest which the pharaoh himself had a hand in planting, as well as a very large number of ferocious lions that were used as guards. If a traveler was not familiar with the few secure roads through the forest to the gate of the city, he would most always succumb to the lions' appetites. Every few days the lions were led to the Nile to drink, and would not return until the late evening.

It was on such a day that Moses and Aaron attempted to travel through the forest. But the lions spotted the holy men and extended their heads and necks toward them. However, the lions eyed them

---

[1]- In Hebrew Mekilta RS, 86 Moses met Aaron in the wilderness, and advised Moses to send his family back to Median. From L.O.J. II, 329 and endnote Moses 151.

[2]- Ara-Tha 157-160, probably from storytellers or Hebrew lore.

with fear and turned and ran away in confusion, stumbling over each other until they reached their home in the forest. Moses and Aaron continued through the forest until they reached the pharaoh's grand city gate, and there they waited for one week. A guard asked them if they did not realize whose gate they loitered beneath. Moses answered, "This gate, this land and all of the occupants belong to the Lord of the Universe, and the people within are his servants." The guard was surprised by these words and was shocked that anyone would speak in such a manner. He informed his superior, who did the same, until the pharaoh was told, "There are two men at the gate saying the most ludicrous things, that their Lord is not you." The pharaoh had them enter and they were brought before him.[1] When asked who he was, Moses answered, "I am a messenger from the Lord of the Universe. It is only right for me to say nothing except the truth about God. I have brought Divine signs from Your Lord, so send the

Exd 5:1  Israelites with me." 7:104-105*

the pharaoh then recognized Moses and said, "Did we not raise you as a child among us, and did you not spend several years of your life among us? Yet you have committed this deed; you are ungrateful." Moses said, "I was misguided and fled from you because I feared you. My Lord has bestowed discretion on me and set me up as an emissary. Is this the favor you have shown me, to have enslaved the children of Israel?" The pharaoh asked Moses, "What is the Lord of the

Exd 5:2  universe?"* And Moses answered, "The Lord of heavens and earth, and all that lies in between, if you will be convinced." 26:18-24  The pharaoh was incredulous, and chided those around him listening to the rhetoric that Moses must be not of sound mind. Moses continued as if he did not hear the pharaoh's comments, and the pharaoh then threatened to put Moses in jail if he "should adopt any god but me." "Even if I bring you clear and convincing proof?" 26:29-30  asked Moses. And the pharaoh allowed that Moses should bring whatever evidence he had to prove his case.[2] Moses cast down his staff and it

Exd 7:10  became an enormous snake* extending from one side of the palace

---

[1] - Ara-Tha 160-161.
[2] - Ara-Tha 157-160.

to the other. Its opened mouth reached up the palace walls high enough that Egyptians outside the walls could see its head. When the snake approached the pharaoh as if to swallow him, he leaped from his throne in a panic. This fright left him in such torment that he needed to use the toilet forty times, not to mention the incident on the throne itself.[1] The pharaoh claimed that he was unlike other people, he was immune to disease and existed on a diet of bananas which, they thought, had no fiber. Prior to his encounter with the snake, thanks to his unusual diet of pure bananas, he only went to the toilet once every forty days. He used that as a proof of his divine nature.[2]

When the snake was near to the pharaoh, he called to Moses, "I beg of your God, and for the sake of nursing you as a baby, to keep this snake away, and I promise to believe in you and send you with the Israelites." Moses captured the snake and it changed back into a staff. He then put his hand inside his shirt, and when he brought it out it shone with an intense light that pierced the eyes and blinded the pharaoh.

When the pharaoh wanted to acknowledge Moses' faith, his vizier "Hāmān" came to him and said, "You are a known and worshiped god. Do not be a follower to a slave." So the pharaoh told Moses he must have some time to think over his decision. God revealed to Moses to tell the pharaoh that if he believed in God, the pharaoh's age will be reversed, and he would get younger and reign for a very long time. But Hāmān advised the pharaoh to reject the offer, as it was not equal to being worshiped by his people as a god. He further suggested the use of black hair dye should the pharaoh want to appear younger.[3]

### Sorcery vs the Power of God

Pharaoh went to his council and told them that Moses was a clever magician who wanted to drive them from their lands, and he

---

[1]- Rep. by *Qutada, As-Siddi, Ibn 'Abbas*; pub. by Taf-Bagh 7:107, Ara-Tha 162-163, Tar-Kath I:251, Taf-Tab 7:107. Humor is a rare commodity in Islamic literature but here we find an exception.

[2]- Rep. by *Ibn 'Abbas, Wahb* and *As-Siddi,* pub. by Ara-Tha 162; Taf-Tab & Taf-Khaz 20:20.

[3]- Pub. by Taf-Bagh & Taf-Khaz 20:44; Ara-Tha.

should be killed, "Let *him appeal to his Lord, I fear he will change your religion or cause havoc in this land.*"40:26 The councilmen suggested killing both of them. But a man from the court called Ezekiel, who was a believer but had hidden his faith, said, "*What, will you kill a man for merely saying, 'My Lord is God?' He has brought you enlightenment from the Lord. If he is a liar, then his lies will turn against him. If he speaks the truth, then what he threatens may afflict you. God does not guide anyone who is a preposterous liar. You have control as masters on earth, But who will support us against God's wrath should it ever come to us?*" The pharaoh said, "*I am only showing you what I see myself, I am guiding you along the path of normal behavior.*"40:28-29 The councilmen decided to make Moses and his brother wait, and recruits would be sent into the cities to bring back every clever magician. They told Moses, "*Have you come to us to turn us out of our lands through your magic? If so, we counter with our own magic. Make arrangements to meet us in a convenient place that neither side will break.*"20:57-58 Moses agreed and it was decided to meet on Decoration Day, the spring festival, and they were to appear early in the morning.[1]

Exd 7:11        The pharaoh summoned every magician in Egypt.[2]* The position of chief magician was jointly held by two brothers in southern Egypt. When they received the summons they went to their father's grave to ask for his advice. They explained to him that they were needed by the pharaoh to deal with two men and, although these men had no arms or supporters, they had a staff that was capable of swallowing wood, stones and iron. Their father's advice was to steal the staff while the owners slept, as magicians are bereft of their powers at that time. Should the staff still be active though its owners slept, then one could discern that the power comes from the Lord of

---

[1]- Pub. by Ara-Tha 162-163 from undocumented sources, probably Jewish lore.

[2]- The number of the sorcerers summoned by the pharaoh is eighty thousand according to *Muhammad bin Ka'b*, or seventy thousand according to *Al-Qasim bin Abi Burda*, or twelve thousand according to *Ka'b*, or nineteen thousand according to *Abu Umama*, or fifteen thousand according to *Ibn Ishaq*.

the Universe, and no one can fight that power. The chief magicians went to steal the staff, but it fought them, and they beat a hasty retreat. The pharaoh had, however, through his recruits, gathered more magicians, seventy thousand in all, which he narrowed to seven thousand, then seven hundred and finally, seventy master magicians. These men were appointed to confront Moses and were promised to be paid handsomely, as well as being given the prestige of becoming part of the court should they defeat Moses.[1]

On the appointed day,[2] everyone from the court showed up to watch the spectacle, and so did Aron and Moses with his staff. They said, *"Watch out for yourself, do not invent any lies about God lest He blot you out through torment. Anyone who invents things will be disappointed."* 20:61 The magicians gloated that *"today you shall see magic the likes of which you have never seen before."* 20:58 Moses allowed the court magicians to begin first. The magicians displayed the rods and ropes taken from some sixty camels' loads before the pharaoh and said, *"By the pharaoh's majesty, we will be victorious."* 26:44 The rods and ropes appeared to the spectators to be snakes, and Moses became afraid. God told him, *"Do not act afraid, you will not lose, throw down what is in your right hand and it will swallow anything that your adversaries have produced. What they have produced is simply a magician's trick, and no magician really succeeds."* 20:68-69

Moses threw down his staff, and it became an ominous and enormous snake with four short, strong limbs, larger than a camel with a powerful tail that could smash into pieces anything it came in contact with. It stuck its head above the city walls and its eyes looked like two flames, its nose blew poison, and the hair on its head looked like spears. The branches of the staff became an open mouth, twelve cubits in lengths, and it attacked and swallowed the magicians' snakes.* The Egyptian onlookers ran away, creating a tremendous    Exd 7:11-12

---

[1]- Rep. by *'Ata*, pub. by Ara-Tha 164. See also Taf-Tab 7:112.
[2]- *Ibn 'Abbas* said it was the first day of the spring festival.

disturbance, and twenty five thousand people died in the stampede.[1]
When the sorcerers realized they were up against no ordinary
magicians they dropped to their knees, saying, *"We believe in the
Lord of the Universe, the Lord of Moses and Aaron."*26:47-48 The
pharaoh was furious and said, *"You believe in his God before I permit
you to do that. He must be your chief who has taught you magic, I'll
cut your feet and hands and crucify you all."* They answered, *"We
will never choose you before He who created us and these signs which
we have now seen. Decide what you will do, your decision may only
affect what happens in this early life. We believe in our Lord, so He
may forgive our mistakes as well as the magic you have compelled us
to perform. God is better and more enduring."*20:71-73 These people
ended their lives as martyrs, while the pharaoh continued with his
rejection and wrongdoing.

## The Plagues

Moses and Aaron went back to the Israelite camp, and the
pharaoh asked the Egyptians to increase the burden on the Israelites,
which they did. It was not unusual for an Egyptian to tell an Israelite
to clean his house, feed the animals and bring him water from the
Nile, all in one day, and without any food. Later in the day the
Israelites were expected to work elsewhere for their meals. The
Israelites complained to Moses, who told them, *"Seek help from God
and be patient, the earth belongs to God. Anyone He wishes from
among His servants will inherit it, and the outcome belongs to those
who heed."* They countered that, *"we were oppressed before you came
to us, and we will be again after you leave us."*[2] Moses said,
*"Perhaps Your Lord will wipe out your enemy and you will be lords
over this earth, so He may observe how you act."*7:128-129

The pharaoh and his people refused to believe and continued
in their rejection, wrongdoing and oppression. Moses called to His
Lord and said, "Lord, your slave pharaoh has oppressed the people of

---

[1]- Taf-Bagh 7:117.
[2]- In Exd 5:7 the Israelites acted as forced labor gathering mud and
straw to make bricks. See also Exd. 5:21.

this earth. His people deceived Your covenant and renounced the promise. Lord, punish them in such a way that it will be a lesson to my people and other nations that will follow them." God sent them one punishment after the other. The first was a flood which devastated homes and temporarily damaged the land, so the fields were not suitable for planting.[1] Even though the water reached the necks of the Egyptians, not one drop touched the Israelites nor their property. The deluge lasted seven days until they asked Moses to ask his God to relieve their misery, and they promised to believe and send with him the Israelites. But the Egyptians did not do what they promised, and, as a result of the water, the Egyptians ended the year with a good crop and said, "This flood was a blessing."

But before the harvest was gathered the locusts came and devoured everything that had been planted. This was God's second punishment, and was very destructive; the insects ate the trees, fruit, the Egyptians' doors, ceilings, and clothes, leaving only the rusty nails in the floorboards.[2] But the Israelites once again were left unharmed, and once again the Egyptians begged Moses to speak to God and have Him relieve their agony. In return they promised to believe in Moses and his religion, and to release the Israelites so they might go with Moses, but once the locusts had been dispatched and life had returned to normal, the Egyptians forgot their promise.

One month later the third punishment was meted out. Moses walked to a great sand hill at Heliopolis and struck it with his staff. Ticks[3] swarmed over the Egyptians' farms and fruit trees and into their foodstuffs, into their clothing and onto their bodies, They attacked their hair down to the scalp, ate at their eyebrows and eyelashes, leaving their skin covered in sores as if there had been a epidemic of smallpox. For the third time the Egyptians begged for mercy and pledged to accept the faith of Moses. But once the scourge of the ticks had passed, the Egyptians decided "only a sorcerer can

---

[1]- In Exd 9:22-26 the thunder and hail were the seventh plague.

[2]- In Exd 10:12-15 the locusts were the eighth plague.

[3]- In Arabic it is the 'qummal', which is a type of insect. *Ibn 'Abbas* maintained it was the weevil but *Mujahid, 'Akrama* and *Qutada* explained it as the baby locust. *Ibn Jubayr* said it was the tick. In Exodus, lice were the third plague 8:16-19, and the flies were the fourth.

change sand into an army of insects. Why should we surrender to
him after he has destroyed our produce and our livestock? What else
can he do? We will never believe in him or follow him." And the
Egyptians returned to their old ways.

That continued for one month until Moses stuck his staff into
the banks of the Nile, directed it upstream, then down and released a
torrent of frogs into the city which inundated every facet of their
lives. The frogs took over their courtyards, buildings, their cooking
ware, and every time an Egyptian opened a food container he found
frogs inside. Frogs surrounded the people to such an extent that they
would take food from the mouths of the Egyptians, making speaking
and eating near impossible tasks. The frogs would extinguish their
fires by leaping into the flames, and great numbers of the amphibians
lay dead on their roads, making the city stink.[1] The Egyptians
surrendered and pleaded with Moses to intercede with his Lord for
relief. God granted them a one-month respite, but when the
Egyptians forgot their promise Moses was instructed once again to
strike the banks of the Nile.

Having done so, the fifth punishment commenced, with the
water in the Nile as well as in the smaller streams, inlets and wells
turning into blood. As with the previous punishments, only the
Egyptians were affected by the wrath of God. The Egyptians and
Israelites might drink from the same water, but only the Egyptians
swallowed blood. An Egyptian woman asked an Israelite woman to
first take some water in her mouth and pour it directly into that of the
Egyptian's. But once the water entered the mouth of the Egyptian, it
had turned to blood. The Nile was watering the farms with fresh
water, but should any Egyptian attempt to slake his thirst with the
water it would be turned into blood.[2] The pharaoh became so parched
he tried to chew some tender and juicy branches, but the juice left him
with only a bitter and salty taste in his mouth. After a week of
drinking blood the Egyptians again asked Moses to seek God's
mercy, and Moses with his staff returned fresh water to the Nile. But
the Egyptians refused to honor the pledge they had made to Moses.
Moses was exasperated with the Egyptians and found no matter what

---

[1]- Frogs are the second plague in Exd 8:1-15.
[2]- Blood is the first plague in Exd 7:17-18.

the punishment, they became more determined to remain as unbelievers, and continued to reject God.[1]

## The Tower of Egypt

In spite of the very powerful status of the pharaoh, he was worried that the people would believe and follow Moses, so he commissioned his vizier Hāmān to build a high, brick tower so he might get close to heaven and see if Moses was telling the truth about his God. Hāmān hired fifty thousand workers who labored day and night, and it was completed in seven years. It was the highest building ever made at that time, and when it was done God did not give the pharoah a chance to walk on the tower. God sent the Angel Gabriel who hit the tower with his wing, and the tower collapsed on the pharaoh's camp, killing two million of his people. Everyone who worked on that tower either died or became disabled.[2]

## The Exodus

Moses and Aaron told God, *"Our Lord, You have given the pharaoh and his councillors much wealth and splendor in worldly life. Our Lord, is this so they may lead us from your way? Our Lord, wipe out their wealth and firm up their hearts so they may not believe until they see painful torment."* God answered, saying, *"Your appeal has been answered, so act straight away and do not follow along the way of those who do not know.[3]"*10:88-89.

The pharaoh and his councillors acquired immense sums of wealth, consisting of gold, silver, rubies, pearls and diamonds in vast amounts. God revealed to Moses, "I shall invest the Israelites with the jewels of the pharaoh and his people to enjoy in the Holy Land. Gather your people together and recite My Name, worship Me, and borrow the jewels of the pharaoh and his people for that special day of celebration. They will allow you to borrow them, as they are in

---

[1]- Taf-Bagh, Taf-Tab & Taf-Khaz 7:133; Ara-Tha 168-173; Tar-Kath I:265.

[2]- Taf-Bagh 28:38; Ara-Tha 167.

[3]- Rep. by *Sa'id bin Jubayr, Qutada, Ibn 'Abbas, Muqatil, Ad-Dahhak, Mujahid* and *'Ata.*

dire circumstances, afraid of suffering." The pharaoh did lend some jewelry to Moses, which stayed with the Israelites when they left Egypt.* The jewels that remained with the pharaoh and his family were turned into worthless stones, as did the money in their hands.

Exd 12:35

Before leaving Egypt Moses asked where Joseph was buried, but the Israelites claimed not to know. He then came upon an old lady who said she knew of the burial site. In return for this information, she wanted Moses to grant her whatever she would wish for. Moses accepted the proposal after consulting with God, and the old lady told him he would find Joseph buried in a marble sarcophagus at the bottom of the Nile. After asking God to part the water, Moses was able to remove Joseph's watery tomb, and it was carried to be buried in the Holy Land.* The old lady's request was to accompany Moses to wherever he would be in Heaven.[1]

Exd 13:19

## Moses and the Israelites Cross the Sea

God directed Moses to see that the Israelites should gather, every four families in one home, and slaughter a baby ram whose blood should be used to mark their doors.* God said, "I will instruct my angels to torture your enemy but not to enter any house with blood on the door. These angels will kill the first born child of every supporter of the pharaoh, but you will be safe.* Take My people, lead them to the sea and wait for My order." The Israelites obeyed God's instruction, and in the morning seventy thousand children whose families were sympathetic to that of the pharaoh had been killed. The Egyptians were preoccupied with the burial of their children, while Moses and his people, numbering six hundred and twenty thousand, not including the very old and young, moved toward the sea.* The pharaoh learned of the exodus and said, "This was Moses' plan; they killed our young and walked away of with our money." God told Moses, "Travel with My servants at night, for you will be pursued." 26:52. The pharaoh sent recruits into the cities: "There are a few dissidents; agitators against us, we are completely forewarned." 26:53-56

Exd 12:12-13

Exd 12:12-13

Exd 12:30-32

---

[1]- Taf-Bagh 2:50; Ara-Tha 174.

The pharaoh followed the Israelites with one million, seven hundred thousand horsemen, each brandishing a spear and outfitted with a helmet.* The Israelites were alerted to the advancing army Exd 14:6-7 by billowing clouds of dust rising above the horizon. They complained to Moses, "Where is the victory you promised us? The sea is in front of us, and if we proceed we drown. The pharaoh's army is behind us, and should it reach us we will be annihilated."* Exd 14:10-12 When Moses reached the sea, a fierce storm hit and the waves swelled menacingly. Joshua bin Nun asked where they should cross, and Moses chose a spot. Joshua crossed the sea riding on his mount with the sea water not higher than the horse's hooves. Ezekiel, the Egyptian believer, attempted the same crossing but he sank. Moses did not know what to do when God called down, *"Strike the sea with your staff."* 26:63* Moses did so but nothing happened. God told him Exd 14:16 to strike again and say, "Sea, split apart." The sea split into twelve roads, and Ezekiel on one of these roads was waiting for them. God sent the wind and sun to dry out the uncovered seabed so the Israelites were able to easily traverse the sea. The tribes utilized the twelve roads, one road for each tribe, but became afraid when they were surrounded by a huge wall of water. God opened up windows in the wall so the tribes might see and speak to each other, which they did until the last of the Israelites crossed the parted sea. [1]

When the pharaoh reached the sea, he told his men it had split due to his majesty and ordered them to proceed. But his cavalry balked, and would not cross. The Angel Gabriel appeared on a mare in heat, and began to cross. The pharaoh's horse caught the scent of the mare and chased her into the sea, with the entire army in pursuit.[2] Once there, God closed the sea, and, with the Israelites looking on, drowned the Egyptian army.* When the pharaoh realized he was Exd 14:23-28

---

[1]- Pub. by Taf-Khaz 2:50. In the Hebrew writings the sea opened unto twelve paths, one for each of the tribes. The water between the paths became as transparent as glass, and each tribe could see the others. Mekilta Beshallah 5,31a-31b.

[2]-Taf-Tab 10-90; In Hebrew Mekilta 52, to lure the Egyptian cavalry into the sea the Lord caused the steeds to swim into water and the rest of the cavalry followed. The legend of Gabriel's mare is related to the legend of the heavenly mare told in Mekilta RS 51-52.

about to die, he said, "I *believe there is no deity but the one whom the Israelites believe in. I am now a believer.*" Gabriel answered him saying, "*You say this now, but you have disobeyed before and been a mischief maker.*"10:90-91 Gabriel reached into the sea and brought out mud which he forced into the mouth of the pharaoh so he could not repeat his words and have God grant him mercy.[1]

The Israelites heard the rush of water and Moses confirmed that the pharaoh and his army were drowning. But as they were skeptical as to the pharaoh's demise, God had the sea spit out the pharaoh's body clad in his suit of armor for all of the Israelites to see.[2]

---

[1]- Taf-Tab and Taf-Bagh 10:90-91; Ara-Tha. The story of forcing mud into the mouth of Pharaoh came from hadith pub. by *At-Tirmidhi.*

The drowning of the pharaoh and his army is remembered each year with sadness by the Mandeans on the day of *Ashuriyyah,* the first day of the month of *Sartanah,* (July). The Mandaeans believe that the Egyptians were the followers of the Mandaean (true) religion, while they believe the Jews were worshipers of the Roha, an evil spirit. Moses and his people crossed the sea after he struck it with his staff which was given to him by the Roha. The pharaoh and the Egyptians followed them using the same trick–striking the sea with his sceptor, but the pharaoh's mistake was not remaining in the split sea until his army had in total passed through. Once he left, the ocean closed, killing all his army. From Sabian legends 15,26-27. The Mandaean is a gnostic religion and predate Christianity, and their writings reflect their persecution by the Jews of Palestine till they were driven away from that land. Most of the Mandaeans to-day live in Iraq with a few residing in Iran.

[2]-Pub. in Taf-Bagh 2:50 and most tafsir books from different sources including the Arabiclegend of Moses. The story of the recovery of the pharaoh's suit of armor is from *Ibn 'Abbas,* rep. in most tafsir books from different sources including the Arabic legend of Moses. In the Hebrew literature there is disagreement about the fate of the pharaoh from being drowned with his army, to his being the lone survivor to see the power of God, to his never dying but standing at the gate of Hell. See end note 54 of Moses in the Wilderness, L.O.J. In the Qur'an the pharaoh and his court are "*Engulfed in the worst torment and have been exposed to Hellfire every morning and evening.*" Q 40:45-46.

The last-minute confession of the pharaoh is mentioned in many Hebrew writings, including Prike De Rabbi Eliezer 43.

## The Israelites in the Wilderness

After crossing the sea Moses and the Israelites passed a bedouin tribe who worshiped idols, and this impressed the Israelites who asked Moses to make them such an idol. Moses refused to accept idolatry and said, "*You are acting ignorantly. What these people are doing is doomed and absurd. How can I seek other than God a deity for you while He has preferred you above all others, and saved you from the pharoah who had imposed the worst torment on you? They slaughtered your sons and spared your daughters.*" 7:138-141

The Israelites found themselves in the desert, under a scorching sun, with little to eat or drink, and complained to Moses, "You took us out of civilization and brought us to this wilderness with no relief from the hot sun." God sent them clouds of glory* Lev 9:16 which gave them shade and which moved with them as they crossed the desert. God also provided them food called manna, a honey-like substance that fell from the trees, and was collected every morning. The Israelites tired of the manna and told Moses that they were craving meat in their diet. Quails appeared by the dozen at the camp, and the Israelites were able to catch them by hand. God told them to collect enough food for one day, but on Fridays they should store enough for two, as neither manna nor the quails would be provided on Saturdays. The Israelites found that saving any more than what God had recommended would spoil and be inedible.* When the Exd 16:13-26 Israelites were in need of water Moses struck a special stone with with his staff, and twelve springs would burst forth, providing them fresh water.[1]* Exd 17:5-7

The stone has a history of its own. The Israelites were in the habit of bathing nude, but Moses was shy and chose to bath in seclusion, which caused rumors to spread that he was not a man. On one occasion, while he bathed, he put his clothes on a stone which took flight and ran away with his clothes. Moses jumped from his

---

[1]- Ara-Tha 216; Taf-Khaz 2:57; Sah-Mus #1610. The story of the stone of water was mentioned in Num. 20: 7-12. In Pseudo-Philo, Book of Antiquities, 10:7, 11:15, it is mentioned that the Israelites brought forth a well of water that followed them anywhere they went. In 1 Cor. 10:7, 11:15, it was said that a rock of water followed the Israelites in the desert. It was similarly mentioned in Tosefta Sukkah 3:11.

bath and chased the stone, shouting, "Give me my dress, stone!" As he pursued the stone he passed a group of Israelites who saw there was nothing unusual about Moses' genitalia. The stone stopped, Moses retrieved his clothing and began to strike the stone, causing twelve holes to form. The Angel Gabriel came to him and said, "Moses, God is telling you to keep this stone, a stone which contains a miracle." And this was the stone that gave them water. The Israelites were now secure with their food and water supply, but still were not able to make new clothing for themselves, so God kept their clothes new and the children's clothes would grow with them.[1]

## On the Mount of Sinai

Moses had promised his people that after leaving Egypt they would be given a book which would explain to them what they should and should not do. In the Sinai they asked Moses to produce the promised book, and God asked Moses to prepare himself for the occasion by fasting for 30 days. After fasting, he climbe Mount Sinai to the place called "*Al-Toor*," where God asked him to fast for ten Exd 34:28  more days.* There were seventy "veils of lights" between God and Moses, all removed but one and God talked to him. The Devil saw this and traveled underground until he appeared between Moses' feet, saying, "It is I, the Devil who is talking to you." Moses became confused and asked God to reveal himself. God said, "You cannot see me, no mortal can see me in this earthly life; if he does, he shall die." Moses replied that, "My Lord, I hear Your words and long to see You; to see You and die is better for me than to live not seeing You."[2]

When Moses requested to see God, God sent fog, thunder, lightning and darkness around the mountain where Moses sat. The angels of the first Heaven paraded around Moses, their blessings becoming as loud as claps of thunder, followed by the angels of the second Heaven who descended onto the mountains as if a pride of rampaging lions. Moses, frightened and covered with goose bumps, wailed, "I should not have asked to see God. Does anything save me

---

[1]- Taf-Tab 2:57 quoting *Wahb*; Taf-Bagh 2:57; Ara-Tha 217: Qis-Kis 240.
[2]- Rep. by Wahb and *As-Siddi*, pub. by Ara-Tha 178; Taf-Bagh & Taf-Khaz 7:143.

now? If I leave this place I will be burned, if I stay I will die." The archangel told him, "Moses, be patient for what you have asked, you have seen only a small part." The angels of the third Heaven then descended with loud rumblings, their colors those of flames and their voices echoing as if a great army was approaching. Moses was terrified and was sure he was going to die, but the chief archangel made him stay where he was and see what he was afraid to see. The angels of the fourth Heaven descended some colored and some snow-white, but louder than the preceding angels, followed by the fifth contingent sounding like nothing Moses had heard before. He was becoming more and more fearful and confused, but could do nothing but accept the onslaught of angels. The angels of the sixth Heaven descended, each one carrying a long spear burning with a flame brighter than the sunlight. The head of each angel had four faces, and Moses joined them in their praise and said, "Lord, remember me, do not forget Your servant, I am not sure that I will survive this." And the archangel answered, "Moses, your fear is growing and your heart is nearly torn from your chest; be patient for what you have asked for." God then commanded the angels of the seventh Heaven to carry down His throne and have Moses gaze upon it. When the glory of the throne appeared, the angels of all the Heavens sang in unison, "Praise the Holy, the King, the Lord of Majesty, who never dies," and the mountain began to shake and crumble, causing Moses to lose consciousness, and be without his soul. God raised the rock, which Moses was sitting on, to protect him from being burned, and gave him back a living soul. Moses woke up and said, "I believe that You are my Lord, and that none can see You and remain alive. Whoever looks at Your angels will have his heart torn from his chest in fear. How great You are and Your angels, You are the Lord of Lords. God of Gods, King of Kings, nothing can compare with You. I repent to You, praise to You, You are Lord of the Universe."[1]

---

[1]- Rep. by *Ibn Ishaq, Ibn 'Abbas & Wahb*. Pub. in Taf-Tab 7:143; Taf-Bagh & Taf-Khaz 7:143; Ara-Tha 178. Although in Exodus 24:9-11, Moses, Aaron, Abihu and seventy Israelite elders went up the mountain and saw the God of Israel on a pavement of sapphire stones, the understanding is that they saw the glory of God because God's face cannot be seen. See Mekilta Bahodesh 4,65b. Moses prayed for God to show him His glory and God answered, saying, "You may not behold my glory or you will perish. As a compromise Moses went into a cave,

When God's glory shone on the mountain, every drop of water on earth became fresh and sweet, every sick man became well, the thorns fell from the trees, the land became green and was filled with flowers, the fire of the Zoroastrian was extinguished, and all the idols fell.  God released a minuscule amount of His glory from behind seventy thousand veils, and the mountains, once smooth and solid were now broken down and covered with sharp peaks and caves. [1]

**The Torah**

God sent the Angel Gabriel to Paradise to cut from an emerald green tree nine boards, ten by ten cubits in measurement.  He then sent Gabriel to bring Him nine branches from the holy sidra tree which were of a pure light, and that light became a pen,  longer than the distance between heaven and earth. God wrote the Torah to Exd 31:18 Moses on these boards by His hand,* while Moses heard the squeaking of the pen *"In the tablets God gave Moses instruction and analysis on everything."*  7:145  And God commanded Gabriel to deliver the tablets to Moses on the mountain, but due to the heavy burden of the covenant Gabriel was unable to move them.  God supplied him with as many angels as there were letters in the Torah, and it was carried to the mountain and presented before Moses, but the mountain cracked from its weight. God commanded Moses to take the tablets to his people and enlighten them as to its contents. But Moses could not carry it, and prayed to God for direction.  God said, *"Moses, I have selected you ahead of mankind to carry My messages and My word, so accept whatever I may give you and act grateful,"*  7:144 and God made it easy for Moses to carry the tablets.[2] But when Moses brought the Torah to his people they refused to accept it or abide by its demanding commandments.  At God's order, Gabriel held a mountain above their heads and said, "Take the Torah which has been provided to you with care. If you refuse, this mountain will land on you ."  They acknowledged the threat and

---

and God, with His angels, passed by in front of the cave.  Moses concealed himself, and if there were a needlepoint opening Moses would have perished.

[1]- Taf-Bagh 7:144;  Ara-Tha 180.
[2]- Ara-Tha 180.

informed Moses that they would obey and accept.[1] After Moses' own exposure to the glory he could see an ant, perched on a rock, on a dark night ten miles in the distance.[2]

## The Ten Commandments

With the Torah God also gave Moses the Ten Commandments. They are summarized in three verses of the Qur'an: "*Come close, I will recite what your Lord has forbidden you:*

*Do not associate anyone else with Him.*

*And [show] kindness towards [your] parents.*

*Do not kill your children because of poverty; we shall provide for you as well as for them.*

*Do not indulge in shocking acts which you may practice either openly or keep secret.*

*Do not kill any person whom God has forbidden, except through* [due process of] *law. He has instructed you in this so that you may use your reason.*

*Do not approach an orphan's estate before he comes of age, except to improve it.*

*Grant full measure and weight in all fairness. We do not assign any person to do more than he can cope with.*

*Whenever you speak, be just, even though it concerns a close relative.*

*Fulfil God's agreement. Thus has He instructed you so that you may bear it in mind.*

---

[1]- Rep. by *Ibn 'Abbas, Mujahid, Qutada, Abul-'Aliya, As-Siddi, Ata,* and *Ibn Jarij,* pub. by Ara-Tha 183; Taf-Tab 2:63; Tar-Kath 1:293; Taf-Khaz 2:63. We find the legend of lifting the mountain above the Israelites in Hebrew Mekilta. From L.O.B. 382.

[2]- Rep. by *Abu Hurayra.* In Hebrew writings, after the receiving of the Torah, Moses' face shone so brightly that even today should his tomb crack, the light emanating from it will be enough to destroy the world. Pesikta Rabbati 21,101a, 101b; Pirke de Rabbi Eliezer 41-end.

*This is My Straight Road, so follow it and do not follow* [other] *paths which will separate you from His path. Thus has He instructed you so that you may do your duty.*" 6:151-153

The Commandments[1] are a part of the "Covenant" which God made with the Israelites, and the following are some rules of the Covenant which were mentioned in the Qur'an and include:

"*Worship none but God.*

*Treat with Kindness your Parents and Kindred, The orphans and those in need*

*Speak fairly to the people.*

*Be steadfast in prayer.*

*Practice regular charity.*" 2:83

"*Shed no blood among you,*

*nor turn out your own people from your home.*" 3:84

"*Make it* [God teachings] *known and clear to mankind and not to hide it.*" 3:187

"*Do not ascribe to God anything but the truth.*[2] " 7:169

## The Golden Calf

When Moses went to collect the Torah, he was to have been gone thirty days, and he put Aaron in charge in his absence. Unbeknownst to the Israelites, Gabriel traveled past their camp but was noticed by a Samaritan living with them, who collected a fistful of dust left in the wake of Gabriel's mare. When Moses did not return in thirty days, the Samaritan said, "Moses is not returning to

---

[1]-These three verses are not meant to be a copy of the Ten Commandments, but they are instructions and guidance to Muslims; yet some mufassirun commented that they are similar to the ten commandments which were given to Moses. In the Bible there are two sets of commandments, the ten ethical commandments mentioned in Exd. 20:1-7 and repeated with some modification in Deut. 5:6-21, and the twelve ritual commandments in Exd. 34:11-26.

[2]- "Covenant" is an agreement between two parties. In this case it was betwee God and the Israelites. The Hebrew word is "b$^e$rîth," which is always translated to English as "covenant." B$^e$rîth is derived from a Hebrew root which means "to cut" in reference to the old tradition of cutting an animal into two parts, and the contracting parties walk between them. In Arabic the word is '*mithaq'* from the Arabic root which means "to tie," because it ties the parties to its contents.

you, and you should make your own god."* Aaron built a fire and Exd 32:1
asked the Israelites to contribute therein the golden jewelry which
had been taken from the Egyptians. They did so, and the Samaritan
threw the purloined dirt from Gabriel's mare onto the molten metal.
From this came a golden calf that mooed and the Samaritan said,
*"This is your god and the god of Moses."* 20:88 The Israelites loved and
worshiped their golden calf.*[1]                                          Exd 32:2-4

Aaron said to them, *"You have been tested with this calf; but
God the Merciful is Your Lord. Follow me and accept my
command."* 20:90 But they replied that they would continue to worship
the calf until Moses returned. Aaron and a small group of those who
refused to accept the calf as their god segregated themselves, and
Aaron did not want Moses to think he had a part in creating the
conflict. God told Moses while he was on the mountain that his
people had been tested by the adoption of a golden calf that had
a voice and body.* Moses asked, "Who put the soul in the golden      Exd 32:7-8
calf?" When God confirmed that God Himself had instilled the soul
in the idol, Moses said, *"It is only Your manner of testing us, You let
anyone You wish go astray and let anyone You wish be guided. You
are our patron, pardon us and show us mercy."* 7:155 God said, "Moses,
I saw that in their hearts and made it easy for them."[2] Then Moses
returned from the mountain and drew near to his people. He heard the
sounds of their singing and dancing around the calf. His seventy
companions were not aware of the golden calf, and thought a fight
had erupted in the camp. Moses then informed them that they were

---

[1]- Taf-Bagh 2:51; Taf-Khaz 2:51 and 20:88; Ara-Tha 184; Taf-Tab 2:51,
7:142, 20:96.
[2]- As rep. by *Ibn 'Abbas* and *As-Siddi*; but *Qutada* said that the sound
coming from the calf occurred when the wind blew in his anus and out from his
mouth. Exd says that Aaron cast the image of a calf from the jewelry of the
Israelites. In Midrash Shir 13a-13b, the golden calf was alive because of the power
of an amulet of silver leaf with an image of a bull engraved on it by Moses himself.
The amulet was dropped into the melted gold by an old Israelite woman. In another
version from Pirke de Rabbi Eliezer, Aaron found a golden plate engraved with the
divine name of God, and an image of a calf which he dropped in the melted gold,
and the calf's sound was caused by the Devil Samuel who entered the calf and
seduced the Israelites by talking through him. From L.O.B. 400.

listening to the sounds of seduction, and in their absence his people had been seduced to worship an ungodly creature. When Moses saw the spectacle of his errant followers dancing around the idol, he threw Exd 17-19 the tablets to the ground where they crumbled.* Only six of the tablets survived. Moses grasped Aaron's hair with his right hand and his beard with his left and demanded to know why Aaron did nothing to stop the worship of the golden calf. Aaron tried to defend himself and said, *"My blood brother, the people felt I was weak and they almost killed me. Do not allow my enemies to gloat over me, nor place me with the wrongdoers."* 7:150 *"I dreaded you would say, 'You have brought dissention to the Israelites and did not observe my* Exd 32:21-24 *instruction.*[1]*'"* 20:94*

Moses then questioned the Samaritan as to what his motives were, and he told Moses about the dust from the footprint of Gabriel's mare. The Israelites realized how nefarious their deed was and said, *"Unless God will pardon us, it will be our loss."* 7:149 Moses told them their souls had been misguided in their worship of the calf, and they must repent. He told them,"Those who did not worship the calf should kill those who did worship." The calf worshipers accepted their fate and sat outside their homes waiting for the inevitable. Moses cautioned them that those who looked at his attacker or attempted to protect himself in any way would find themselves cursed and their repentance would not be accepted.

The calf worshipers were attacked with swords and daggers, the attackers sometimes killing their own brothers, sons, fathers and neighbors, but having to do so to execute God's judgment. God sent down a black fog so the attackers could not clearly see what they were doing, and the killing continued until seventy thousand lay dead.[2] Moses and Aaron begged God to end the carnage, and God lifted the fog and stopped the killing. Moses was horrified at the thousands of dead bodies strewn over the ground. God reassured Moses, " The

---

[1]-Rep. by *Ibn 'Abbas, Al-Hasan* and *Tamim ad-Dari*. Pub. by all books of tafsir at 20:94.

[2]- In Exd. 32:25 Moses, supported by the Levites who did not worship the calf, attacked and killed three thousand of the calf worshipers. Moses said, "Today you have ordained yourselves for the service of the Lord."

killers and their victims will enter Paradise, and those who were killed are martyrs, those who committed the deed are cleansed of their sins." God commanded Moses to melt the golden calf, grind the molten gold and sprinkle its dust into the water.[1] Moses wanted to execute the Samaritan, but God revealed to him, "Do not execute him because he is generous." Moses spared his life but cursed him, saying, *"Go away, during your lifetime you will tell people not to come near you, and this torment will not be broken. Look at your god to whom you have been so devoted, we shall burn it and scatter its remains into the sea. "*20:97 Moses ordered the Israelites not to speak to or even come close to the Samaritan, who lived out his life in complete isolation.[2]

## The Apology

Moses selected seventy men who accompanied him to the mountain, and there they apologized to God on behalf of all his people for their sin of worshiping the golden calf . To ready themselves for this apology Moses had them fast and cleanse themselves and their garments. A fog enveloped the men as they approached the mountain, and as they entered the cloud and lay prostrate before God they heard God say to Moses, "I am God, there is no deity but Me. I brought you out of Egypt, worship Me, and worship no one else." When Moses finished talking to God, and the clouds of glory had disappeared, his people came to him, saying, " We will not believe you until we see God in person." God then sent a fire from heaven, killing all seventy of Moses' companions. Moses saw this show of force and said, *"My Lord, even though you may have wished to annihilate all of us, as you did earlier, are you destroying us simply because of what a few fools among us have done?*

---

[1]- In Q 2:93, we read that the Israelites were made to drink the calf in their hearts. Most mufassirun interpreted this verse to mean that the worship of the calf had been absorbed into their heart, but a few like *As-Siddi* and *Ibn Jarij* went with the biblical version that Moses ground the golden calf, scattered the dust on the water and forced the Israelites to drink from it. Exd. 32:20.

[2]- Rep. by *Ibn Jubayr, Mujahid, 'Akrama, Ibn 'Abbas, As-Siddi & Qutada*. The whole story had been reported by Taf-Bagh, Taf-Tab & Taf-Khaz 2:54 and 7:148-154; Ara-Tha 187.

It is only Your manner of testing: You allow anyone You wish to go astray, and let anyone You wish to be guided. You are the patron, so pardon us and show us mercy, You are the best pardoner." 7:155 He then asked God how he could be expected to return to the remaining Israelites after so many had been killed at God's command. Moses pleaded with the Lord until He brought them back to life, one after another, while they watched, astounded at what was happening.[1]

### The War of the Israelites

In one of the Israelite wars against their neighbor, God asked them to enter a new town they had acquired by kneeling down, as a sign of being humble, in gratitude to God for helping them capture the city. God also asked them to say "*hittah*" when they entered the town. The wrongdoers altered the words. 2:59 and they did not take this command seriously. Rather then kneel, they crawled on their backsides and said not "*hittah*" but "*hintah*." As a result God imposed torture on those who did not obey.[2]

### The Land of the Giants

God promised Moses and his people that they would be given the Holy Land which was inhabited by the "Amalekite" tribe, a giant people descended of Amalek.[3] God assured Moses that the Amalekite

---

[1]-This story is an interpretation of Q 2:55-56. "You said, 'Mose, we will never believe you until we see God openly. The thunderbolt caught you while you were looking on, then we raised you up after you had died, so you will be thankful.' " from Taf-Bagh & Taf-Khaz 2:55-56 and 7:155; Ara-Tha 188. In Exd 32 Moses went back to the Lord the next day, asking for forgiveness to all Israel.

[2]- Rep. by *Ibn 'Abbas, Qutada, Al-Hasan, Mujahid,* and other scholars. Pub. by Taf-Tab2:58-59; Taf-Khaz 2:58-59 and 7:161-162. This story must be of Hebrew origin since 'hit' in Hebrew is sin, and 'hittah' is wheat. In the Hebrew story, probably they were supposed to repent for their sins (hit), but according to *Ibn Mas'ud* they changed the wording to mean, 'black barley inside pierced red wheat grain.' *Al-Mawdudi* commented that is probable that the place mentioned in this verse is Shattin, which the Israelites conquered–according to the Bible–during the last year during the life of Moses. After the conquest the Israelites became decadent and God smote them with a plague from which 24,000 died. Num. 25: 1-9.

[3] Thebiblical Amalek is the son Eliphaz, the grandson of Esau, and the chief of an Idumean tribe. Gen. 36:12; 36:16.

would be subdued and the Israelites would soon inhabit the Holy Land.  Moses was told to pick one leader from each of the twelve tribes and entrust them with the responsibility of making recruits ready for the upcoming fight with the Amalekite.  Moses sent these leaders into the Holy Land to act as spies.*  When the hapless spies Num 13:1-2 entered the Amalekite lands they met with the giant Og, who was carrying firewood on his head.  Og picked up the spies, hung them from the firewood, and brought them back to his wife, saying. "Look at these people who claim that they will fight us."  He put them in front of her and told her he was going to smash them with his foot.  But his wife said, "Better to send them back to their people where they can tell them what they saw." And he released them.   Og was 23,333 cubits in height. His mother Ong was Adam's daughter and the first woman to sell her body. She too was a giant, and every finger of her was three cubits in length and had two nails as sharp as a sickle. At the time of the flood the water did not exceed Og's knees.

After Og released the twelve spies, they were able to explore the unusual land they found themselves in.  They found that it took five of them to carry one bunch of grapes, and one pomegranate shell could be used as shelter for four or five Israelites.  They departed the Amalekite land, apprehensive about what their finding would mean to the public, and decided to report only to Moses and Aaron.  The leaders, with the exception of Joshua and Caleb, were not able to keep their mouths shut, and soon all the tribes learned of the ferocity of the Amalekite people and how foolish it would be to engage in a conflict with them.  Hearing this, the Israelites cried, "To die before in Egypt or die here in this wilderness is better than to lose our children and property in the spoils of war to these giants."[1]*          Num 14:1-3

Moses said to them, *"My people, remember God's favor toward you when he planted prophets among you and set you up as kings. He has given you what no one else in the world has ever been given. My people, enter the Holy Land which God has assigned to you. Do not turn your back on it lest you be sent away as losers." They*

---

[1]-Rep. by *Ibn 'Umar*. Pub. by Ara-Tha; Taf-Bagh & Taf-Khaz 5:12. *Ibn Kathir* comments on the story of Og and the giants of the land, "This is Jewish lore and invention of the unknowledgeable Jews and it is not truthful." Tar-Kath 1:278.

*said, "Moses, there are dangerous people there and we will never enter
it until they leave."* But Joshua and Caleb tried to encourage them
and said, *"Enter the land, and you will be victorious; you should rely
on God if you are believers."* But their encouraging words had no
effect and they said, *"Moses, we will never enter it at all so long as
they remain in it, you go and fight, both you and Your Lord, we will be
waiting here."* When Moses realized he was getting no help from his
people he said, *"My Lord, You have only myself and my brother.
Please distinguish us from among such perverse folk in your
judgment."*5:20-25

The clouds of glory appeared once again, and God revealed to
Moses, "How long will these people disobey Me, and how long will
they ignore My signs and miracles? I will take their lives and give
you another people stronger and more numerous than these." Moses
said, "My God, if You kill these people, the other nations who hear
will say that You did this because You could not make them enter the
Holy Land, so You killed them in their wilderness. Your patience is
prolonged, your favors are profuse, and you forgive sins. Forgive
these people and do not punish them." God said, "I forgive them by
your prayer, but the Holy Land will be *proscribed for them for forty
years. They will wander around the land of the wilder ness. Do not*
Num 14:10-23  *worry about such a perverse people."** 5:26 & 14:33-34

### Korah (Qārūn)

Korah was a wealthy and handsome cousin of Moses who,
after Moses and Aaron, was known both for his extensive knowledge
of the Torah and his ability to recite it. He was said to be the richest
man in history, whose keys to his treasures would have overburdened
a squad of strong men. The keys were carried on sixty mules, and for
each key there was a treasure. Originally made of iron, they soon
became too heavy and were replaced by wood, which in turn were
replaced by cowhide.

Korah made his money from his work in alchemy, the science
of turning copper into gold. Moses knew of this process and taught it
to his sister Mariam, who taught it to Korah. Korah behaved in a very
arrogant fashion toward the Israelites. He and his servants arrived at

a parade dressed in all their finery, in saffron-dyed clothing and on white donkeys, with their saddles colored crimson. Following him were one thousand horsemen and six hundred concubines, resplendent in red and laden with jewels, and riding cream-colored mules. This show of conspicuous display made some along the parade route envious, and they said, *"If only we had the same as Korah, who has been extremely lucky."* Those who had been given the knowledge said, *"It will be bad for you, God's recompense Is better for anyone who believes and acts honorably."* 28:79-80

Moses assigned Aaron and his descendants to the Israelite priesthood. The Israelites would bring their offerings to Aaron who would place them on the altar; a fire would come from the sky and burn these offerings. Korah complained to Moses that, while Moses had the leadership and prophecy, and  Aaron was given the priesthood, he, Korah, was left with nothing. He reminded Moses that he was as proficient in reciting the Torah as Moses was and was not content with his lot in life. Moses countered that God had told him to assign the priesthood to Aaron, but Korah was not convinced and said, "I do not believe you, show me proof from God."*Moses Num 16:3 had the tribal leaders bring him their staffs and, after marking each with their respective owners' names, he placed them inside the temple tent. The next morning they found that Aaron's staff had sprouted green leaves. But this miracle did not convince Korah, who thought Num 17:5 this trick no different from that of a magician. He went away angry, and grew more arrogant and defiant, building an ostentatious home with a red-gold door and the walls covered in gold plate. Although Moses was not pleased with Korah's behavior, he did not wish to create any conflict, as they were cousins.

God ordered the Israelites to pay alms to Moses, and Korah made a special arrangement to pay one percent of his money and cattle. But when Korah calculated just how much he owed to Moses, he became stingy and wanted out of their agreement. Korah went to his people and said, "You have obeyed Moses in everything he asked of you. Now that he wants your money, what will your answer be?" They answered, "You are our elder and our leader, we will do whatever you think we should." Korah told them of his plan to "bribe a prostitute and claim that she slept with Moses." Korah knew that this would not be acceptable to the Israelite people, who would reject

Moses, and Korah paid the prostitute one thousand coin, and hoped this would rid him of Moses. The next morning as Moses was preaching to the Israelites and reminding them of the code of penalty, Korah asked him if the code applied to Moses himself. When Moses replied in the affirmative, Korah accused him of consorting with a prostitute. Moses said, "Bring her here and ask her if this accusation is true." When the prostitute was brought before Moses, he said, "I ask you, in the name of God, who split the sea, and brought us the Torah, to speak the truth." The prostitute felt she could only speak the truth and said, "They bribed me to say that we slept together." Hearing this, Korah realized he was in trouble while Moses prostrated himself before God and wept, "Lord, this enemy of yours hurt me and wanted to scandalize me. My God, if I am Your prophet be angry for me and give me control over him." God told Moses, "Get up, the earth will obey whatever you order it to do." And Moses stood up and said, "God set me against Korah as much as He set me against the pharaoh. If you are on Korah's side, stay with him, but if you side with me, stay away from him." Everyone but two men stepped away from Korah.* Moses then said to the earth, "Earth, take them." They sunk in to their heels. And Moses again said, "Earth, take them." They continued to sink into the earth and began to plead with Moses to have mercy upon them. Korah begged Moses to relent seventy times, but Moses was unmoved and the earth continued to swallow them.* God told Moses that his heart was very hard, and even after crying for mercy seventy times, no mercy was shown. He said, "I swear by My Majesty, if they had called Me, I would have answered them."

Num 16:26-27

Num 16:31-33

     Korah and his companions were sinking into the earth about a man's length every day but would not reach bottom until the day of judgement. The Israelites said, "Moses prayed against Korah so as to gain control over his house, money and treasures." When Moses learned of this, he asked the earth to sink Korah's house and possessions. After that, God said to Moses, "I shall never allow the earth to obey any one anymore."[1]

---

[1]- From Taf-Bagh 28:76; Tar-Kath I:309; Ara-Tha 188-192.

## Moses and Al-Khadir

One day, Moses asked God, "Lord, whom of Your servants do You love the most?" God answered, "Those who keep praising Me, and never forget Me." Moses continued questioning, "Whom of Your servants is most capable of ruling?" And God replied, "The one who rules, not by his emotions but by justice." "My Lord," asked Moses, "whom of Your servants is the most knowledgeable?" God told him, "the one who seeks knowledge of others for himself, looking for a word that might guide him, or keep him away from damaging his soul." Moses asked God if there was anyone on earth who was more knowledgeable than Moses himself and God told him of a man called *Al-Khadir*. He could be found on the beach, at the rock where the fish will escape, at the junction of the two seas.[1]

Moses told his assistant Joshua, *"I shall not give up until I reach the junction of the two seas, even if it will take forever."*18:60 On their way they stopped for a rest, and while they slept a salted fish they had brought along for food came to life and jumped into the sea. The men awoke and continued their walk until they felt hungry and Moses told Joshua, *"Bring the food, as we have experienced much strain on our journey."*18:62 Joshua found there was no fish and said, "I think our lunch has escaped into the sea!" Moses exclaimed, *"That is exactly what we are looking for."* 18:64 And they retraced their steps until they reached the place at which they had slept, at the junction of the two seas. There they met *Al-Khadir*, dressed in green, standing and praying on a green rug, floating on the water.[2]

---

[1]- Rep. by *Ibn 'Abbas*, pub by Ara-Tha 192.

[2]- *Al-Khadir* is an Islamic personality surrounded by mystery, and has no parallel in either Jewish or Christian literature. There is disagreement between the Islamic scholars on whether he is a prophet or just a holy man, but the miracles that are built around him are many. The sufis considered him their highest spiritual teacher and immortal. The leaders of the sufi orders claim to have met and learned from him. *Al-Khadir* meets with Elijah, another immortal prophet, once a year in Mecca during the Hajj. In some legends he lived at the time of Alexander the Great. (the two-horned king). They both went looking for the spring of immortality in the land of darkness, but only *Al-Khadir* found that spring and washed himself from the spring, becoming immortal.

Moses greeted him and said, "My Lord sent me to you, to be your companion and to learn from you. *Al-Khadir* answered, *"You will never have any patience with me! How can you show any patience with something that is beyond your knowledge?"* 18:67-68 But Moses assured him that he would be the soul of patience and would not disobey him in any matter. *Al-Khadir* permitted Moses to accompany him on one condition, *"If you follow me, do not ask me about anything until I talk to you about it myself."* 18:70

They walked along the beach until they saw a ship, and *Al-Khadir* asked the captain to take them on board, which he did. Once they were in the middle of the sea, *Al-Khadir* hit the ship's bottom with an axe and broke one of the boards. As the sea water rushed in, *Al-Khadir* closed the hole with a piece of his dress. Moses was astounded and cried, *"Have you pierced this ship to drown her crew? Why have you done such a peculiar thing?"* *Al-Khadir* said, *"Did I not say that you would soon lose patience with me?"* Moses countered with, *"Do not take me to task for what I have forgotten, nor weigh me down by making the case too difficult for me."* 18:71-73

Later, after their sea voyage came to an end, the two men chanced upon a youth. To Moses' surprise and horror, *Al-Khadir* kicked the youth to death. Moses screamed, *"You committed a terrible deed by killing an innocent soul."* *Al-Khadir* again reminded him, *"Did I not tell you that you would not have any patience with me?"* Moses apologized and said, *"If I ever again ask you about anything, do not allow me to accompany you, and it will give you an excuse to have me leave."* 18:74-76        Their travels continued until they reached a town, and although they were hungry and tired, the town people refused them food, water and shelter. They found a dilapidated stone fence, which *Al-Khadir* rebuilt, and there they spent the night. Moses questioned why *Al-Khadir* fixed the stone fence for the stingy townsfolk but did not ask for payment. *Al-Khadir* answered, *"This means a parting between us, yet I shall explain to you something of what you have no patience for. As for the ship, it belongs to poor men who worked on the sea. I damaged it because there is a king that seizes, by force, any ship in good shape. The parents of* the youth I killed are good believers, but their son was a thief who had these parents cover for him. God did not want him to further burden his good parents with his arrogance and disbelief, and was to replace him with a more pure and tender child. The fence belonged to two orphaned boys living in the city, and underneath it lay a treasure which had belonged to their late father. Your Lord wanted them to come of age and claim their treasure as mercy from Him. I did not do it of my own accord. These are the explanations of what you showed no patience for.[1] " 18:78-82

**Moses and the Cow**

The body of a murdered man was found at the Israelite camp. A cousin was accused by the victim's family of the crime, which he denied. When the Israelites failed to solve the murder, they asked for Moses to assist them. Moses told them that God had commanded them to slaughter a cow, but they were skeptical and reminded Moses of the unsolved murders. Moses answered that, "I seek refuge with God, lest I become so ignorant." The Israelites realized Moses was serious and said, "Appeal to Your Lord for us, and clarify what kind of cow He meant." Moses described the cow, "She should not be worn out, nor a heifer, but of an age in between. Now do as you are ordered" But the Israelites continued to press Moses for more information. "Appeal to Your Lord for us and tell us what color she should be." Moses said, "She should be of a beautiful bright yellow color" But originally Moses simply stated, "Slaughter a cow, any cow will do." The more the Israelites persisted in asking for details, the more difficult they were making it for themselves to procure such a cow. They continued and said, "Appeal to your Lord for us and have Him explain exactly what this cow should be. There are all kinds of cows, and God willing, we need to be properly guided." Moses attempted a further explanation, "He says she should not yet have

---

[1]- Details of the story rep. by *Ibn Abbas* and pub. by Sah-Bukh # 3400; 3401 and all tafsir books.

*been broken in to plow, nor to irrigate, and she should be sound with no blemish on her.* " At last the Israelites ceased to question Moses, and they set about searching for the cow. They did manage to locate this very unique bovine, but its owner demanded a very high price, enough gold to fill its hide, which the Israelites had no choice but to pay.

Moses said, "God commands you to touch the body of the murdered man with a part of the cow." And when they put the cow's tongue to the dead body, he came to life, stood up, pointed toward his murderer and said, "This is the one who killed me." He then fell to the ground, dead. Moses said, *"This is how God revives the dead, and He is showing you His signs so you may use your reason. "*2:67-73 After this incident, God revealed to Moses the roles of purgation of blood guilt.[1]

## Death of Aaron

God revealed to Moses that the time of Aaron's death was at hand and he should take Aaron to a certain mountain where he will die. Upon their arrival they saw a large tree shading a house in which was found an inviting bed enveloped in a pleasant scent. Aaron found the bed irresistible and told Moses that he must lie on the bed, but worried that the rightful owner might discover him enjoying this bed. Moses said, "Do not worry, I will look after everything." Aaron asked Moses to lie beside him so they would be found together in the same bed should the owner appear. They lay together until Aaron felt death creeping into his body, and spoke to Moses, "You deceived me." After Aaron's death, God removed the tree and the house containing Aaron.

---

[1]- From almost all tafsir books. Although this story has no parallel in Hebrew books, the roles of the purgation of blood guilt in Deut. 11 said that if a body of a killed man is found in open country, and no one knows who killed him, the distances to the towns near to the body are measured, and the elders of the nearest town should take a heifer that has never been worked, and never pulled a yoke, to a wadi with running water, and there break her neck. The elders should then wash their hands over the heifer and declare that their hands did not shed this blood, nor did they witness it.

When Moses returned to his people without Aaron, he was accused of killing him. God ordered his angels to take Aaron's body and pass through the Israelite camp telling of the true version of Aaron's death. Moses' story was then believed, and the angels carried Aaron's body to a secret place seen only by a bird, the Egyptian vultures, who were then made both deaf and voiceless.[1]

## The Death of Moses

The Angel of Death came to Moses and said, "Answer Your Lord," but Moses responded by striking the Angel in his face, puncturing his eye. The Angel of Death returned to God, complaining, "Lord, You sent me to Your servant who does not want to die: he struck me in my eye." God restored the angel's eye and told him, "Go back to my servant and tell him, 'If you want to continue living, put your hand on the back of a bull. You will have as many years to live as hairs your hand picked from that bull.' " Moses then asked the angel, "And what after that?" And the Angel told him. "Then you shall die." Moses was resigned and said, "Why should I not die now?" Then, "Lord, let me die close to the Holy Land." And with that, Moses died.[2]

## Another version of the Death of Moses

As Moses was walking in the wilderness, he recognized a group of angels digging a grave and went to them. He had never seen such a grave before and asked, "Angels of God, for whom are you digging this grave.?" They answered that it was for a pious servant. Moses wondered if this person was highly valued by God, and they said, "Prophet of God, would you like this grave to be your resting place?" Moses said he would, and they told him to "lie down, direct yourself to the Lord and breathe easily." Moses did so, God collected his soul, and the angels covered his grave with dirt. Moses lived for one hundred and twenty years[3].

---

[1]-Taf-Khaz 5:26; Qis-Kath 2:196.
[2]-Rep. by *Abu Hurayra*. Pub. in Taf-Bagh 5:26; Taf-Khaz 5:24; Ara-Tha 219; Tar-Kath I:317; Sah-Mus # 1613.
[3]-Rep. by *Wahb*. Pub by Ara-Tha 220.

### The Story of Ezekiel

Ezekiel was an officer in the court of the pharaoh who was a believer in Moses' teachings but disclosed them to no one. He cautioned the pharaoh against confronting Moses, but when the sorcerers announced their belief in public, Ezekiel joined with them and was killed as a result. His wife was the princess' hairdresser, and, like her husband, was a believer. While brushing the hair of the princess she dropped the comb from her head and she picked it up, saying, "In the name of God." The princess asked if she was referring to her father, the pharaoh, but the hairdresser told her, "I am speaking of my Lord, and the Lord of your father." The princess told her father and the hairdresser was threatened with punishment if she did not retract her statement. The hairdresser again stated her belief and she was, along with her children, burned to death.[1]

### The Story of Asiyah bint Muzahim

Asiyah was an Israelite who became the wife of the pharaoh but was a believer who worshiped God secretly. When the royal hairdresser was put to death she witnessed the torturous burning from her window and also saw the angels taking her soul to Heaven. This strengthened her belief, and when the pharaoh boasted of this incident, she asked him, "Woe to you, are you not afraid of this God?" The pharaoh said, "Are you as mad as that hairdresser?" She replied, "I am not mad, but I am a believer in God, both my Lord as well as your Lord and the Lord of everyone." The pharaoh summoned her mother to put some sense in her, threatening that if she refused to reject Moses' God she would meet the same fate as the hairdresser. But Asiyah never rejected her belief and the pharaoh ordered her to be stretched between four stakes and tortured to death. Her last words were, "My Lord, build for me a house in Your Heaven.[2] " 66:11

---

[1]- Ara-Tha 166.

[2]- From Ara-Tha 166; Taf-Bagh & Khaz 89:10. Asiyah is one of the perfect women of Islam, the others being the Virgin Mary and *Fatima*, the Prophet's daughter.

**The End of the Giant Og**

    Og walked toward the Israelites with the intention of killing them all by taking the top of the mountain and crushing the army. But God sent a bird to peck a hole in the mountain top, and it broke apart, encircling Og's head as a necklace. When Moses saw this he jumped and attacked the giant with a spear, piercing him in the heel, which killed Og.[1]

---

[1]- Rep. by *'Awf Al-Bakali* and *Ibn 'Abbas.* Pub. by Taf-Tab; Taf-Khaz 5:12; *Ibn Kathir* published it but then denounced the story, saying it was from Jewish lore and had no truth in it.

# 10     King David / *Dāwūd*

*David, We have placed you as an overlord on earth.*
— Qur'an 38:26

## Introduction

David was known in pre-Islamic Arabia, not as a biblical figure, but as an Arabian personality. He was both a king and a blacksmith, famous for inventing an armor made of rings which proved to be very efficient in battle and *Turfah bin al-ʿAbd*; *Ḥusayn bin al-Ḥamām al-Mirrī; Umayyah bin Abiṣ- Ṣalṭ* and *Al-Aswad bin Ya ʿfar* all pre-Islamic poets mentioned David's armor in their poems. The Qur'an says that God softened the iron for him, and this unique Arab tradition combined with the stories of Solomon, and the fact that neither name has been found in archaeological digs in Palestine, nor anywhere else, raises the question of the identity of these two figures. The Arabian-Islamic story of David was later mixed with biblical tradition to confer a complete life story of David.

Historians have two opposing views concerning the United Kingdom of Israel and focusing particularly on the personages of David and Solomon. The so called maximist historians state that their biblical stories should be taken as a history until it is proven otherwise. They profess that David and Solomon were kings of the lands of Israel with Jerusalem as their capital, while the minimalists maintain that these two figures as kings of Israel were legends, as real as King Arthur and the Round Table. David is considered by Muslims to be one of the thousands of prophets sent by God, and God revealed to him the book of *Zabūr* / Psalms, one of the four books of revelation mentioned in the Qur'an.

# Samuel, Saul & David

Although the Qur'an does not mention Samuel by name, there is a story about an unnamed prophet who came after Moses and was asked by the Israelites to appoint a king for them, *"Appoint for us a king, and we will fight for God's cause."* The prophet said, *"Is it not possible if you were commanded to fight that you will not fight?"* They answered, *"How could we refuse to fight for the cause of God, knowing we were turned out of our homes and away from our families?"* But when they were commanded to fight, all but a small 1Sam 8:5-22 *group turned back, and God was aware of those who were the evildoers.* 2:246\*

Moslem scholars identified this prophet as Samuel, but it is clear from these Qur'anic verses that pre-Islamic Arabs did not know Samuel. The Qur'an does not mention his name because it is the entire story and not the name which is important, and which the Qur'an stresses. But early mufassirun wanted to know more about this facinating personality, and they took that from the two Books of Samuel.

Samuel was the miraculously firstborn son to a woman passed childbearing age. He was called Samuel, meaning 'God heard 1Sam 1:20 my call,'\* and was brought to Eli, the high priest of Israel, where he learned the Torah. One night, as they both slept, the Angel Gabriel called to him, in the voice of Eli: "Samuel!" and he awoke and was frightened. When he questioned Eli, he was told to go back to sleep only to be called by name again. Eli assured Samuel it was not he who had called his name and told Samuel to first perform his ablutions and pray before returning to sleep. He did so and for the third time was aroused from slumber by a voice calling his name. He answered, "I am here." And Gabriel then appeared and told him God 1Sam 3:3-11 had chosen him to be a prophet of the people of Israel.\*

After a long life of prophecy, Samuel was asked by his people to find a king for them—like other nations have. Samuel was reluctant to do that until they promised him that they will obey and fight with their king. He showed them a cane and told them that the one matching the height of that cane would be the king.[1] The only man who matched that height was Saul. Once he was identified, Samuel poured the holy oil from a horn on his head.* The oil actually *1Sam 10:1* bubbled out of the horn and poured itself on Saul. Samuel told the Israelites, *"God has appointed Saul as your king."** But they com *1Sam 10:24* plained that, *"How can he reign over us when we are better suited than he to reign, and he is not even gifted with ample wealth?"** *1Sam 10:27* Their prophet told them, *"God has chosen him above you, and has *1Sam 9:2* gifted him abundantly with knowledge and physical strength.** God grants His authority to whomever He pleases. God is Boundless and Aware."* As a sign of his authority, the Ark[2] shall come to them containing serenity from the Lord, as well as some relics, which Moses' house and Aaron's house have left behind. It will be carried by angels; *"In that there will be a sign for you, if you are believers."* 2:247-248

The people of Israel used to take the Ark onto the field of battle to secure victory for them, but at the battle of Ebenezer in the time of Eli, the Israelites were defeated and their enemy, the Philistines, captured the Ark.* The Philistines put the Ark in their *1Sam 4:2-11* temple which hosted their grand idol, and placed the Ark under the idol, but when they came next day, they found the idol under the Ark. They again positioned the idol above the Ark and nailed his feet to it,

---

[1]-From Taf-Tab, Taf-Bagh, & other tafsirs at 2:247; Ara-Tha 235. There are other Islamic versions of the appointment of Saul reported by Wahb which matched the biblical version; Saul went with his servant looking for his father's lost donkeys, and stopped by Saul's house to ask their whereabouts. But once inside, the oil in the horn bubbled, and Samuel checked Saul's height by measuring him with a cane and they were the same. Samuel anointed him with the holy oil and proclaimed him the king of Israel.

[2]-The Ark of the Covenant is a wooden chest made to certain specifications, and containing two tables of stone, the pot of manna, and Aaron's dry branch that had budded. It was the most sacred relic for the Israelites, and hosted inside the Holy of the Holies, the most sacred part of the Temple.

but the next day the idol –with both hands and feet amputated–was under the Ark, and all other idols were knocked down. They took the Ark out of the temple and put it on a street corner, but the people who lived in that area developed neck pain and most of them died. They moved it to another town, but the town was attacked by vicious mice that killed the townspeople. They took the Ark into the desert and buried it in a ditch, but anyone getting close to it was affected with hemorrhoids and stomach pain, so it was unearthed and hoisted up onto a house for ten years and seven months.[1] But everyone who came in contact with it was burned, and the people of the city suffered from all kinds of illnesses and disabilities; their sheep died and their 1Sam 6:1-14 women were affected with the plague.*

After all this suffering, the Philistines decided to send the Ark back to Israel, and it was put on a cart and pulled by two oxen who did not stop until they reached the land of Israel, where they broke 1Sam 6:1-14 their yokes and returned home.*The return of the Ark was considered a sign from God that He had chosen Saul as their king.[2]

God revealed to Samuel that he must command King Saul to mobilize an army and fight his enemy the Philistines. After the Israelites saw the return of the Ark, they were optimistic about their victory and volunteered in great numbers for the draft. But Saul cautioned that he did not want anyone with unfinished business, those who were in debt, nor any newly married man to join the army. Under 1Sam 13:2 these conditions, he raised an army of eighty thousand men.*[3] Saul

---

[1]- In the Bible, the Ark stayed in captivity for seven months only. 1Sam 5: 7,8.

[2]- Rep. by *Wahb*, pub. by Ara-Tha 237; Taf-Tab, Taf-Bagh and Taf-Khaz 2:248. There is no connection in the Bible between the return of the Ark and the appointing of Saul. In some Hebrew writings, Saul was a soldier in the army of Israel when the Philistines captured the Tables of the Low, and he walked sixty miles to the camp of the Philistines and rescued the holy tables returning to Shiloh the same day. He was helped in this task by an angel. Tehillim 7,63; Tosifta - Targum 1Sam. 4.12. From L.O.J. IV, 65 and footnote Samuel 48. *Al-Mawdudi* in his tafsir, stated that the Qur'an alludes to the return of the Ark on the cart. The cart which delivered it was driverless and it was the angels that had custody of it and delivered it to the Israelites.

[3]- Ara-Tha 238; Taf-Tab, Taf-Bagh & Taf-Khaz 2:249. In the Bible, Saul chose three thousand Israelites, keeping with him two thousand at Michmash and the hill country of Bethel. He put one thousand with his son Jonathon in

led his army to meet the enemy on a hot day, and when they became thirsty, Samuel said, "God is testing you with a river we will cross. You are permitted to take only one fistful of water to quench your thirst, those who take more should leave this army." This test reduced Saul's army to four thousand soldiers. Those who limited themselves to the one fistful of water were well satisfied, while those who drank more found not only was their thirst not diminished, but their lips turned black, and no amount of water could relieve their parched throats. They stayed at the river, too cowardly to fight, and said, *"We have no way to prevail over Goliath and his troops."* Those who passed the test knew they were to meet God and said, *"How often has a small detachment defeated a larger one? God stands alongside the patient.*[1] " 2:249

A shepherd named David, his father Jesse and twelve brothers were among those who remained in Saul's army which marched onward and made their camp close to the Philistine army.[2]  Goliath, the Philistine hero, sent a message to Saul, suggesting they fight man to man with the victor taking the other's k ingdom.* Saul was disturbed by this proposal, as Goliath was a very strong and tough opponent. Many times before, Goliath defeated an army on his own. His iron helmet alone weighed three hundred pounds, and his white horse was as powerful and able to endure as much as his master. Saul announced to his camp that whoever killed Goliath would marry Saul's daughter* and share in his kingdom, but Goliath was very much feared in the camp. Saul asked Samuel for help and was given a clay tube (tandoor), and a horn filled by holy oil. God said, "You will recognize the man able to kill Goliath when the oil is placed above his head it begins to bubble and it spills over but does not drip on his face. He will also be able to easily pass through the tandoor." Saul summoned the strongest and most powerful men in his army, but they failed the test. Samuel said to Saul, "God revealed to me that the one who will slay Goliath is the son of Jesse. He will become king after you, for now he is a shepherd." Jesse presented his sons to

1Sam 17:25

1Sam 17:25

---

Gibeah of Benjamin, and sent the rest home to their tents. 1Sam 13:2.

[1]- Ara-Tha 238; Taf-Tab, Taf-Bagh & Taf-Khaz 2:249.

[2]- In the Bible only the three eldest sons of Jesse, who had eight sons, had followed Saul into battle. 1Sam 17:12-13.

Samuel, but not one of them could enter the tandoor. Jesse was asked if he had any more sons, and was adamant that he did not. But God knew he lied and told Samuel, who said, "Jesse, God has impeached you." Jesse confessed that he did in fact have another son, David, but he was too young, too small and was off shepherding, so should not 1Sam 16:6-13 be considered. Samuel went looking for David.* and he found him crossing the wadi with his sheep, carrying them above the water, two at a time, rather than risk losing them to the wadi's flow. Samuel said to himself, "This man is merciful to animals, he must also be merciful to people." And David passed both the holy horn and tandoor tests.[1]

When Saul met David he said to him, "Kill Goliath and you will marry my daughter and rule my kingdom," and David accepted the challenge. As he walked toward the front, he heard a stone calling to him, "David, carry me. I am Aaron's stone, and was used once before to kill a king." David picked up the stone and then heard a second stone call, "David, carry me, I am Moses' stone, and he used me to kill a king." He put the second stone in his bag when a third stone called out to him, "David, I am the stone that will kill Goliath." 1Sam 17:40 And David now had three stones.[2]*

The two armies lined up for the fight, and Goliath stepped forward, challenging anyone for one-to-one combat. Saul gave David a horse, a shield and a weapon, and told him to accept Goliath's challenge. David stepped proudly forward, stopped and went back to Saul, saying, "Let me fight him in my own way. If God does not want me to win, this weapon will not help me." Saul agreed and said, "Fight him in any manner you see fit." David threw down his weapon and 1sam 17:38-39 shield* and walked toward Goliath carrying only his slingshot and his bag. Goliath, mounted fully armed, questioned whether David was to be his opponent. When David allowed that he was, Goliath asked, "Are you coming to me armed with a slingshot as if you are fighting a dog?" "Yes, you are worse than a dog," answered David. Goliath threatened that he would "divide what remains of your body among the wild beasts and birds." David retorted, "I will fight you in the name of God, Who will spread your flesh between the birds and

---

[1]- From Ara-Tha 240; Taf-Tab, Taf-Bagh & Taf-Khaz 2:251.

[2]- In the Bible, David picked five stones from the wadi and put them in his bag. In the Hebrew legend, these five pebbles turned into one.

beasts."* David took a stone from his bag and continued, "In the Sam 17:43-46
name of the God, the God of Abraham", and put the stone in his
slingshot. He took the second stone saying, "In the name of God, the
God of Isaac," and again readied his slingshot. When he picked up
the third stone and said, "In the name of God, the God of Jacob," the
three stones became one.[1] David fired the stone from his slingshot
which was carried by a divine wind; it pierced Goliath's helmet, went
through his brain, and exited from the back of his head. The stone
proceeded to kill thirty fighters, then broke apart and continued its
rampage until every man in Goliath's camp lay dead.[2] David
approached the fallen Goliath, took his sword, and cut off his head,
triumphantly carrying it back to the Israelites,* and proffered it befor 1Sam 17:49-52
Saul. The Israelites reveled in their victory.[3]

## David and Saul

Saul married his daughter to David* who had to provide a 1Sam 18:17
dowry of three 1Sam 19:25 hundred foreskins taken from the killed
Philistines. *Saul came to despise David because of his popularity as 1Sam 18:17
a hero of the Israelites. Saul attempted to kill David, but David ran* 1Sam 19:10
and hid in the mountain with other worshipers of God. Saul became
very violent and had everyone whom he believed to be on David's
side killed, including Jewish priests.[4] But God changed Saul's heart
and he became extremely repentant. He would walk every night in
the graveyard crying, "Does anyone know a way for me to repent?"
His incessant wails brought a voice from the graves, "Saul, is it not
enough that you robbed us of our lives? Now we must listen to your
constant cries?" Saul became more and more depressed, and even his
baker felt sorry for him. Saul asked him if he knew of any priest who

---

[1]- In Ps-Philo 57,61.5, David wrote on seven stones the names
of Abraham, Isaac, Jacob, Moses, Aaron, his own name and the name of the
Almighty.

[2]- In the Hebrew Tehillim 78,350, the pebble which David threw at
Goliath penetrated the metal helmet. From L.O.J. IV, 87-88 and endnote David 42.

[3]- Rep. by *Wahb, Ibn Ishsq, Mujahid, Ibn Zayd and Ibn Jarij.* Pub.
by Ara-Tha 241; Taf-Tab, Taf-Bagh & Taf-Khaz 2:251.

[4]- In the Bible, Saul slaughtered eighty five priests of the Lord at Nob
because they hid David, then helped him to flee. He also put the sword to the men,
women, children, oxen, donkeys and the sheep of the city of Nob. 1Sam. 22:18-19

could help in his repentance, and the baker told him that he was like
a king who spent a night in a town and had an ominous feeling about
roosters, so he had them all killed. When he wanted to sleep, he
asked his men to awaken him when the rooster crows, but they
informed the king that there were no roosters left.

Saul became more depressed, and the baker said that if Saul
would swear not to harm that person, the baker would find him
someone who might help. Saul swore, and was taken to a priestess
who was spared from death once before with the baker's help. The
priestess was the only one left who knew the most holy name of God,
and upon seeing Saul, the woman was frightened, but when she
learned the reason for the visit she said, "I do not know of any way
for Saul to gain repentance, but let us go to the grave of the prophet
Samuel." At the gravesite, the priestess prayed and called to Samuel,
using the most holy name of God. Samuel, peace be upon him, came
from the grave, shaking himself free from dirt. Seeing the priestess,
the baker and Saul standing before him, he said, "Is it the day of
Resurrection already?" "No," answered the priestess, "but here is
Saul, asking if you know of any way he can repent." Samuel asked
Saul what he had done, and Saul confessed he had committed all
manner of heinous sins. Samuel found that Saul had ten sons[1] and
told him, "If you want to repent, you should give up your crown and
go with your children to fight the enemy for the sake of God. Keep
your children in front of you, until they are all killed, then step
forward to be killed yourself." Samuel then returned to his grave.
Saul was feeling very melancholy and was afraid that his sons would
not do as Samuel suggested. But when his sons learned of the story,
they asked him, "Are you going to be killed after us?" When he
answered that he would, they said, "It is no good for us to live if you
are dead; we are ready to do what it takes for you to repent." Saul
and his children did go to the holy wars, and, one by one, they were
killed, with Saul the last to die. Saul's killer went to David and told
him that he had killed his enemy and David said, "You will not go on
living after him," and beheaded him.[2]

---

[1]- The biblical Saul had only four sons.

[2]- Pub. by Ara-Tha 242; Taf-Bagh & Taf-Khaz 2:251. In the Bible, at the
last battle between Saul's Army and the Philistines, Saul's army was defeated and

## King David

Muslims considered David both a king and a prophet.[1] God inspired him with the Book of Psalms, and he is famous for the way he praised God. He was able to chant the psalms using seventy different tunes, and often did so while walking through the wilderness with all the priests of the kingdom following him. The people would follow the priests, with the jinn behind them, and the demons following the jinn. Beasts would approach to listen, and overhead the birds would offer shade with their wings. The flowing water would stand still and the winds would die. The Devil created musical instruments that copied David's chants, and used this to attract people in the same way that David's songs did. God honored David and favored him; when he walked through the mountains chanting and praising God, the mountains responded by joining with him in song.

He was also honored for being wise and having the ability to act as a judge in a dispute among people. Two Israelites came to David and asked him to render a decision. One of the men claimed that the other had stolen his cow, a charge that the accused denied. David said he would need some time to think over the situation. When, after four successive nights in which God revealed to him in a vision to "kill the accused," David summoned the accused and told him of his dream. The man said, "Are you killing me without a trial?" David answered that he was going to execute God's command. When the man realized he was about to die, he confessed to a murder which had been committed sometime before.[2]

God further favored David by bestowing upon him the "judgement chain," a chain as strong as iron, with the color of fire, its links made from precious stones and pearls. The chain connected the

---

the Israelites fled, and three of Saul's sons were killed. Saul himself was wounded badly. Afraid he might be taken by his enemy, he asked an Amalikite to kill him and he did so. Then taking his crown and armlet, he brought them to David. David mourned Saul and killed the Amalikite. 2Sam 1:5-16.

[1]-In the Hebrew Mekilta, Bo 2a, it is mentioned that although the psalms are not part of the prophetic section of the Bible, David is nevertheless a prophet. See also Seder 'Olam 20. From L.O.J. IV, 84 and endnote David 24.

[2]- Rep. by *Ibn 'Abbas*, pub. by Ara-Tha 247; Taf-Tab, Taf-Bagh & Taf-Khaz 38:20.

milky way with the zodiac, and came to an end at the prayer site of David. The people of Israel used this chain to judge their differences, the one who was able to hold onto the chain had judgment on his side. A rich man from Israel loaned a precious pearl to his friend, and sometime later asked him to return it. But the friend claimed he had already returned the pearl, and therefore no longer possessed it. They argued and then agreed to accept the judgment of the chain. Before they went to the chain, the friend, who still had the pearl, hid it inside his cane. Once at the chain, the friend asked the pearl's rightful owner to hold his cane for him, and said, "God, you know that the pearl has been returned, now help me to hold the chain." And he held onto the chain with both hands; but the next morning, they found that God had retracted the chain.[1]

God also honored David by giving him the ability to soften iron in his hands. He worked with it as if it were wax or mud, without having to heat it nor pummel it with a hammer. God taught him to make body armor, and he was the first to make body armor from rings instead of plate. He would sell every piece of armor for four thousand coin, and used the money on himself, his family, and would donate some to charity. Though he was a king, he would have preferred to live by working with his hands. David was able to endure much in the worship of God, and would fast every other day and pray all night.[2]

### David's Sin

David asked God to grant him the same divine honor which his ancestors Abraham, Isaac and Jacob had been given. God reminded David that those men were sorely tested, as none before had been, but David persisted: "Test me as you tested them, and honor me as you honored them."[3] God advised David that on a certain day and

---

[1]- Rep. by *Ibn Abbas*, pub. by Ara-Tha 246; Taf-Tab, Taf-Bagh & Taf-Khaz 2: 251.

[2]- The story of David's ability to work with iron came from the Qur'anic verse 34:10. David's famous shields are mentioned in many pre Islamic poems.

[3]- See the story In Hebrew writings in Sanhedrin 107a; Tehillim 18, 157; 26, 216. From L.O.J. IV, 103 and endnote David 92.

date he would be tested and he should take heed when that day
arrived. David closed his door, retreated to his prayer site, and read
the psalms. While he did so, the Devil entered his room in the shape
of a dove. David attempted to catch it, but it flew out the window,
while David followed it with his eyes.[1] As he gazed out his window
he saw a beautiful nude woman taking a bath on her roof.* She    2Sam 11:2
She caught sight of David and quickly gathered her long hair around
her naked body. David was infatuated with the woman, and found out
she was Bathsheba, daughter of Eliam, and the wife of Uriah who was
a soldier fighting in the army of Israel.* The general commanding    2Sam 11:3
the army was Joab, David's nephew, and David sent a message to the
general to have Uriah sent to the front, where he was killed.* After    2Sam 11:17
Bathsheba's period of mourning, David married her and she gave
birth to Solomon.[2]

   Shortly thereafter, God sent two angels in the shape of men to
see David, but as it was his day of worship, his guards prevented
them from seeing him. They scaled the walls, and when they
surprised David praying in his hall they said, *"Fear not, we are two
disputants, one of whom has wronged the other. Decide now between
us with the truth, and treat us not with injustice, but guide us toward
the even path. This man is my brother and has ninety nine ewes, and
I have but one. Yet in harsh tones, he tells me to turn over my one ewe
to him."* David said to both of them, *"He has undoubtedly wronged
you by asking for your ewe, many partners try to take advantage of
one another, except for those who believe and perform honorable deeds,*

---

[1] - As to David's wish to be considered as one of the great prophets,
see the Hebrew Tehillim 18,139; Pesahim 117b, Zohar I, 82a. For Satan's
appearance in the form of a dove see Sanhedrin 107a; Tehillim 18,157.

[2] - Ara-Tha 248-250; Taf-Tab, Taf-Bagh & others at 38:21. The Hebrew
books explained David's sin by maintaining that David's nature did not permit him
to commit such sins, but God himself brought him to commit that sin so he could
say to other sinners, "Learn how to repent from David." 'Abodah Zorah 4b-5a. The
warriors of Israel at that time used to give their wives a valid, written divorce to be
used only if the warrior died in battle. And Uriah died, so his wife Bathsheba was
divorced when David slept with her. Uriah brought the death penalty upon himself
when King David commanded him to sleep with his wife and he refused. Shabbat
56a. From L.O.J. IV, 103 and endnote David 92.

*and such as those are few indeed.* 38:21-24  I will not let you take advantage of your brother, and if you do, you will be punished." The Angel said, "David, you are the one who should be punished. You had hundreds of wives while Uriah had only one, yet you sent him to be killed and took his widow." The two angels disappeared and 2Sam 12:1-13 David then realized who they were and realized that he had sinned.[1]*

He immediately fell to the ground and bowed for forty nights, crying until grass grew around his head and blisters covered his forehead: "David sinned a sin that is bigger than the gulf between east and west. My Lord, if You do not have mercy on David and forgive him, his sin will be talked about by everyone who comes after him." After forty nights Gabriel came to him with a message: "David, God has forgiven you." David said, "I know that God can forgive any sin, and I also know that He is just. What shall I do on the Day of Judgment when Uriah asks to be a judge against me, the one who caused his death?" Gabriel was unable to answer this question, but God answered David: "Go to Uriah's grave and ask him for forgiveness." David did as he was told and called to him at the grave site. Uriah answered David's call with, "I am here, who are you who has

---

[1]- Ara-Tha 248-250. In the Bible, after David saw Bathsheba bathing on the roof he sent for her and she came to him. He slept with her, she returned to her home, and when she found she had conceived, told David she was pregnant. David then sent for her husband Uriah from the battlefield and asked him to sleep with Bathsheba, but Uriah refused while his comrades were still at war. David sent him back to the war and asked his general, who was also his nephew, to put him in harm's way, assuring his death. After Uriah's death, David made Bathsheba his wife. 2Sam 11. But attributing both murder and adultery to David was not acceptable to Moslem scholars, and the Qur'an did not mention anything about David's sins – only the poor and rich man parable and David's repentance. Mufassirun came with many different 'sins' for David, and I mentioned above those most critical of David. Other stories are less critical, such as: 'David saw a woman of his people and loved her and asked her husband to divorce, which he did, and David married her.' Another version is that 'the woman was not married, just engaged, so David's minor sin was that he requested to marry an engaged woman.' Other mufassirun mention different and minor sins having nothing to do with Bathsheba : 'When David listened to the first litigant he came to a conclusion before hearing the second party.' or 'David thought that the two litigants came to kill him; and realizing his mistake, asked for forgiveness.' Or 'David was at prayers when a man and woman came to him in an argument, and David was temporarily attracted to the woman and forgot his prayers.'

interrupted the pleasure of my sleep and awakened me?" David stated his name and Uriah asked, "What brought you here, prophet of God?" "I come asking your forgiveness for what I did to you," said David. When Uriah asked what it was that David had done, David confessed that he had caused his death. Uriah replied, "You caused me to enter Paradise, how can I be unhappy about that?"

God revealed to David, "You should let him know that you married his wife." When David returned to the grave, Uriah asked him, "What more do you want, have I not forgiven you for what you did to me?" David said, "Yes, you did, but what I did not tell you is that I sent you to die so I could marry your wife, whom I loved." When Uriah did not respond, David took some dirt from the grave and put it on his head, saying, "Woe to me on Judgment Day when judgment will be enforced, woe to me when I will be dragged, with my face in the dirt, with the other sinners to the Hell fire, woe to me when the angels of torture will put me with every wrongdoer in Hell." David heard God saying, "David, I forgive all your sins and have mercy on you." But David said, " But Uriah did not forgive me?" God answered, "On Resurrection Day I will give him unimagined rewards and ask him, 'My servant, are you satisfied?' and he will answer, 'Yes, My Lord, I am very satisfied, but You are giving me more than what I deserve.' And I will say, 'This is compensation for your forgiveness of My servant David.' Uriah will then forgive David."[1]

David recognized that God had forgiven him and prostrated himself before the Lord in repentance. God told David that *"I have made you a viceregent on earth, so judge between men with truth and justice, and follow no whim which will lead you away from God's path. Those who stray from God's path will suffer severe torment."*38:26 After David's repentance, he cried over his sins for thirty years, both night and day. After that he divided his time in four ways: one day was set aside to hear people's grievances, one day was reserved for his women, and one day was left exclusively for David to praise God in the wilderness. The fourth day he stayed in his prayer chamber.[2]

---

[1]- Rep. by *Wahb,* pub. by Ara-Tha 252; Taf-Bagh & Khaz 38:24.

[2]- Rep. by *Shu'ayb bin Muhammad,* pub. by Ara-Tha 253.

When David went to the wilderness his praising of God rang
out with his cries, his dulcet tones as melodious as those of a flute.
Accompanying him were the trees, the mountains, the beasts and the
birds, and their tears filled the wadis. David would continue to the
oceanside where the whales, fish and all manner of sea creatures
would join him in his lamentations.  Once it was announced that
anyone wishing to join David in his praising God could do so. Four
thousand monks clothed in sackcloth and carrying staves came, sat in
the prayer hall, and began to wail with David.  He was so overcome
with emotion, he collapsed after his tears soaked the floor on which
they sat.  His son, Solomon, came and carried David from the hall.
David dried his tears, washed his face and said, "My Lord, forgive me
for what you see."

David, after his sin, would congregate with sinners and tell
them, "Come to David, the sinner." He would only drink that which
was mixed with his tears, and to eat he would mix dry rye bread, salt
and ash with his tears saying, "This is the food of sinners."  Before
his sin he would pray one half of every night, but after his sin he
prayed all night and fasted every day.[1]

**David and Solomon**

This story shows the difference between David and Solomon and
their manner of adjudication.  David was asked to settle a dispute
between a farmer and a shepherd.  The shepherd's sheep trespassed
on the farmer's land and devoured the entire crop, and David ruled
that all the sheep should be turned over to the farmer for
compensation.  When Solomon heard of the decision he let it be
known that he would have found a different solution. As a result,
David asked Solomon to judge the dispute.  Solomon said, "I would
have the farmer keep the sheep for one year, and during that time,
receive the benefits of the wool, milk and newborn lambs.  Further,
the shepherd should work on the farm, plowing and planting until the
land was returned to its condition before the sheep damaged it.  At the

---

[1]- Rep. by *Wahb*, pub. in Ara-Tha 254;Taf-Bagh & Khaz 38: 25. The
extremely exaggerated theme of this story was necessary to balance his severe sin
in the mind of the readers, but most mufassirun did not agree with it and instead
comment how ridiculous this story is.

end of the year, the shepherd will take back the sheep, and the farmer his land."[1]

## Solomon Proclaimed David's Heir

God brought David a book from Heaven with a golden seal. The book contained multiple questions, and God told David that if his son, Solomon, could answer them all, he would be next in line to be king. David summoned seventy priests and had Solomon sit with them. He told his son about the Heaven-sent book, and that the questions contained therein would determine Solomon's ability to serve as king, after David's passing. Solomon said, "You may ask me anything that comes to your mind." And the questions began:

Q- What is the nearest thing and what is the thing most far away?

A- The nearest thing is what is coming in your life, and the most far away is what has passed from it.

Q- What is the most cheerful thing and what is the most gloomy?

A- A living human body is the most cheering, and a dead human body is the most gloomy.

Q- What is the best thing in life and what is the worst thing in life?

A- Belief after disbelief is the best thing in life, and disbelief after belief is the worst thing.

Q- What is the most simple thing and the most complex thing?

A- Faith is the most simple thing and doubt is the most complex one.

Q- What are the two objects that stand still, and what two objects are constantly in motion?

A- Sky and earth are the objects which stand still while the sun and moon are the always moving objects.

Q- What are the two companions and the two enemies?

A- Day and night are the two companions, while life and death are the two enemies.

Q- What is the ride which takes man to satisfaction, and the one which takes him to dissatisfaction?

A- Clemency at the time of anger takes you to satisfaction, while rage at anger takes you to dissatisfaction.

---

[1]- Rep. by *Ibn Abbas and Qutada*, pub. by Ara-Tha 257; Taf-Tab, Taf-Bagh & Taf-Khaz 21:78.

The book's golden seal was opened, and Solomon's answers matched those made in Heaven. But the priests were not yet satisfied, and had one more question to ask. If Solomon could answer correctly, he would be accepted as the heir. "What is the thing, if right, makes everything in man right, and, if it is wrong, then everything is wrong?" Solomon answered, "Man's heart."[1]

## The Death of David

David had a special maid who would close and lock his doors, give him the keys, and leave him to his worship every night. One night, after giving David his keys, she saw a man inside the house and asked him who he was, and how he was able to gain entry, she explained that he should be careful, as the owner would brook no intruders. He said, "I am the one who enters the homes of kings without their permission." David was standing up in prayer, and what he heard shocked and frightened him. He had the maid show the man to his prayer room and asked him "Who let you in, at this time without permission?" The stranger answered, "I am the one who enters the castles of kings without their permission." When David asked if he was the Angel of Death, the Angel answered, "Yes, I am." "Did you come to preach or are you bringing bad news?" asked David. The Angel confirmed that he was the bearer of bad news, and David wanted to know, "Should you not let me know in advance, so I can be ready to answer?" The Angel of Death said, "I did warn you many times, but you paid no attention. Where are your father, your brothers, your mother, your neighbors and maids?" "They are all dead," answered David. The Angel chastised David, saying, "Did you not know that your turn would come as well?"[2]

---

[1]- Rep. by *Abu Hurayra*, pub. in Ara-Tha 257.
[2]- Rep. by *Abu 'Amr al Farabi*, pub. in Ara-Tha 259.

# 11    Solomon / *Sulaymān*

> We bestowed Solomon on David. How favored was such
> a servant.
>
> – Qur'an 38:30

## Introduction

The story of the biblical Solomon is described in 1 Kings 1-11, and 2 Chr. 1-9, and according to these writings he was the third king of Israel which flourished in Palestine. He was born circa 1035 B.C.E. succeeding his father, King David, by age 18 and reigned for forty years. Biblical writers claim Solomon's kingdom extended from the Euphrates to the border of Egypt (1Kings 4:21), and under his guidance the first half of his reign was a time of peace and prosperity for his kingdom. Most of the biblical stories concerning Solomon concentrate on his personal affairs and his life style. He surrounded himself with all the luxury and grandeur befitting a great king of the time (1Kings 4:22-28; 10:25-29), including one thousand women between wives and concubines from multiple ethnicity, (1Kings 11:13). Solomon established a large but efficiently run forced public service program (1Kings5:13-16), which constructed many palaces (1Kings 7), but his major public accomplishment was the building of the Jerusalem Temple to house the Ark of the Covenant (1Kings 6) , although his forced labor policy was one of the factors which eventually led to the decline and breakup of his kingdom, as dissent grew among the laborers.

Writings in the Bible concerning his international affairs are scanty, though it is said he married the daughter of the Egyptian pharaoh (1Kings3) and entered into an alliance with Hiram, King of Tyre who assisted in the building projects with shipments of both cedar trees and skilled labor (1Kings 5:1-12), as well as with the

construction of sailing ships bound for Africa where much profit was
to be made from trade (1Kings 9:26-28; 10:22). There is, however,
no historical confirmation of the above events.

Solomon is remembered for his wisdom, and his fame spread
throughout every surrounding nation. He composed three thousand
proverbs and his songs numbered one thousand and five. He spoke of
trees, from the cedars in Lebanon to the hyssop that springs from the
wall. He also spoke of the beasts and fowl and creeping things and
fish (1Kings 4:32-33). Along with the men who came from these
lands to listen to Solomon and hear his words of wisdom (1Kings
4:34) was the Queen of Sheba who was filled with amazement by all
she saw and heard, and exchanged gifts with Solomon before
returning to her kingdom (1Kings 10:1-10; 11:13).

The writers of Solomon's chronicles saw his demise stem
from his love of the plethora of foreign women he kept and for whom
he built 'high places' (temples) for the gods they worshiped. They
believe his heart was turned toward these other gods (1Kings 11:8),
which angered the Lord. After his death the kingdom was divided.

The above describes the Solomon of the Bible, a prosaic
Solomon, realistic though perhaps not historically accurate. But there
was another Solomon who we call "the apocryphal Solomon," a man
of many wonders who controlled demons and used them in his
building projects, dominated wild beasts and birds; his power
emanating from a ring on which was depicted a magical diagram.
The apocryphal Solomon is found in 'The Testament of Solomon,'
written in the third century C.E. 'The Book of King Solomon,' which
was quoted in Zohar, from the 'Book of Recipes,' contains
instruction on concocting magic potions, and this possibly was the
book in which Hippolytus (160-236 C.E.) writes that Hezekiah hid
and kept these writings from circulation. Josephus, in 'Antiquities
8,2,5,' writes that God granted Solomon a mysterious and special
knowledge to be used against the demons for the benefit and healing
of man, including the ability to compose incantations to relieve illness
and exorcisms to drive out demons.

In 'Targum Sheni to Esther,' Solomon ruled over the wild
beasts of the earth, as well as the devils, the spirits of the night, and
he understood the languages of all of these; he even talked to the

trees. Theodoret (393-458 C.E.) refers to the existence of Solomon's medical texts and praises his medical knowledge.

In addition to these two different Solomons, we need to add a third, the Arabic Qur'anic Solomon, a priest "prophet king," with an Arabic name and a kingdom which neighbored the southern Arabian kingdom of Saba', "Sheba." He garnered obedience over the winds and the jinn, two connected powers in the mind of the Arabian people. He also had the obedience of birds, even understanding their talk and raising falcons which was and still is considered a sign of power in Arabia.

But what is most important in understanding the Qur'anic Solomon is not just what the Qur'an said, but what it does not say. The Qur'an does not connect Solomon and his father to the Israelite tribes; as a matter of fact the only time the term "children of Israel," is mentioned in conjunction with David is in Verse 5:78, which says that David cursed the disbelievers of the children of Israel. Nothing in the Qur'an connects Solomon to the land of Palestine and it mentions nothing of his private life or interstate busines, internal affairs of state, or about building the temples or palaces.

Both David and Solomon are praised for their wisdom, judgement, knowledge and repentance. Solomon has a special favor given to him by God, which no one before nor no one after shall have. The Qur'an does not elaborate as to what favor was granted but most probably it was the combination of both king and prophet in one person.

In pre-Islamic Arabia, the same poets who wrote of David mentioned Solomon, and gave him different names, which coincide with the rules of rhythm in Arabic poetry. *An-Nābigha,* in his poem praising the Arabian King of Hira, *An-Nu'mān,* told of Solomon who used jinn to build the city of Tadmor, while *Al-A'shā* included Solomon in his poems and noted the extent of his empire, stretching from Syria to Egypt. *Al-Aswad bin ya'far* called him *'Sallām'* and *An-Nābigha* called him *'Salīm, '* and both wrote of his skill in the making of ring armor, an art usually ascribed to his father, David.

The Arabic name Solomon, *'Sulaymān, '* is the diminutive form of the name *'Salmān, '* which means 'in Peace,' from the Arabic root 'slm.' His wife's name, *'Al-Jarāda, '* means 'locust' in Arabic. The story of Solomon in the Bible and in rabbinical literature contain many Arabic connections, e.g. his story in the Arabian land of *'Ād* and the legendary king *Shaddād* mentioned in Jewish lore and the story of Solomon and the Arabian Queen of Sheba. Abraham Jogel said that Solomon wrote his scientific works in a language other than Hebrew, and we know of the existence of many original Solomonic Arabic books, like Kitab al-Nakhlah which translates to Hebrew as 'Sefer ha-Tamar,' and the book of 'Miftah Sulayman' or The Key of Solomon.

Most Qur'anic strories regarding Solomon are ambiguous, although the ambiguity was solved by giving these stories biblical or rabbinical background. This Qur'anic profile of Solomon did not survive intact, and soon the three differing Solomons combined in the early Islamic oral tradition, in the books of tafsir and the books of "The Stories of the Prophets." His control over the winds developed into a flying carpet and the royal visit of the Queen of Saba' became a power struggle ending in a love story where the queen exposed her legs to Solomon. And of course, stories from the biblical and apocryphal Solomon were introduced, such as the building of the temple, his temporary loss of power and his death.

In the Qur'an, King Solomon, son of David, is a man granted many astonishing powers, who had the capability of controlling demons and jinn (Q34:12-13), and whose army consisted of humans, jinn and birds, (Q27:17). He was able to understand the talk of both birds (Q27:16) and ants (Q27:19). One of his courtiers was a powerful but good demon (Q27:39), and another one is a man who had the knowledge and power to bring the throne of the Queen of Sheba to Solomon in the blink of an eye (Q27:40). But, according to the Qur'an, Solomon did not use magic to achieve these wonders; on the contrary, this was an exceptionally unique and special power granted exclusively to Solomon by God as a great favor. It was given to no one before Solomon nor would it be given to anyone after Solomon. The difference between magic and divine miracles is not in the type of wonders but in what authority lies behind these marvels, being derived either from a divine or devilish source. Some mufassirun were captivated by this figure who had the power to seemingly do anything, which they added to the Qur'anic version of the stories of wonder, whether attributable to Solomon, or not.

I now will introduce the Islamic Solomon, the combination of the three personalities and not just the Qur'anic one.

# The Story of Solomon

God gave Solomon the ability to understand the language of all animals and birds in particular. After hearing the song of a bird, Solomon would translate it for his companions, and the following are examples of bird sayings:

**The wood pigeon**: "What you begot will die, and what you have built will fall."

**The peacock**: "As you judge, so you will be judged."

**The Hoopae**: "Those who show no pity will not receive any."

**The shrike**: "Sinners, repent your sins."

**The sandpiper**: "Living creatures will die, and material possessions will become obsolete."

**The swallow**: "Provide good deeds, you will find them when in need."

**The pigeon**: "The glory of my supreme Lord, is filling the earth and heavens."

**The turtle dove**: "Glory to He who will never die."

**The sky kite**: "Everyone will die, save Him."

**The sand grouse**: "Those who keep their silence, keep their safety."

**The sparrow**: "Glory to the One mentioned everywhere."[1]

One spring, a skylark laid her eggs on the road used as Solomon's procession route. The male was not pleased and chastised his mate, "Did I not prohibit you from this? When Solomon's procession passes by, our eggs will be destroyed." When Solomon heard that, he sent a jinni to protect and cover the eggs with his feet. And when the procession marched down the street the eggs remained safe. The skylark couple were very touched by the mercy of the king, and to thank him, flew to his palace and presented him with gifts, the

---

[1]- From Ara-Tha 261; Taf-Bagh and Taf-Khaz 27:16. Rep. by *Ka'b*. This legend was built on the Qur'anic verse quoting Solomon "We *have learned the birds' speak*" 27:16.

male giving a locust and the female giving a date. Solomon prayed
for them and stroked their heads. It has been said that the crest of the
lark was created by Solomon's touch.[1]

On another occasion, Solomon and his army of soldiers, jinn
and birds were on the march and came to the valley of the ants. An
ant from the valley cautioned the others, *"O ants, enter your
dwellings lest Solomon and his armies crush us, without even
noticing."* 27:18 God granted that these words would reach Solomon,
perhaps by the winds carrying the words of the ant to him. Solomon
had the ant brought to him and asked, "Why did you warn the ants
about my army? Do you not know that I am a just prophet? Why did
you say Solomon and his armies would crush you?" The ant who was
called Takhia, responded, "Prophet of God, did you not hear the rest
of my statement—'without even noticing it'? By 'crush', I did not
mean bodily harm, but the crushing of souls. I was worried that when
they will see what God gave you, they would wish for it or become
preoccupied watching you, instead of praising God." Solomon
wanted the ant to preach to him further. The ant asked Solomon if he
knew why his father was called David, and when Solomon answered
in the negative, the ant explained, "Because he cured the wounds of
his heart."[2] And it went on to explain the naming of Solomon. "You
are at peace," the ant told him, "you have reached your position by the
serenity in your heart, and God made the wind serve you to tell you
that everything in this life is like the wind." Solomon smiled and
laughed at her preaching, saying, *"My Lord, help me to be grateful for
your favors which you have bestowed on me and my parents, and help
me to work toward the righteousness that will please you, and admit
me, by Your grace, among your righteous servants."* 27:19

---

[1]-From Ara-Tha 262, Islamic Arabic lore.
[2]- David's Arabic name "Dawud" sounds close to the ward "dawa" which
means to heal.
[3]- From Ara-Tha 263; Taf-Bagh 27:17-18. Rep. by *Al-Sha'bi, Ad-Dahhak
and Muqatil.*

**Solomon's Control of the Spirit World**

God gave Solomon control over the jinn, demons, birds and beasts. To control the jinn and demons God assigned an angel with a whip of fire to work with Solomon, and whenever his commands were not obeyed, the angel would strike the offender with the whip, which would burn the offender to ashes. Jinn and demons worked hard for Solomon. They built for him palaces, public baths, mills, and they invented glass and soap. They even dug a river through his land. Another group was assigned to work as divers, and they dove throughout the seas and sought out pearls, coral and other types of precious marine gems. Still others worked as miners and searched for rubies, emeralds and other precious stones.[1]

**The Magic Carpet**

Solomon's demons wove a carpet of gold thread and silk, measuring one by one league, and when he wanted to travel he would sit in the middle of the carpet on a gold throne, surrounded by three thousand chairs made of silver and gold. The prophets sat on the gold chairs and the priests sat on the silver, surrounded by the common people, around them the jinn and demons, and above them all, birds flew to give them shade. The west wind carried the carpet in one day a distance equal to one month of land travel. It has been said that Solomon and his army flew to Iraq, where he prayed the afternoon prayer in the city of Balakh, then on to the Turk land, then to China, then India, and on to the land of Makran and Karman. From there he went to Persia and stayed for a few days, then back to Tadmor, a new marble city built for him in Syria by the demons.[2]

---

[1]- Ara-Tha 270, see Q 38:37-38 & 27:17. For Solomon's dominion over spirits and demons in Hebrew writings see L.O.J, IV 149-154.

[2]- Ara-Tha 261; Taf-Bagh & Taf-Khaz 21:81; Taf-Tab mentioned the story without a carpet. "The wind carried them," and he referred it to *Ibn 'Abbas*. These legends were built on the Qur'anic verse 34:12, which said that God made the wind obedient to Solomon. Tadmor is the Arabic name for Palmyra; the legend of building Tadmor by Solomon came from the Bible 2Chr 8:4.

## The Font of Melted Brass

One of the privileges God granted to Solomon was the font of the melted brass. God brought forth from the earth melted brass which ran for three days in Yemen, and it is said most of the brass in use today came from that spring.[1]

### The Story of the Glass Dome

Solomon, surrounded by his retinue, the jinn, birds and animals, gazed out over the waves and into the sea, and felt that he should know what lay at the bottom of the sea. He summoned his chief diver and had him assemble one hundred divers. The field was narrowed to thirty of the best, then down to ten, and finally three divers were brought before Solomon. Solomon chose one and told him to dive to the bottom of the ocean and discover what lay at the bottom. The diver stayed below for quite some time, and when he eventually emerged he told Solomon, "At first I saw nothing but water and fish. Then an Angel appeared and asked what I was doing. I explained that the prophet of God, Solomon, sent me to dive to the bottom of the sea, and the Angel told me, 'Go back to Solomon, pay him my respects, and tell him that forty years ago some sailors sailed this sea, their ship suffered some damage, and in the process of repair a hammer fell overboard. That hammer is still sinking, and has not yet hit bottom.' "[2]

Solomon was full of wonder upon hearing the diver's tale. Suddenly, a glass dome appeared in the sea, and when Solomon had the divers bring it to the shore, the dome's double doors opened and out stepped a young man dressed in white. He was dripping wet, and Solomon asked him whether he was human or jinn. The young man claimed to be human, and explained how he came to be in such a state. "Prophet of God, I was very considerate to my late mother. I fed her and had her drink from my own hands, doing everything

---

[1]-This story came from the Qur'anic verse 34:12: "We *made a font of molten brass to flow for him.*" The Bible mentioned that Hiram from Tyre was commissioned by Solomon to do bronze works for him. Hiram cast many bronze works such as pillars, capitals, pomegranates, stands, molten sea and many other works. 1Kings 7:13-51.

[2]- From Ara-Tha 270; reported by *Wahb*.

possible to make her happy. When she was about to die, I asked her to pray for me. She looked at the sky and said, 'My Lord, You know how good my son has been to me. Allow him to worship You in a place where the Devil and his followers can have no effect on him.' Then she died and I buried her. One day as I strolled along the beach, I saw this dome, and when I entered, it closed on me. Since then, I spend my life enclosed in the dome, being pushed by waves." "But how do you eat and drink?" asked Solomon. The young man told him, "Every night a white bird visits me with white stuff in its mouth. It is released to me and satisfies my need for both food and drink." Solomon asked how he knew day from night, as the sea is dark. "There are two strings in the dome, one white, one black, and during the day, the white one is longer; during the night, the strings are reversed." Solomon asked the young man if he would like to stay with them, but he apologized and asked to be returned to the sea. He went back to the dome which closed him in, and the waves pushed him deep into the sea.[1]

**The Glass City of Solomon**
        Jinn and demons built a glass city with dimensions of ten thousand by ten thousand cubits, and one thousand stories high. The first floors were stronger than iron, while the top ones were transparent as water, and everything outside was visible, including the sun and moon. A large white dome crowned the top floor where, at night, a white flag flew, from which a light shone and illuminated the horizon and lit the army camp. The city was built on a thousand columns, and each column was carried by ten demons. The city accommodated Solomon, his army, his servants, the priests, and in the lower floor stabled his horses. This glass city was Solomon's home, where he slept and ate, and where, at his command, the wind would carry the city anywhere he wished to go.[2]

**The Throne of Solomon**
        Solomon commanded the demons to build an imposing throne for him. He requested that it be so great that when he sat in

---

[1]- Ibid.
[2]- From Ara-Tha 271.

judgement, no one coming before him would give false testimony. It was constructed from elephant tusks and inlaid with rubies, pearls, sapphires and diamonds.  Four golden palm trees adorned each corner, with leaves made of rubies and sapphires, and on two of the trees were golden peacocks, and facing them were two golden eagles. On either side of the throne sat golden lions  decorated with emeralds. On the palm trees hung red gold grape leaves, the grapes made from rubies and arranged so that the vines formed a canopy over the throne. When Solomon set foot on the  throne, the throne's golden creatures seemed to come to life.  The eagles and peacocks spread their wings, the lions stretched their legs and hit the floor with their tails while the eagles perched on the palm trees and sprayed him with musk and ambergris.

Solomon would call the meeting to order and read from the Torah, which was opened for him by a golden pigeon laden with pearls, and resting on one of the columns.  One thousand leaders from Israel sat on gold and silver chairs, covered with precious stones on Solomon's right side, while in silver chairs to his left sat one thousand jinn leaders.  During the hearings, as a witness would testify, birds flew overhead, and the throne shook with the movements of the lions, eagles and peacocks.  The commotion was so great that those testifying, were terrified and would only speak the truth.

When Nebuchadnezzar, the Assyrian, invaded Jerusalem many years after the death of Solomon, he took the throne to Antioch.  As the king was not familiar with the intricacies of the throne, Nebuchadnezzar found himself thrown to the floor by the movement of the lion's paw.  His leg was injured and he was left with a limp that stayed with him until the day he died.  The throne remained in Antioch until his descendants returned it to Jerusalem, but it remained untouched.  It was placed under a holy rock whence it has disappeared, and no one is cognizant as to its whereabouts.[1]

---

[1]-From Ara-Tha 272; reported by *Wahb* and *Ibn Maymuna*. The description of Solomon's throne in Hebrew writings can be found in Targum Sheni 1.2, 5-7; Abba Gorion 4-, from L.O.J. IV 157-160. The stories of the glass dome, the glass city, and the throne have no Qur'anic origin, and are mentioned only by story tellers.

**Solomon's Horses**

Solomon inherited one thousand horses from his father, David, and they were the best of the Arabian horses. He was extremely proud of them, and admired them frequently. One day after his noon prayer he was viewing the horses, and he became very occupied with their beauty; overwhelmed by their number until the sun had set, he missed the afternoon prayer. No one of his court dared to remind him of his indiscretion, but once Solomon realized what he had missed he became very upset and asked the grooms to return the horses. He then had them slaughtered as a sacrifice to God to repent for his dalliance.[1]

**The Building of the Temple**

God blessed the descendants of Abraham, and their numbers grew. David wanted an accurate count, and formed a committee to take a census, but they were ineffectual in completing the challenge and ultimately announced their failure. God sent the Angel Gabriel to David and revealed to him, "David, you know My promise to your father Abraham. When I commanded him to sacrifice his son, and he obeyed, My blessings extended to his descendants who were to multiply until their numbers equaled the stars in the sky. But no one but I will know the exact count. However, as you are proud of their numbers, I swear that I will test them in a way that will decrease their size and take away your pride. You will have your choice of three

---

[1]-This story was discussed in most tafsir books and came from Q 38:31-33, but these thre verses generated much controversy in their interpretation. The above is *Muqatil's* version, but *Al-Hasan* mentioned that these horses came from the sea and they were winged. *Al-Kalbi* maintained that the horses came from Nasibin, when Solomon conquered that city. *Ka'b* mentioned the same story but said there were only fourteen horses. Not all mufassirun accepted the killing of the horses. *Al-Razi* maintained that Solomon did not harm the horses, but actually donated them to his cavalry for the war effort and branded them with a special brand. *Az-Zahri* explained it by saying Solomon had the horses cleaned after the parade. Even those who say he killed the horses did not make it a good and non-selfish act. *Ka'b* said that after killing the fourteen horses God punished him by dethroning him for fourteen days, see Ara-Tha 268; Taf-Tab & Bagh 38:34. According to the Bible, David was the first to form a cavalry in Israel (2Sam 8:4). Solomon enlarged the force and increased their number (1Kings4:26) by importing horses from Egypt (1Kings 9:33).

disasters: a three-year famine, an attack and defeat from your enemy for three months, or a natural disaster lasting three days.

David gathered together the people of Israel and gave them God's news. As they did not want to die by starvation, nor die a dishonorable death at the hands of their enemy, they chose a natural disaster as their test. David asked them to prepare to die, and they took their last ceremonial bath, wore their death shrouds and gathered together at the site of the Temple, not yet built. There, with their families around them, they pleaded with God to show them mercy, but God sent them a plague which killed one thousand of them in one day and night. On the second day, David lay prostrate on the ground, bowing to God, and said, "My Lord, I am the one who sinned, why should Israel suffer? If You have more punishment, place it on me, and pardon the people of Israel." God accepted his prayer and stopped the plague. David saw the angels sheath their swords and ascend a golden ladder from the holy rock at the site of the Temple.

David said, "God put his mercy on you and the plague ceased, so renew your thanks to him." They asked how they should show their gratitude, and David told them, "Build a temple on this spot where you received God's mercy." They began building the rock edifice from stones which David and the righteous Israelites carried on their backs. They completed the foundations but their construction came to a holt when they found they were unable to move one more stone. God told David, "This is a holy place and you have much blood on your hands. But Solomon, your son, will build it, though its dedication and good deeds will be credited to you.

When David died and Solomon became king, God commanded him to finish the temple. Solomon summoned his people, the jinn and demons, and each was assigned a different task. He began building the city with marble, gold, and clear white crystals which the jinn and demons brought from the mines. The city was laid out in twelve sections, each section representing an Israelite tribe. After the city's completion, work was begun on the temple. The demons were sent to various places to acquire and utilize different building materials. Some mined gold, silver and rubies; others dove for pearls; some cut marble; and some sought out musk and ambergris. Generous quantities of everything were needed. The temple was made of white, yellow and green marble, while the columns were constructed of alabaster. The ceiling was from gold plate set with precious stones, while the floor was tiled with sapphires. When finished, there was no structure on earth more lovely, nor one with more light than the temple. He gathered together the priests of Israel and informed them that the temple had been built for the glory of God. And they must celebrate as they had never celebrated before. A thousand camels, twenty-five thousand cows and four hundred thousand sheep were sacrificed for the occasion. Solomon made an offering on the holy rock and said, "God, You gave me this kingdom, and made me its overlord. You honored me when I was nothing, praise be to You. God bless whoever visits this temple and prays in it. Forgive him of his sins as he was the day he was born. Grant him serenity in his heart, heal him when he is sick, and enrich him when he is poor. God, if You accept this petition, give me a sign so I can be sure of your acceptance." Immediately, a fire fell from the sky, took the offering, then turned back from where it came.[1]

### Sakhr, the Demon and the Shamir Stone

The builders found that, due to the hardness of the marble, it was very difficult to shape the stone, and the noise from the polishing became very annoying. Solomon summoned the jinn who said the solution lay with Sakhr, the demon. Solomon sent a message to Sakhr requesting his presence by means of a letter stamped with his seal, which flashed like lightning. Anyone seeing Solomon's seal responded immediately to his inquiry, as an astonished Sakhr did after receiving the summons. Solomon sent ten messengers to return with Sakhr, and they reported to Solomon that during the trip Sakhr derided people along the way.

When questioned about this, Sakhr explained, "Prophet of God, I was not making fun of them, but I laughed in wonder from what I observed. We passed a river and saw a man and his mule. The man gave the mule a drink from a clay pot, then tied the mule to the pot while he stepped away to make his toilet. The mule kicked and broke the clay pot, and I laughed at the stupidity of the man who thought that the clay pot would hold the mule still. I then passed a

---

[1]- From Ara-Tha 273, rep. by story tellers.

man having his shoe repaired by a shoemaker. I heard him ask for a four-year guarantee for the shoe repair, but the man forgot that the Angel of Death can strike at any time. I laughed at his ignorance and mental deficiency. I next passed an old woman seer who would tell people their future. She herself had little to eat, and yet did not know that under her own bed lay gold buried long ago. I then passed a man who cured his chronic illness by eating a great amount of onion. In spite of the deleterious effect onion can have on some conditions, including affecting the brain, he prescribed onion for every affliction. I found this hilarious and laughed. Then I passed a bazaar and found garlic, the best medicine sold by the bulk, and black pepper, a lethal poison sold by the ounce. I saw people sitting together asking God for His mercy and blessing; some of the people left and others took their place. Then God's blessing came down and blessed the newcomers. I laughed in wonder at God's destiny."

Solomon asked him, "With your tremendous experience, do you know of anything that can carve these stones and gems easily and without noise?"[1] Sakhr answered, "Yes, prophet of God, there is a white stone, the 'shamir', which will accomplish the task, but I do not know where to mine it. However, the smartest bird in the world is the hawk, and if you put the hawk's chicks inside a box made of the gems, the mother hawk will locate the shamir stone, and break open the box. This was done, and it took the hawk a day and a night to find and bring a shamir stone to break open the box. Solomon had sent the jinn with the hawk, and they recovered enough of the shamir

---

[1]- A similar story in Hebrew lore involved Asmodeus, the king of the demons who was captured by Solomon's chief man, Benaiah. After his capture, and on his way to Solomon, Asmodeus acted in a peculiar way because of what he saw around him. He later explained his strange behavior to Solomon in stories similar to those of Sakhr. When he was asked about the shamir, Asmodeus answered that it was given by God to the angels of the sea, and they entrusted the moorhen with it. Solomon's people covered the moorhen's nest with glass, and when she was unable to reach her young the moorhen brought the shamir to break the glass. Solomon's people shouted and scared the moorhen, and she dropped the shamir which Solomon's people caught. The shamir, according to Hebrew lore, is a hard stone used by Solomon to carve the stones used in building, as the Torah prohibited the use of iron tools in erecting an altar, from L.O.J. IV 166-169.

stone to complete the cutting, shaping and polishing of the building materials.[1]

### Solomon and the Queen of Sheba / *Saba'*

Her name was *Balqīs*, the daughter of King *Al-Bashrakh*, a great king in control of all Yemen, who felt that the border princesses would not make a suitable wife so instead married a jinn named *Rayhānah*. And she bore him *Balqīs*. After the death of her father, a dispute arose between *Balqīs* and a man who wanted the throne, which was settled by dividing the kingdom in two, each one ruling his and her domain. But *Balqīs'* rival behaved in a disreputable manner, forcing women to copulate with him, and remaining in power despite attempts to oust him. When *Balqīs* heard these stories she proposed marriage to him, which he readily accepted as he had wanted to marry *Balqīs,* but thought she would have refused his offer. He then made an official proposal, and though her courtiers were surprised, she formally accepted and the wedding took place. After the ceremony, when they were alone, she plied him with wine until he became intoxicated. *Balqīs* then cut off his head, put it on a pole, and placed it outside his door. She then returned to her palace, and when the people saw what she had done they realized that the marriage had been a ploy to rid them of the tyrant, and she was asked to be queen of all Yemen.

After her coronation she built a palace on a hill near *San'a.* Her palace had five hundred columns with ten cubits between each, the columns connected with a ceiling made of marble. It was joined together with lead, and gave the appearance of being carved from a single piece of marble. The ceiling was square, and on each corner was a golden dome, while at the entrance to the city was built a tower of white, green and red marble. Its sides, as well as the offices of the courtiers and walls of the palace, were covered in gold, silver and gemstones. *Balqīs'* throne was made of gold, and imbedded with rubies and emeralds. Its back was made of silver, also studded with gems, while each leg was set with a different stone-rubies, emeralds,

---

[1]- Ara-Tha 275. These stories about the building of the temple, the demon Sakhr, and the Shamir stone have no Qur'anic origin, and are borrowed from Jewish lore.

and pearls. *Balqīs* and her people worshiped the sun, which they bowed to at sunrise and sundown.[1]

## The Hoopae

The hoopae was the bird in Solomon's army which was responsible for locating water when Solomon traveled. He was called Yafur, and had the ability to see underground water as others would see water in a glass.[2] He was able to detect the water's depth and would advise Solomon who would then send the demons to extract the water. One day, as the hoopae was flying high above the earth, he was attracted by the green in the garden belonging to Queen *Balqīs*. He landed in the garden and there he met a Yemenite hoopae called Afir. Afir asked Yafur where he came from and Yafur answered, "I come from Palestine with my master Solomon, son of David." Afir then asked who Solomon was, and was told by Yafur, "The king of all jinn, humans, beasts and the winds." Yafur then questioned Afir about where he came from. "I am local, from these lands, and our queen is *Balqīs*, who has great power. She controls all Yemen with twelve thousand officers, each having twelve thousand soldiers." Together, the two hoopaes explored the Yemenite kingdom and Yafur was late in returning to his camp.

Solomon was searching for water and for the hoopae. When he found him absent he exclaimed, *"I shall punish or even slaughter that bird unless he has a good excuse for his absence."* 27:21 A hawk was sent to find and bring back the hoopae, and as the hawk reached an altitude which enabled him to look down on the earth as if it was a plate, he spotted the returning hoopae. He swooped down upon Yafur but retreated when Yafur begged for mercy. They flew together to Solomon who was seated on his throne. Yafur raised his head and lay his tail and wings on the floor in an act of submission before Solomon, who angrily asked him where he had been. *"I have acquired some new information from Saba' which will be of interest to*

---

[1]- Ara-Tha 276; Qis-Kath II 290 and after.

[2]- Rep. by *Ibn Abbas*. The skeptic *Nafi' bin al-Azraq* asked *Ibn 'Abbas* how is it that the hoopae does not see a bird trap hidden under a little dirt? Pub. by Taf-Tab 27:20; Qis-Kath II 289.

*you. I found a woman ruling there, who has everything, including a splendid throne. Both she and her people bow, not to God, but to the sun. The Devil has made their actions seem attractive, and has diverted them from the proper way. They have no guidance and do not bow before God, who brings forth what is concealed in heavens and earth. He knows what you hide and what you reveal. There is no deity but God, Lord of the splendid throne."*

Solomon said, *"We shall see whether you have told the truth,"* and wrote a letter to the Queen of Sheba. *"In the name of God, the mercy-giving, the merciful,* peace be upon those who follow His guidance. *Do not act haughtily toward me, and come to me committed to peace."* 27:22-31 He put his seal on the letter and told the hoopae, "Take this letter of mine and deliver it. Leave for a short while, but be observant should they send something to me."

It was early in the morning and the queen was in her palace awaiting the sun. It appeared each day through a high window, and there the queen would bow. The hoopae appeared in that window and its wings blocked the sun. She looked up to see why the sun was late and encountered the hoopae who threw down the letter. When Queen *Balqīs* read the letter she realized that a king that had the obedience of birds was a mighty king. She asked for a meeting of her council, and told them of the important letter she had received. She wanted the council's opinion on the matter, as she never settled anything without their recommendation. They advised her, *"We possess strength and can be extremely violent, while authority rests with you. So attend to whatever you command."* She answered, *"Whenever any king enters and then plunders a town, they turn the most important men among them into the lowest. I will send a gift and shall be watching for what the emissaries bring back.[1] "*27:33-35

---

[1]- From Ara-Tha 277; Taf-Bagh & Taf-Khaz 27:20; Taf-Tab 27:3. Rep. by *Ad-Dahhak, Ibn 'Abbas; Akrama, Muqatil, Qutada, Wahb.*

## The Gift of the Queen

Queen *Balqīs* sent a mission headed by *Al-Mundhir bin 'Amr* and with him were five hundred slave boys and five hundred slave girls. She had the boys dress as girls with gold bracelets, necklaces and earrings, and the girls dress as boys and enter on horseback. The boys rode mules adorned with saddles of gold and set with precious stones. The girls were instructed to speak in masculine voices and vice versa. She also sent five hundred gold bricks and five hundred silver along with a crown set with pearls, rubies and a great amount of musk, ambergris and sandalwood. Inside a locked box she enclosed a precious and rare non-pierced pearl, and a bead pierced with a curved hole. A letter accompanied the gifts: "If you are a prophet as you claim, you should be able to discern what the box contains before opening it." She told the head of the mission, "If the king looks at you in anger, you will know he is just a king. Do not let him scare you; I am more powerful than he. But if you find him smiling and not unkind, he must be a holy prophet. Listen to him carefully and bring back his response."

The hoopae listened to what the queen had said and took the information back to Solomon. Solomon planned a very detailed reception to the impending mission. He commanded the jinn to construct a hall, nine miles long, made of gold and silver, that would lead to his throne. He then summoned the most amazing land and sea creatures, and positioned them on the walls of gold and silver, where they ate and where they defecated. He asked the jinn to bring their children, and had them assemble on either side of the hall, along with four thousand chairs for his people, and had the jinn, demons, beasts, lions and birds line up on either side of him.

When the Sabaean mission arrived and saw the animal droppings on the walls of gold and silver, they threw away their golden and silver gifts. As they approached Solomon they encountered the demons and were scared, but they had been told not to worry, so they passed by and went on to find jinn, beasts, humans, and lions until they reached the throne.

Solomon greeted them with a smile on his face, and asked the purpose of their visit. *Al-Mundhir bin 'Amr* told Solomon about their visit and gave him the letter. Solomon read the letter and asked for the locked box. He then shook the box and the Angel Gabriel appeared and told him what it contained.  Solomon said, "There is a precious non-pierced pearl and a bead with a curved hole in this box." The ambassador said, "You are right; may I ask you to pierce the pearl and thread the bead?"  Solomon asked those around him if anyone knew how to accomplish this, and although the humans and jinn did not, the demons said, "Only the termites can do this." A termite was brought before Solomon and it ate its way through the pearl, leaving a hole in the middle.  In return for the termite's assistance, it asked that its sustenance would now be found in the trees, and so it was.  When Solomon asked if anyone could thread the bead, the white worm answered, "I will do this, Prophet of God." It took a thread by its mouth and passed through the bead.  For its reward, the worm asked for its sustenance to be found in fruit, and so it was.

Solomon watched the male and female slaves washing their faces and hands, and determined that the females used one hand to scoop the water and the other to splash it on their faces, while the males used both hands to do the task.  The Queen also sent a staff which had been passed down through her dynasty.  She asked him to decide which end was up when it was part of a tree.  He did so by throwing the staff high in the air.  He said, "Whichever end hits the earth first will be the lower end."[1]  The last query she put to Solomon was in the form of a cup.  It was to be filled with water, neither collected from the sky nor from the ground.  He had a herd of horses run until there was enough sweat to collect and fill the cup.

Although the Sabaean mission was impressed by this show of force, luxury and wealth, the same could not be said of Solomon's impressions of the Sabaeans and the gifts they proffered.  He said, *"Will you furnish me with wealth? What God has given me is better than what He has given you, though you seem content with these gifts."* He told the ambassador, *"Go back to your people, for we shall come with armies you cannot resist. We shall expel you, as the most evil people, and you will be humiliated."*27:36-37

When the Sabaean mission returned home and the queen was told about the wonders they had seen, and what Solomon said, she

---

[1]- The lower part of any branch of a tree is heavier than the upper part.

decided, "He is more than a king, and we cannot fight him." She sent him a letter announcing her intention to visit Solomon in the company of her officials in order to learn about him and his faith. Her throne was then secured behind seven locked doors, with guards surrounding it and with her viceroy in charge of its protection, under strict instructions to let no one close to it. The queen was ready for the journey, traveling with twelve thousand army chiefs, each in command of one hundred thousand fighters. Solomon saw the reflection of sunlight from the queen's caravan and set the stage for another one of his tricks. He asked his council, *"Which of you will bring me the queen's throne before they come to me, committed to peace?"* A giant among the jinn said, *"I am both strong enough and trustworthy to carry it, and will have it here before you rise from your council."* But this did not satisfy Solomon, who wanted the throne immediately. *Asef bin Berkhia*, a man who had knowledge of the Torah and knew the most holy name of God, said, *"I shall bring it to you in the twinkling of an eye."* *Asef* called God, using His most holy name to bring the throne. At once, God sent angels who transported the throne beneath the earth until it appeared before Solomon, all in the twinkling of an eye. On seeing the throne, Solomon exclaimed, *"This is by the grace of My Lord, as a test, to determine whether I am grateful or ungrateful. Those who are thankful give thanks only on their own behalf, while to those who are thankless My Lord is transcendent and generous."* Solomon continued, *"Disguise her throne, let us see whether she is guided and will recognize it or whether she receives no guidance."*

The queen arrived, and was asked whether her throne was like the one before her. *"It does appear to be similar,"* she replied. Solomon said, *"We were given knowledge before she was, and have become believers.* 27:38-42"[1] But he did consider her answer a wise one. In preparation for the queen's visit, Solomon had the jinn build him a crystal palace with water running beneath it, stocked it with fish, and had his throne placed inside. The reason behind the new building

---

[1]- From most tafsir books at 27:27-42.

was the fear on the part of the jinn that the queen, being part jinn herself, would marry Solomon, who would then learn from her the secrets of the jinn. This would place the jinn in danger of becoming slaves forever, so they described the queen to Solomon as a crazy woman with horrible legs and cloven hooves for feet. Solomon was not convinced of what the jinn said, but wanted to see for himself, as well as test her mind, so the palace was built. When the queen saw the water and fish, she assumed it was a pool of water, and gathered up her skirt, baring her legs in order to walk through. Solomon paid attention to her movements and saw shapely legs and feet, though he was not pleased to see hair on her legs. He then explained to her that his hall was made with glass slabs, not water, and asked her to adapt to his faith. The Queen acquiesced, saying, *"My Lord, how I have wronged myself! I commit myself peacefully, along with Solomon, to God, Lord of the worlds .27:44"*[1]

After the queen's conversion, Solomon wanted to marry her, but hesitated because of her hirsute condition, and asked his counselors for a solution. They suggested that she shave using a blade, but Solomon did not want her legs marred by any cuts, and asked the jinn for another answer. They were of no help, but the demons invented the 'norah,' a lotion composed of lime and arsenic which removed the hair. Solomon and queen *Balqīs* were married, and she kept her lands and title as Queen of Sheba. Solomon was very much in love with her, and ordered the jinn to build three forts—*Salḥīn*, *Ghamadān*, and *Banyūn*—in her lands for her use. Solomon would visit her each month and would stay for three days.[2]

### God tests Solomon

Solomon was told about a great kingdom found on the far off and unreachable island of Sedon. Though impenetrable to others, Solomon, accompanied by his army of jinn and humans, flew on the wind, landed on the island, killed the king and captured the inhabitants, one of whom was princess *Jarādah*, the beautiful daughter of the slain king. Solomon was very attracted to her. He

---

[1]- From most tafsir books at 27:44.
[2]- Ara-Tha 280-287; Taf-Bagh & Taf-Khaz 27:23.

kept her for himself and asked her to adopt his faith, and she did so but only out of fear, and had no true belief in his religion. Solomon loved her more than any of his other wives, and she became his favorite, although her position did not make her happy. She was constantly in tears, and when Solomon asked her why, she told him, "When I remember my father and how powerful he was with his majestic kingdom and then recall what happened to him, I cannot help but cry." Solomon countered that, "But God gave you a kingdom which is mightier than your father's, and guided you to the real faith." "What you say is true, but I cannot help myself. Would you please ask your demons to erect a statue of my father to stand in the palace, and perhaps seeing his face will make me feel better?" asked Jaradah. And the demons did complete the statue which was kept near the princess, who dressed it in her father's garments. Unbeknownst to Solomon, when Jaradah and her slaves were alone they would worship the statue.     This continued for forty days until the news reached Solomon's advisor, the holy man *Asef bin Berkhia*. He had the privilege of gaining access to the king at any time of the day or night, and went to him, saying, "Prophet of God, I am getting old and soon will be gone. I would like to give a sermon before my death, a sermon describing the past prophets and their achievements." Solomon arranged for the sermon, and a congregation awaited *Asef*, who spoke of earlier prophets and how God had blessed them. He then praised Solomon's early life, his wise deeds, his piety and God's satisfaction with him, but fell short of any mention of Solomon's current life. Solomon was angry at this, and after the sermon sent for *Asef*, asking him, "When you spoke of past prophets you praised them throughout their life; however, my life appears only to deserve praise during my early years. What have I done to deserve this slight?" *Asef* answered, "Because of your love for a woman, not God, but another has been worshiped in your home."

Solomon was incredulous, but *Asef* assured him that it was the truth. Solomon told *Asef*, "I realize that you would not say something as grave as this unless you know of what you speak." Solomon went to his palace, discovered the idol, smashed it and punished his wife and her slaves. He asked for ritually clean clothes, garments woven by virgins and untouched by any menstruating women. He went to the wilderness where he ordered himself and his garments covered with cinders, which he sat in as a gesture of humility, and asked for God's forgiveness for what had occurred in his home. He remained there all day, and when he returned that night he removed his ring which held much power and left it with his daughter Āminah. This ring was a ruby brought from Heaven and given to him by the Angel Gabriel, and within it was the power to control his kingdom. He was not to have the stone touch him unless he was ritually cleansed.[1]

While he was in his bath, the sea-devil ʾSakhrʾ came to Āminah disguised in the shape of Solomon, and asked for the ring. Sakhr put it on his finger, and when he sat on Solomon's throne the humans, jinn, demons and birds submitted to his authority. After Solomon finished his bath, he went to his daughter and asked for his ring, but his features had changed, and Āminah did not recognize him. He insisted that he was indeed King Solomon, but she retorted, "You are a liar, you are not Solomon, he has already been here, retrieved his ring and is sitting on the throne." Solomon stormed out on the street, proclaiming, "I am King Solomon!" but his subjects thought him crazy, laughed at him and threw dirt at him. He realized that this was punishment for his mistake, so he went to the seashore where he worked for the fishermen, taking their fish from the sea to the market, and for his services he was paid two fish a day. This continued for forty days until the priests of Israel and Āṣef bin Berkhia began to have doubts about the man who appeared to them as Solomon. They questioned his wives about anything unusual that they had noticed, and they said, "He sleeps with us during menstruation, something he has never done before."

The devil realized he had been discovered and ran away, throwing the ring into the sea, where it was swallowed by a fish. This fish was caught by a fisherman which was then given as remuneration to Solomon. As Solomon was cleaning the fish in preparation for his dinner, he discovered the ring, placed it on his finger and bowed his head to God. His powers returned, and he knew this was a punishment for allowing an idol to be worshiped in his home. Solomon commanded the demons to search for Sakhr, and bring him

---

[1]- From Ara-Tha 287-289.

to the throne. Once found, Solomon had him secured inside a hollow rock encased in lead and iron, and then threw him into the sea. [1]

## Solomon and Sorcery

Before Solomon, sorcery was fashionable with the people of Israel, and sorcerers used to claim that they had connections with demons who channeled through them their magic skills. Solomon prohibited the work of sorcery under the threat of death, and collected all their books burying them under his throne, but after his death the Devil–who presented himself in a human form–told the people of Israel about the buried books, and claimed that Solomon used sorcery from these books to control people, demons, beast and birds. Solomon became known as a sorcerer, and sorcery became common among the Jews until the revelation of the Qur'an when God exonerated Solomon from the evil of sorcery in Q 2:102 *"They followed whatever the devils recited concerning Solomon's control. Solomon did not disbelieve but the devils disbelieved teaching people Magic."*[2]

---

[1]-From Ara-Tha 287-291; Taf-Bagh,Taf-Khaz & Taf-Tab, and most other tafsirs at 38:34. *rep. By Wahb* and *As-Siddi*. Sakhr here has a different personality from sakhr who taught Solomon how to get the shamir; this represents two different demon stories incorporated into this compound story. This legend was built on the Qur'anic verse 38:34, "We *did try Solomon, We placed on his throne a body."* In <u>Hebrew</u> writings, Asmodeus challenged Solomon to remove his magic ring, and when he did so, the demon snatched Solomon with his wings and threw him four hundred leagues, and Asmodeus usurped Solomon's throne. Solomon stayed dethroned for three years, wandering and begging for food, but he kept claiming to be king, though people thought him to be a lunatic. Later, he worked as a cook for the king Ammon and married his daughter Naamah. The king banished the couple to the desert, but they found their way to the shore and bought a fish, finding inside the stomach of the fish the magic ring. Once Solomon wore his ring, his power was restored and he was transported to his capital, where he regained his throne. <u>'Emek ha Melek</u>14d-15a & 108c-109d, from L.O.J. IV 169-171 and footnote Solomon 91.

[2]- Taf-Bagh, Taf-Khaz, Taf-Tab, and other books of tafsir at 2:102.

## The Death of Solomon

It was Solomon's habit to watch new plants growing in the temple, plants which would speak to him and explain to what species they belonged and what special properties they may have. Solomon would then cut the plants and use them according to their own instruction, either for food or medicine. On one occasion while Solomon was praying, he saw a new plant growing. It told him it was a carob[1] plant, and was an omen for the destruction of the temple. Solomon knew that God would not destroy the temple while he lived, and understood that his death was imminent. Solomon asked the Angel of Death if this was true and was told he had but one hour left. He had the demons build him a glass room with no door, and it was there, at fifty-three years of age, that Solomon's life ended while he was standing, leaning on his cane. The demons and jinn were working very hard for Solomon, building shrines, images, basins as large as reservoirs, and cauldrons fixed in their places. The demons had been tortured by Solomon at his whim, releasing some and commanding others to carry heavy rocks for construction. The demons complained to the Devil, *Iblīs*, that they could not continue at the grueling pace set by Solomon, and the Devil placated them by letting them know that it would not continue much longer. When the demons and jinn walked by the glass room, they would see Solomon apparently standing and praying, and their fear of him would keep them toiling. Nothing indicated his demise until a wood worm ate through his cane and he fell down. Realizing that Solomon had been dead for some time, the demons and jinn felt cheated that they had been worked so hard out of fear of a dead man. The humans realized that, contrary to what the demons and jinn had said, they did not know the unseen, or they would not have continued to suffer such humiliating torment. Once the demons were free, they showed their gratitude to the wood worm by supplying it with water and mud inside its wood tunnels.[2]

---

[1]- In Arabic, Carob 'kharub' and destruction 'kharab' sound similar.

[2]- From Ara-Tha 291; Rep. by *Ibn 'Abbas*. Ibn Kathir published the story and commented that this story is a Jewish lore and should not be believed nor disbelieved.

# 12    Jonah / *Yūnus*

*Jonah was an emissary.*

– Qur'an 37:139

## Introduction

The book of Jonah in the Hebrew Bible is the oldest surviving account of this story. The author of this book is anonymous but the literary and theological consideration of the story in addition to its language and historical background made the biblical scholars believe it was written in the post-exilic period. The author talked about Ninevah, not in its historic boundaries–three miles wide as shown in archaeological discoveries–but in its legendary image after the destruction, presented as a great city with a population more than 120,000. (Jon 4:11) Ninevah was destroyed in 1612 B.C.E.

Jonah, son of Amittai, was a Galilean prophet from Geth-hepher, and lived in the eighth century B.C.E. He was a contemporary of King Amaziah (2 King 14:25). This means that the story of Jonah was known in oral tradition long before it was written in the Book of Jonah. Unlike all other Jewish prophets Jonah was sent to preach, not to the people of Israel, but to the idol-worshiping people of Ninevah. Biblical scholars who commented on this explained it as a reflection of the new force in the belief of the people of Israel, shifting from particularism to universalism. But what contrast with this explanation is that we do not see this universalism in the contemporary writings. Most probably the story of Jonah was originally a well known legend in Ninevah concerning a Ninevan prophet or 'seer' who was swallowed by a big fish and survived the ordeal.

# The Story of Jonah

The biblical story of Jonah began with God asking him to go and preach in Nineveh. But Jonah tried to flee from the presence of the Lord, and went instead to Jappa, where he boarded a ship bound for Tarshish. As they sailed, a storm threatened the ship and the sailors cast lots to find whose sin was responsible for the calamity. Jonah confessed to attempting to run from the presence of the Lord, thereby admitting his guilt. Jonah suggested that he should be thrown into the sea and, after some hesitation, his shipmates agreed, and he was left to the mercy of the ocean. Jonah was swallowed by a large fish and stayed there for three days and three nights until the fish spewed Jonah onto dry land. God asked him for the second time to preach in Nineveh, which he did. Jonah relayed to the people of Nineveh the threat of God that in forty days the city would be destroyed. To his surprise this was believed by both the people and their king and they repented. God then changed his mind and did not wreak havoc on the city as had been promised, which prompted Jonah to feel both betrayed by God and angry at him. He left the city and sat by the shade of a wall, and God grew a bush next to Jonah to provide more shade, but he was desolate to find the bush dead the next day. God said, "You are upset about the bush, which you did not grow yourself and had for only one night. Should I not be concerned about the great city of Nineveh with more than one hundred and twenty thousand persons and many animals?"

The summary of the segments in the Qur'an story of Jonah has nothing in it to suggest a different sequence of events, and some mufassirun agree with the biblical sequences, but the most famous Islamic story of Jonah has different sequences and reads as follows.

Jonah was a righteous man who worshiped God and lived at the foot of a mountain near the town of Nineveh. The people of Nineveh were pagans who worshiped idols, and Jonah had little patience or tolerance for them. But God commanded that Jonah should preach to these people, and threaten them that unless they repent they would be tortured. Jonah did so, but as no one listened to his admonitions he soon gave up, and asked God to begin the torture. God informed Jonah that he had not tried hard enough, and instructed him to preach for forty days; if after that the people of Nineveh showed no repentance, then the torture would commence. Jonah returned to Nineveh and began to preach, and on the thirty seventh day he warned them, "You have only three days left to repent, or you will be tortured. Your colors will begin to change, which will be a sign of the coming torture." When the people of Nineveh saw that their colors were changing, they remembered that Jonah had never lied to them before, and they decided to watch Jonah and see if he had plans to leave the city as the fortieth day approached. On the last day, the city awoke with a thick, smoky black cloud hovering overhead which blackened their roofs, and they hurried to find Jonah who had already left the town. At that moment the people of Nineveh felt repentance in their hearts and announced their belief in God. They separated all mothers from their children, including the animals which caused so many cries that God heard their pleas for mercy and suspended the descent of the tortuous cloud.

Jonah left Nineveh and waited outside the city for a sign of the impending destruction. When nothing happened he thought he could not return and have the people think him a liar, so he walked away from Nineveh against the wish of God. Thinking God would not reach him,[1] Jonah walked to the seashore and found a ship captain who agreed to take him along on a voyage. But once Jonah stepped onto the ship the vessel could not move, though ships on either side were leaving the port. A sailor said that their delay was due to a runaway slave and they drew a lottery to determine who it was. Three times the lottery determined that Jonah was the runaway slave who saw no choice but to throw himself into the sea. When Jonah went to throw himself from the ship, he saw a whale with his head above the water waiting for him with an open mouth. Jonah went to another side of the ship where he again found the whale awaiting him.

---

[1]- Many mufassirun did not accept that a prophet would go against God's command and maintained that Jonah walked away from Nineveh's request and believed there would be no punishment.

He soon realized this was a divine arrangement, so without hesitation he threw himself overboard and was swallowed immediately.

God sent the whale which swallowed Jonah, but the whale was advised that Jonah was not food, and that Jonah was to find a home inside the whale. The whale swam with Jonah inside him through the seven seas. Jonah was able to hear the prayers of the sea creatures and it reminded him to pray, and he cried from the depths of darkness, *"There is no deity but You, glory to You, I have been a wrongdoer."* 21:87 The angels in Heaven heard Jonah's prayers and informed the Lord that they heard "a weak and unidentifiable sound emanating from an unknown land." God told them that the sounds were coming from a disobedient servant called Jonah, and that He had imprisoned Jonah in a whale. The angels were surprised and exclaimed, "Jonah, the righteous man, who every night and day dedicates his good work to You?" When God confirmed this, the angels attempted to mediate for Jonah's forgiveness.

After three days[1] in the whale, God commanded that the whale should disgorge Jonah, who found himself on land–weak, and with his skin burned away like a plucked chicken. God gave him a pumpkin[2] bush which gave him protection from the sun, and which kept the flies away from his skin. God also provided him with a doe for fresh milk. The following day Jonah found the pumpkin bush had died, and he shed tears for its demise. God announced, "You cried for a plant which died, but you had no tears for the thousands I was about to destroy?"

Jonah then met a young shepherd and asked where he had come from. The shepherd answered that his home was in Nineveh, and Jonah told the young man, "When you return to your people, tell them you have met Jonah." The shepherd said, "You know I cannot say that without proof." Jonah answered, "Let your witness be this spot, this tree and this ewe" pointing to one of the shepherd's ewes. The shepherd returned home and told the king of his meeting with

---

[1]-There is disagreement among mufassirun about the duration of Jonah's stay inside he whale from three to forty days.

[2]-The name of the bush in the Qur'an is *'yaqtin'*, which is explained by most mufassirun to mean a squash or pumpkin bush; but others, like *Sa'id bin Jubayr*, maintained it is any bush. In Hebrew text it is *'qiqayon.'*

Jonah, and the king cautioned the shepherd that without proof he would be put to death. The shepherd asked for a few people to accompany him, and they traveled to the area where he had last seen Jonah. He asked, "Was I here before with the man known as Jonah?" The ewe, the tree and the land all said, "Yes."

The ewe also told them that Jonah had walked down to the wadi, and they did the same where they found him. They knelt before him, kissed his feet and asked him to return with them to Nineveh. After some resistance he did return and stayed with his family for forty days. The king abdicated and appointed the shepherd as the new king, and, with Jonah, left the city, traveling –as two ascetics– throughout the lands.[1]

This is the most famous Islamic story of Jonah. The adoption of this modified sequence of events by the mufassirun, even when they pointed out the differences between this and the biblical account proved that the Islamic stories of prophets developed independently of the biblical stories, and the Mufassirun adopted biblical segments only when it did not change the major event in their stories. The Qur'anic verse Q37:147 says, *"We sent him as a missionary to more than one hundred thousand people."* This section of the Qur'an came after Jonah's ordeal with the whale, but the mufassirun who insisted on the modified consequences explained that verse as a referral to his original mission.

The Bible did not explain why Jonah fled from the Lord and would not obey His instructions, but in the Hebrew Midrashim, Jonah was sent before to proclaim the destruction of Jerusalem, but the people there did repent, and there was no destruction of the city, and Jonah became known among the people of Israel as the false prophet. He realized this might happen again in Nineveh, and he fled.[2]

---

[1]- Taf-Tab, Taf-Bagh, Taf-Khaz and most other books of tafsir at 10:98, 21:87 & 37:139.

[2]- Pirke de Rabbi Eliezer 10 ; Midrash Jonah 96. From L.O.J. IV, 247 and endnote Jonah 27.

# 13     Short Stories

*We have sent messengers befor you, some of whom We have told you about, while We have not told you about others.*

                – Qur'an 40:78

     In this chapter I discuss different kinds of short stories. There are stories of prophets briefly mentioned in the Qur'an with very few details, the details provided later by mufassirun, either from biblical and or rabbinical sources, or from oral traditions. There also are brief stories with no names, and here again the mufassirun added the names and details at a later time. And finaly, there are stories introduced into Islamic literatures after the time of the Prophet.

# Enoch / *Idrĩs*

The Qur'an mentions the prophet *'Idrĩs'* first in 11:58, by listing him as a pious person, and again in 19:56-57, saying, "Mention in the book [Qur'an] Idris, he was truthful and a prophet and we elevated him to a high place." Idris was identified by most Mufassirun with 'Enoch,' the great grandfather of Noah, and his 'elevation' was interpreted as his ascension into Heaven. According to the mufassirun, *Idrĩs* was a man of many accomplishments; at a time when all cloth was woven, he was a tailor, and the first to sew a set of clothing and wear them. He was the first to write with a pen, the first to invent an armory, and the first to practice the sciences of both astronomy and mathematics. As to his elevation into Heaven, the following are two different versions of the story. The first is reported by *Ka'b.*

### The Story as told by *ka'b ul-Aḥbãr*

As Idris walked under the hot sun, he spoke to God: "Walking under the heat of the sun is very enervating for me, but what of the angel, who carries the sun for what is equal to five hundred years of walking in one day? My Lord make that job easy for him." And the next day when the Angel went about his duty of carrying the sun for the day's illumination, he found it to be surprisingly light in weight and mild in heat. When he questioned God, the Angel was told that the change came in response to the prayer from His servant *Idrĩs.* The Angel wanted to meet *Idrĩs* so that they might be friends, and when they were brought together, Idris asked the Angel to mediate on his behalf and delay his death so that he might have more time to worship God. The Angel of the Sun took *Idrĩs* with him and left him in Heaven at the place where the sun rises, while he consulted the Angel of Death. The Angel of Death explained that while it was not his place to delay someone's time of death, he would review his book and reveal the time of death so that the person might prepare himself. After the reading, the Angel of Death said, "Strange, you are speaking of a man who may never die, because, according to this book, his death will occur only in Heaven where the sun rises." The Angel of the Sun realized where he had left *Idrīs*, and when he returned, *Idrīs* was dead.

### The story as told by *Wahb bin Munabbih*

The angels became accustomed to receiving frequent good deeds in the person of *Idrīs*–many more, in fact, than the rest of the population–and this so impressed the angels that the Angel of Death requested permission to visit him, which God granted. On the third day when the angel told *Idrīs* his true identity, *Idrīs* asked the Angel to collect his soul for one hour, so he might experience death. The Angel fulfilled his request, and *Idrīs* then asked to be taken to Paradise so he might experience the wonders there, and with God's permission, this was done. *Idrīs* asked to visit Hell, which was also allowed, as was a visit to paradise. But when the time came to leave Paradise, *Idrīs* refused to leave, and clutching the branch of a tree declared he would "never leave this place." God sent another angel to settle the dispute, and *Idrīs* explained his plea: "God said, 'Every soul shall taste death' 29:57 and I've tasted it. He also said, 'Everyone of you will enter Hell,' 19:71 and I have done that. In speaking of Paradise, God said, 'They will not be evicted,' 15:48 and I am not leaving." God revealed these words to the angels: "With My permission he entered Paradise, and with My command, he shall not leave it." Idris is said to abide in Heaven "Paradise" as does Jesus.

# *Hārūt* and *Mārūt*, The Angels

According to Q3:7, two types of verse are present in the Qur'an: the first being clear and easy to understand while the second type is a of a more ambiguous nature which is understood only by those scholars who have attained a high level of knowledge in Qur'anic study. A good example of the latter type of Qur'anic verse is 2:102, which introduces the angels, called *Hārūt* and *Mārūt*. Because of the specious aspect of this verse, any verbatim attempt at translation will be unsuccessful and the following is but one of many interpretations of the verse.

"Harut and Marut are both angels who descended into Babylon with knowledge revealed to them [by God]. There, they taught the people how to perform magic spells, but they did so with a warning that this kind of knowledge is actually a test and it would be blasphemous to practice these skills. Nevertheless, people did learn harmful things from the angels—the ability [for instance] to create discord between a man and his wife—although in reality harm happens only with God's permission."

Around this verse, many stories were born, such as the one reported and published by Tafsir *At-Tabarī*:

The angels of Heaven said, "Our Lord, You created humans to obey and worship You, yet they commit all manner of sins: disbelief, murder, theft, adultery, corruption and drinking." The angels kept up their incessant criticism without allowing any defense to be presented, until God asked the angels to chose two from among them who were to be assigned to earth as humans, and there they would be perhaps able to prove their accusations. *Hārūt* and *Mārūt* were the chosen angels, and God sent them to earth in human bodies with human desires and gave them clear instructions: to worship only God, to not commit murder, to not steal, to not commit adultery and to not drink. Once on earth, because of their angelic knowledge and honesty they were hired as judges in the city of Babylon where, in the beginning, they were most competent and settled disputes with veracity and impartiality. One day, a very beautiful and concupiscent woman named Venus appeared in their court to swear a complaint against her husband. Both *Hārūt* and *Mārūt* were overcome with carnal desire, and both asked her to sleep with them, which she agreed to, but only on the condition that her husband would be killed. After an initial hesitation on the part of the angels, they acquiesced and her husband was killed. When they asked that she now fulfil her part of the bargain, she refused, unless they would teach her the secret word which they used to ascend to Heaven and descend to the earth. They told her the word, and as soon as she learned it she whispered it and ascended into the sky, which prompted God to make her forget the word, causing her to be stranded, unable to return to earth. *Hārūt* and *Mārūt* attempted to ascend to Heaven but found their efforts fruitless and remained on earth where they realized the magnitude of their sin. When they asked God's forgiveness, they were given two choices: delay their punishment until the Day of Judgement and then be tortured for eternity, or to serve their sentence in this life until the Day of Judgement, which is what they chose. They were tortured in a deep well of fire in Babylon, hung upside down by their feet waiting for the Day of Judgement to receive their salvation. As for Venus, God changed her into a planet and she remains suspended in the sky. After this incident, the angels of Heaven ceased their criticism of man and began asking for his forgiveness."

**Comment**

There is no doubt that this story was derived from a Jewish source, and a similar theme is found in an unknown midrash in Yalkot and Aggadat Bereshit which talked about the two angels Azazil and Shamhazi who descended to earth to live among humans and to show God their superiority to humans. Shamhazi fell in love with a beautiful woman named Venus, and she agreed to surrender herself to him only if he would teach her the most holy name of God which he used to ascend to Heaven. Once she was cognizant of the name, she spoke it and ascended to Heaven not stopping to surrender

herself to Shamhazi. God placed her between the seven planets as
she had kept herself away from sin.[1]

Early mufassirun, in their rush to find a biblical parallel to
every name in the Qur'an, accepted this story without reservation, but
mufassirun of the publishing era rejected it. *'Iyād al-Qāḍī, Al-
shahābī* of Iraq and Imam *Ar-Rāzī* all maintain that this story goes
against the basic Islamic belief. Angels in Islam cannot nor would
not sin under any circumstance because God created them that way.
*Iblīs* the Devil sinned, but he was a jinn and not an angel.

In a different reading version[2] of the Qur'an, *Hārūt* and
*Mārūt* were described as two kings '*malikayn*' rather than two angels
'*malakayn,*' of the traditional Qur'anic reading; this would discredit
the entire story. Some mufassirun, *Al-Alūsī* for example, gave this
Qur'anic verse a symbolic interpretation and warned that it not be
taken literally.

---

[1]- L.O.J. III, 247 and endnote Noah 10.

[2]-According to a hadith of the Prophet, the Qur'an revealed in seven
readings. The differences between these readings are mostly linguistic, reflecting
the different accents of the Arabian tribes, but some readings might change the
meaning of the verses.

# The Man to whom God gave signs,
## but he slipped away from them.

**The Qur'anic version**

*"Relate to them the story of the man to whom We gave our signs, but he slipped away from them. The Devil followed him and he became misguided. If it had been our will he would have risen upwards guided by our signs, but he clung to the earth and he followed his own desires. He can be compared to a dog, who pants when you drive him off, but still pants if left alone. The people who rejected our signs are like that dog, relate this story to them so that they may reflect."* 7:175-176.

The moral of this proverb is: some people will not accept wisdom from others, nor will wisdom come to them if left alone. This is one of many proverbs in the Qur'an, but unlike other proverbs which are not connected to a certain story, most mufassirun maintain that these verses are about a biblical figure, Balaam, son of Bor, the prophet from Aram (numbers 22-24). The following is the story according *to Ibn 'Abbās, Ibn Isḥāq, As-Siddī* and *Al-Kalbī.*

During the war between the Israelites and their neighbors the Amalekites [Moabites], the Amalekites asked Balaam, the priest who knew the most holy of God's names, to curse Moses and his people. "Moses is a strongman, supported by a large army and he comes to kill us, take our land, and settle his people here. We are your people, your cousins and your neighbors. Curse this man who is our enemy and who made our life so difficult, curse him as your curse is always successful." Balaam answered, "Woe to you, for this is a prophet of God, supported by angels and believers. How can I curse them knowing my act will have consequences on me in this life and in the next?"* The Amalekites kept pressuring him until he relented and Num 22:5-13 said he would ask the Lord. But Balaam never cursed anyone if he felt his visions prohibited him from doing so, and this time his visions were clear that he should not put a curse on Moses, though his people

Num 22:16-18 persisted, hoping Balaam would chang his mind.* Ten of the Amalekite leaders then went to Balaam's wife, each laden with gifts–a gold plate filled with silver–and presented them to her. After receiving these gifts she herself went to Balaam and asked him to go to his Lord again, and this time he received no vision, which prompted the Amalekite to interpret this as a sign that he should indeed curse their enemy. Balaam agreed to this, and attempted to ride his donkey up a mountain so that he might survey the Israelite army below. But his donkey stopped and sat down, so Balaam struck her until she stood up, walked a short distance, then sat down again. This pattern continued until the donkey suddenly stopped and began to speak, "Woe to you Balaam, where do you think you are going? Can you not see the angels in front of me, pushing me back? Who are you to curse a prophet of God and his group of believers?" Balaam fell to his knees, crying and begging for God's mercy until the angels Nim 22:21-35 left.* The Devil then appeared and said, "Go and fulfill your plan, if if God did not want you to curse Moses, he would not command his angels to retreat." Balaam once again mounted his donkey and rode to the mountaintop where his every curse was reversed, calling for execrations on the Amalekites, and summoning praise for the enemy. The Amalekites called to him and asked him if he knew what he Num 23:7-10 was doing, and he answered that it was somthing beyond his control* whereupon his tongue was pulled from his mouth and hung down to his chest. Balaam, realizing he had cursed himself, managed to say to his people, "I have lost the rewards of this life and the expectation of the next, our last resort is deceit. Send your most comely women to the Israelite camp as itinerant merchants, and advise them to give themselves to any man who wants them. If only one of the Israelites commits adultery, they will no longer be a threat to you. Balaam's people accepted this plan and sent the women to the Israelites where Cozbi, the daughter of Zur, caught the eye of the Israelite leader Zimri, son of Salu. He admired her beauty and brought her to Moses, saying, "I think you will say that it is a sin to sleep with this woman." And when Moses agreed that it was, Zimri informed him that he was not listening and took the woman to his tent. God immediately sent a plague to the Israelite camp, and one by one they began to die. Phinehas, son of Eleazar, son of Aaron the priest and brother of Moses, was away from camp when Zimri slept with the woman.

Upon his return, finding his people succumbing to the plague and
learning of Zimri's indiscretion, he went to the tent where the couple
lay together and slew both with his spear, then carried the skewered
victims out and displayed them. God then lifted the plague after it had
left seventy thousand dead.[1]*                              Num 25:7-15

## Comment

Balaam, son of Bor, is a real historical figure.  A discovery of
a plaster inscription in Tell Deir Allah in Jordan dating to the eighth
century B.C.E. mentioned his name: Balaam, son of Bor, seer of the
Gods, who received visits from the gods at night and who would in
turn report these visions to his people.

This story is a combination of two stories in the Bible, the
story of Balaam (num. 22-24), and the story of sexual relations
between the Israelites and the women of Moab (Num 25).  These two
stories are written in sequence but are not connected.  Balaam of the
Bible is not a Moabite but "from Aram, the mountains of the east."
The Moabite king Balak sent him to curse the Israelites.  Not all
mufassirun accepted the above Qur'anic verses as relating to Balaam.
Others gave it a contemporary interpretation and maintained that it is
the famous poet *'Umayyah bin Abiṣ-Ṣalṭ'* who is meant by these
Qur'anic verses.  This is the subjective opinion of *'Abdullah bin
'Umar* and *Al-Kalbī*.  *Umayyah* was a contemporary of the Prophet
Muhammad and he followed the faith of *Hanif*, a pre-Islamic
monotheistic religion which followed the teachings of Abraham the
prophet.  *Umayya*h had the criteria to be a good Muslim and was
hoping to be the Prophet, but when Muhammad received that honor
he envied him and refused to accept Islam.

---

[1]- Taf-Tab, Taf-Bagh, Taf-Khaz and others at 7:175. Ara-Tha 209-211.

240

# The Story of Elijah *"Elias"*

## The Qur'anic version

"Elijah was an emissary when he admonished his people, 'Will you not do your duty? Do you appeal to Baal and ignore the Best Creator, God, Your Lord, and your earliest forefather's Lord?' Exept for God's sincere servants, they rejected him, and therefore they will be called up [for punishment]. We left mention of him among later men, 'peace be upon Elijah.' Thus we reward those who act kindly; he was one of our believing servants." 37:123-132.

The story of Elijah was reported and translated by *Ibn Ishāq* and published in Ara-Tha 223; Qis-Kath 2:241; Taf-Bagh & Taf-Khaz 37:123, but was edited as were other biblical translations. Although the Syrian deity in this story–Baal–was very famous in pre-Christian Syria, he had been forgotten by the time of the Qur'anic revelation, and the only reminder of his former renown is found in the name of the city of Baalbek, in today's Lebanon. It is for this reason the story tellers made Baalbek the capital under the reign of King Ahab / *Lajab*, the seventh king of Israel. This story is found in 1Kngs 17:1-18:2. The land of Israel was enduring a two year famine when Elijah met Ahab and proposed that they should offer public sacrifices to determine whether Baal or God is the true God. This was done on Carmel mountain, and as a result of that demonstration , the people fell on their faces crying, "The Lord is the God," and all prophets of Baal were put to death. Nothing in the story of Elijah other than the Qur'anic verse is original Islamic or Arabic narrative.

## The Story of Elisha

Elisha or *Alyasa'* is mentioned in the Qur'an at 6:86 and 38:48 but with little discussion. His story was published and translated from the Bible by *Ibn Ishāq* and nothing in that translation is in the tradition of either an Islamic or Arabic narrative.

# The First and Second Destruction of Jerusalem

**The Qur'anic Version**

"We gave clear warning to the children of Israel in the Book, that twice would they do mischief on the earth and become elated with mighty ignorance, [and twice would they be punished]. When the first warning came, We despatched servants of Ours to inflict severe violence upon you [all]. They rampaged through [your] homes, and it served as a warning which was acted upon. Then We offered you another chance against them, and reinforced you with wealth and children, and granted you more manpower. If you have acted kindly you acted kindly toward yourselves, while if you commited any evil, it was toward [yourselves] as well. When the second of the warnings came, We permitted your enemies to disfigure your faces and to enter your temple, as they had entered it before, and to visit with destruction all that fell into their power. It may be that your Lord may yet show mercy unto you, but if you revert to your sins We shall revert to Our punishment, and We have made Hell a prison for those who reject faith." 17:4-8

These five verses from the Qur'an referred to the destruction of Jerusalem by the Babylonian king Nebuchadnezzar in 586 B.C.E. when the entire population of Jerusalem was carried off into captivity, and also the destruction by Titus in 70 C.E. The best interpretation of these verses came in a long hadith by *Ḥudhayfah*, which mentioned how the Temple in Jerusalem was built by Solomon with help from the jinn, and made of gold, silver, pearls, rubies and sapphires. But when the Israelites disobeyed and killed their prophets, God sent Nebuchadnezzar against them, who, with his army, entered Jerusalem and killed the men, and they enslaved the women and children, and carried the gold and the religious vessels, and all they had pillaged away to Babylon on seventy thousand carts. The Israelites were enslaved and humiliated, but after one hundred years God had pity on them and sent a Persian king to Babylon to free them. The Israelites were freed and the treasures of the Temple restored. God threatened them that if they should return to their lives of sin, so too would return the time of killing and enslavement. Once again, the Israelites began to sin, and God then sent the Roman emperor [Titus], who invaded from both the land and sea, killed many men, stole their women and their gold and all their religious vessels, transporting all he had looted back to Rome on seventy thousand carts.

This is the best historical interpretation in spite of the exaggeration in the number of carts, but for unknown reasons it was not adopted by most mufassirun and Islamic historians, who instead amalgamated incidents of the first and second destructions, ignoring a six hundred and fifty six year time lapse, and adding to it the legend of the 'bubbling blood.'

"When the king of the Jews killed John the Baptist to satisfy the request of a woman, John's blood kept bubbling on the spot where it was spilled. The king ordered dirt to be thrown on the blood, but the blood continued to flow through the dirt until the dirt became as high as a city wall. Sennacherib, the Babylonian king, heard this and sent Nebuchadnezzar and his army to invade Jerusalem. He surrounded the city but only conquered it with the help of an old lady, who taught him how to crack the city walls by invoking the name of John. She took him to where the blood still bubbled and told him, 'Kill from the Jews until John's blood ceases to bubble.' Nebuchadnezzar killed seventy thousand before John's blood bubbled no more."[1]

*Al-tha'labī* realized the discrepancy in that story, and brought attention to the missed time between the two destructions, which he calculated as 461 years. He adopted the story of *Muhammad bin Ishāq*, who reported that Jerusalem was first destroyed by Nebuchadnezzar, while the second destruction, the avenging of John's death, occurred centuries later, and was led by King Kardus[2]

---

[1]- Pub. By Taf-Tab, as repoted by *Said bin al-Musayyib*.

[2]- I did not find the original source of this story, but the names of the Babylonian king and his general sound Parthian. King Kardus could be king Ordes II "57–38 B.C.E." or King Gotarez II "40–51 C.E.". The Parthians invaded Syria and reached as far south as Petra at 40 B.C.E.

of Babylonia and his general, Banurazadan The general saw John's bubbling blood and killed 770 Jewish leaders, then slaughtered 7000 of their wives and children.   When John's blood kept flowing Banurazadan insisted the Jews tell him the story of the blood or he would leave no one alive.  He then heard the story of John, son of Zachariah, who would preach against them and his prediction of the coming destruction, which was not believed, and the eventual killing of John. Banurazadan approached the blood and said, "John, The Lord of both of us knows what has happened to your people . For your sake and for the sake of all who have been killed, quit, or I will leave not one of your people." And only at that time did John's blood finally stop bubbling.

*Ibn Kathīr* also mentioned the amalgamated story and commented, "this is not  true. Because John son of Zachariah came a long time after Nebuchadnezzar, it is possible that the blood was that of a previous prophet or saint."[1]

The story of the bubbling blood was borrowed from legends of the Talmud which were centered around the killing of the prophet and high priest Zachariah, son of Jehoiada, who was stoned to death at the command of King Joash, and who died 'in the court of the house of the Lord' 2Chr. 24:21. Most probably he is the same 'Zachariah, son of Barachias,' that Jesus said was killed between the Temple and the altar. Matt. 23:35; Luke 11:51.   Rabbi Achan mentions the Talmudic legend in which Nebuchadnezzar comes to Jerusalem, sees the bubbling blood, and in answer to his questions is told by the priests that the blood is from the slaughter of calves, lambs and rams, which had been sacrificed at the altar. Nebuchadnezzar slew these same animals, but as their blood did not continue to run, he threatened the priests with bodily harm if they did not tell him the truth. And they then confessed that the blood that still bubbled came from the prophet Zachariah, who had prophesied the calamities they were suffering. Nebuchadnezzar thought he could appease him by killing the rabbis, and when this did not work, killed young boys, still at school.  The blood still bubbled, so he killed young priests and continued until

---

[1]- Qis-Kath I: 329.

ninety four thousand people lay dead.  Defeated, he approached the flowing blood and said, "O Zachariah, you have caused the death of the chiefs of your people, shall I slay them all?"  Then the blood ceased bubbling.[1]

---

[1]- Jerusalem Talmud, Taannith, fol 69; Babylonian Talmud, Sanhedrin, Fol 96. A second point of view concerning the second destruction of Jerusalem comes from the Mandaean book of "Harran Koyetha," which said that after the death of John, the Jews persecuted the Mandaeans, killing them and had their books burnt. When Angel Insh Athra – who raised and taught John – saw the suffering of the Mandaeans, he complained to God.  God ordered Angel Hiwal Ziwa to destroy the rebelling Jews, and Angel Anthra put seven catapults around Jerusalem, loaded them with seven projectiles, and Angel Hiwal positioned seven people at each catapult. Hiwal, seven times, asked the innocent people of Jerusalem to leave the city which they did, leaving behind only the government officials. Angel Athra then ordered the catapults to fire upon the city and within a short time Jerusalem was destroyed.

# The Book of Daniel
## As Translated by *Wahb bin Munabbih*

After conquering Jerusalem and taking its population into exile, Nebuchadnezzar, the King of Babylon, returned home. After some time, he experienced a frightening dream but could not find anyone from among all the magicians and priests to interpret it. At that time Daniel and some of his friends[1] were prisoners in Babylon when they heard about the king's dream. Daniel told the chief of the guards[2] that he could interpret this dream, and the chief, who liked Daniel, had the message passed on to the king and the king, requested his presence before the court.

Once in court, Daniel did not prostrate himself before the king as protocol demanded and when the king asked him about his behavior his reply was, "My God gave me my wisdom and knowledge, and He demanded that I prostrate myself before no one. I was worried that if bowed down to you He would reclaim the knowledge which He Himself has granted to me. He might even take my life." The king admired Daniel's forthrightness and said, "You did the right thing; you obeyed His oath and honored the knowledge He gave you."

The king then questioned Daniel about his dream, and was told, "You saw a statue, the head made of gold, the chest of silver and the abdomen from copper, its thighs made of iron, and the legs from clay. You then saw a huge stone fall from the sky, destroying the statue. The stone then grew larger and larger until it filled the lands from the sunrise to the sunset. You next saw a tree with its roots in the earth and its branches in the sky. You then saw a man holding an axe, and you heard a voice calling him to strike the trunk of that tree so the birds on its branches would fly away and the beasts and pack animals beneath would also take flight but still leaving the trunk intact. Daniel said, "The golden head of that statue is you; you are the

---

[1]- Their names in the Book of Daniel are: Hananiah, Mishael and Azariah. No names are mentioned in the above text.

[2]- His name in the Book of Daniel is Ashpenaz.

leader of and the best of your dynasty. The silver chest is your son who will reign after you, the copper abdomen represents a king who will come after your son, and the two iron thighs are the division of your kingdom into two strong states. And the clay legs are the kings of these two states: two weak kings. The stone which smashed everything is a prophet of God who will be sent at the end of time. His kingdom will grow and extend between the sunrise and sunset. The tree with the bird on its branch, with both beast and cattle beneath and the command that it be cut signifies a temporary end to your reign which will last for seven years during which time God will transform you into a great eagle and you will be a king of great birds. You will then be turned into a bull and you will be the king of the cattle. God will then turn you into a lion and you will be the king of beasts, but your heart will stay a human heart to know that God owns Heaven and earth and He dominates the earth and whoever lives on it. Your vision of seeing the trunk of the tree intact means your kingdom will survive.[1] When Daniel completed his interpretation, the king made him a close advisor and both he and his friends

Dan 2:46-49 received high status in the court of the king.* The Zoroastrian priests were envious over this and told the king that Daniel and his friends

Dan 3:8-12 did not worship the king's god* nor did they partake of the king's food. When the king questioned them about these matters, they said, "Yes, we worship our Lord and we do not eat your food." The king ordered the six of them to be thrown into a pit with a lion,[2] and the king left with his courtiers for food and drink. Upon their return they found them uninjured, with the lion sitting among them and joined by an angel, making their number seven. The Angel hit the king with a stroke of his hand, and in the span of seven years was transformed into an eagle, a bull and a lion, just as Daniel had predicted. God

---

[1] - This is a combination of two dreams in the Book of Daniel; the first one concerns the statue and its destruction in Dan. 2:31-45, while the second dream concerns the tree and the seven years of animal-like life in Dan 4:9-26. The Book of Daniel did not talk about actual body transformation but said that the king will be driven away from human society , and his dwelling shall be with the wild animals. He shall be made to eat grass like oxen and bathed with the dew of heaven.

[2] - In the Book of Daniel, this happened in the reign of Darius, The Mede, because he refused to pray to the king and prayed instead to the Temple of Jerusalem. Daniel alone was placed in the lion's den. Dan 6:10-28.

then returned him back into a man and a king, and once again Daniel and his friends became confidantes of the king.[1]

The Zoroastrian priests envied them and told the king that when Daniel drank wine he could not help but to urinate immediately which, according to their custom, was a shameful act. The king invited them for food and drink and told the guard that the first one to leave the gathering should be struck with a truncheon—even if that person claims to be the king. But God protected Daniel and his friends from the necessity of having to leave, and instead it was the king himself who was so burdened and who walked out into the night. When the guard saw him, he hit him and the king screamed, "I am Nebuchadnezzar." But the guard, remembering his instructions, continued striking the king until he was dead. [2]

After the king's death, his son[3] became king. The sacred vessels in the Temple of Jerusalem which Nebuchadnezzar had brought to Babylon were used by the new king who polluted them with wine and pork, and Daniel and his friends were now out of favor. One day the king saw a hand not attached to an arm which wrote three letters while he watched, then disappeared. He was surprised and did not know its meaning so he brought Daniel, and after first apologizing, asked him to interpret the hand and its letters. Daniel said, "It reads, 'He weighed what is light, He promised and will fulfil, He gathered and will separate.' The interpretation means God has weighed your good deeds and found them to be scant, God has promised your kingdom will be destroyed and it will be so, He gathered for you and your father a great kingdom but today that

---

[1]- This is the first Arabic translation of the Book of Daniel which was done by *Wahb bin Munabbih* and it became the reference for Islamic writing about this prophet.

[2]- This story of the death of Nebuchadnezzar was rep. by As-Siddi. Another version of the king's death, is rep. by Muhammad bin Ishaq who mentioned that the king died from a mosquito which flew into his brain through his nose and which is the same story told regarding the death of Nimrod.

[3]- Nebuchadnezzar II (604-562) was succeeded by his son Evil-merodach, who after a reign of two years was followed by Neriglissar who ruled from 559 to 555 B.C.E. He was succeeded by Nabonadius, (555-539), and at the close of his reign Babylon fell under Cyrus at the head of the combined armies of Media and Persia. The name of the last king in this dynasty from the Book of Daniel is Belshazzar while his name in the above Islamic Arabic story is Philstas.

kingdom will be dispersed.''* Shortly thereafter the king died and the kingdom fell, but Daniel remained in the land of Babylon and died in Susa.[1]

## Comment

The name of Daniel did not come either in the Qur'an or in the hadiths and it is doubtful that Muslims at the time of the Prophet were familiar with him. It seemed that the first Islamic exposure to Daniel occurred when the Muslim army conquered the Persian city of Susa, the place which claimed Daniel's remains, in 638 C.E. It has been reported that a man from the tribe of *'Abdul-Qays* who resided in Susa made a copy of the Book of Daniel and would read and translate it to Arab Muslims at the reign of *'Umar*. But when *'Umar* heard of this he ordered him to stop and to erase the writing.[2] Daniel's name also came from the testament of *'Amr bin Maymūn al-Awdī* who said he saw a man walking into their gathering carrying the Book of Daniel.[3] *Al-Tha'labī* reported that at the time when Muslims subdued the city of Susa under the Command of *Abū Mūsa al-Ash'arī* and confiscated all the royal treasure, they came to a storage house both locked and sealed in lead. After *Abū-Mūsa* opened the door, he found the remains of a dead man in a stone sarcophagus, wrapped in a shroud of golden thread with only his head exposed. When the people of Susa were questioned about the man, they said he was a holy man who lived in Iraq and was famous for his prayers which brought rain in time of drought. When the drought hit Susa, they requested him to come and pray but Iraq asked that fifty men be brought to Iraq as a guarantee that this holy man would return. The people of Susa found him a valuable asset and, as they did not return him, he died there. *Abū-Mūsa* reported this to the Caliph *'Umar,* and the Caliph asked the sahaba if they had any information about this man. Imam *'Ali* responded that he thought this man was Daniel, the prophet and he told *'Umar* the entire story. *'Umar* wrote to *Abū-Mūsa* that they should bury him in a place that could not be reached by the people of Susa. *Abū-Mūsa* diverted a river and buried Daniel

---

[1]- Pub. by Ara-Tha 302-305.
[2]- Al-Khatib al-Baghdadi, Taqyid ul-'Ilm 51.
[3]- Taqyid ul-'Ilm 65.

in the riverbed after changing his shroud and giving him a funeral prayer, and then he returned the river to its original course.[1] Later on a mosque was built on the bank of Karkhe river beside the supposed spot.

Susa was once the capital of ancient Elam, and the Persian Empire, and became a Christian center in the fourth century. The modern village of Shush, with the tomb of Daniel, lies to the west of the ancient site, in the province of Khuzistan, in southwestern Iran.

---

[1]- Ara-Tha 304 -305.

# The Man who Arose from the dead
### after one hundred years.

## The Qur'anic version:

This is the story of a man *"who passed by a town in ruins, and said, 'I doubt that God would revive this town after its death.' God kept him dead for one hundred years, then brought him back to life. 'How long were you asleep,?' asked God. 'Maybe one day, maybe less than a day,' answered the man. God informed him, 'You were dead for one hundred years, but look at your food and drink—they did not age. And look at your donkey—look at the bones and how they have come together and are covered with flesh. You will be a lesson to all people.'* " 2:259.

## The story in detail according to *Wahb*:

When Nebuchadnezzar conquered Palestine, demolished Jerusalem, and killed many Israelites, sending others into exile, the Prophet Jeremiah fled into the wilderness to live among the beasts. When the Assyrian king went back to Babylon with the exiled Israelites, Jeremiah returned to Jerusalem, riding his donkey and carrying grape juice and figs. When he saw the destruction in the city, he said, *"I doubt that God would revive this town after its death."* Jeremiah then tied his donkey using a new rope, and feeling tired, lay down for a nap. God took his soul, the donkey died, and people were blinded from seeing Jeremiah and the birds and beasts were prevented from reaching his body. Seventy years later, God sent an angel to King Cyrus of Persia to tell him, "God orders you to take your people to Jerusalem, and to rebuild it to eclipse its former glory." The king assigned three hundred thousand workers to one thousand leaders, the city was rebuilt, and the people returned and multiplied. Many years after the rebirth of Jerusalem and one hundred years after the death of Jeremiah, God returned his soul and he awoke.  The Angel Gabriel asked him, "How long were you asleep?" Jeremiah thought he may have been asleep a day or even less, but the Angel told him, "You were dead for one hundred years, but look at your food and your drink, neither have become stale." Jeremiah found that his juice was still fresh and the figs in his basket were fresh and dripping with syrup. The rope with which he had used to tie his donkey was still new.  "Look at your donkey," continued Gabriel. Jeremiah saw his donkey's bones miraculously coming together, to be covered with flesh and skin, and then coming back to life.  Jeremiah returned to his village and found his family, sons and daughters and grandchildren all having grown old and not recognizing him.  He then returned the vision of an old lady who remembered him and convinced his family of his identity.[1]

### Comment

Mufassirun have struggled to connect this Qur'anic story with Hebrew legends, and so along with this story there are a profusion of other versions.  The name of the city could be Jerusalem, Salmabad, Dayr Sayrabad, or Dayr Hercules, and the man raised from the dead could be Jeremiah or Ezra the scribe. Those who suggested Ezra are 'Akramah, Qutādah, Ad-dahhāk, As-Siddi, and Ar-Rabī' bin Anas. Ezra is the famous Jewish leader who led the second contingent of exiles returning from Babylon to Jerusalem. The Ezra version ended by describing how he  dictated the Torah by heart to the retainers of Jerusalem, which had been forgotten by that time. But the story of the biblical Jeremiah has no known parallel with our story except for the witnessing of the destruction of Jerusalem.  The biblical Jeremiah then travels to Egypt with Baruch, his servant, and there his name disappears from the Bible. To find an ancient story resembling the Islamic one, we go to the Pseudoepigripha, the Book of '4Baruch', originally written in either Greek or Hebrew in the first half of the second century.

In '4Baruch', on the eve of the Babylonian destruction of Jerusalem, the Lord warned Jeremiah of the impending disaster and instructed him to leave the city with his servant Baruch. Jeremiah

---

[1]- Taf-Tab, Taf-Bagh , Taf-Khaz and other books of tafsir at 2:259.

asked the Lord to save his faithful follower Abimelech, and the Lord instructed him to send Abimelech out of the city on a pretext, the Lord promising that He would preserve him as well. God instructed Jeremiah to go with his people into captivity and leave Baruch with those who were left behind. Abimelech left to gather figs for the sick as Jeremiah instructed him. In his absence, Jerusalem was conquered by the Babylonians and most of its people were placed in captivity. After gathering his figs, Abimelech stopped to rest under a tree and awoke after sixty-six years, his figs still fresh and dripping with syrup. He returned to Jerusalem, but left disoriented until he met an old man who surmised that he must have slept for sixty-six years, and thought perhaps that was God's way of sparing him the sight of witnessing his city's destruction. He also found that Jeremiah was with his people in exile.[1]

Although it is possible that the story of Abimelech in '4Baruch' was the source of the Islamic story-beside the Qur'an, it may also be possible, with the many versions of Jeremiah, that the Islamic version was taken from similar stories, even more closely resembling the Islamic one.

Another Haggadic legend which is reminiscent of the Islamic story is the story of Honi Ha Me'aggel, who once saw a man planting a carob tree. He learned from the farmer that it would take seventy years for the tree to bear fruit. "As my forefathers planted for me, I will plant for my children." Honi sat down for a meal but was overcome with sleep, and when he awoke after seventy years, he saw a man gathering fruit of the carob tree. He realized he had slept for seventy years when he found that it was the farmer's grandson collecting the fruit. Upon his return to his village, Honi found that no one either knew him or believed his story, which caused him endless grief and he died.[2]

---

[1]- O.T.P. II: 413
[2]- Encyclopedia Judaica, Honi Ha Me'aggel.

# The Story of Ezekiel

Although there is no direct mention of Ezekiel in the Qur'an, in Q2:243 there is a story without a name which implicates Ezekiel as the personality detailed.

*"Have you not seen those who have left their homes? There were thousands of them risking death! God told them, 'Die!' then revived them. God possesses bounty for mankind even though most men do not act grateful."*

### The story as published by 'Arāyis al-Tha'labī

A group of the Israelites were ordered by their king to fight their enemy. They numbered in the thousands and were camping in preparation for war, but they acted cowardly.* They told their king Ezk. 11:8 that a plague had broken out in the enemy camp and they would not attack until the plague was under control. God then sent the plague to the Israelites which decimated their numbers and when the survivors began to flee God said, 'Die!' which they did with their lifestock. After three days the bodies began to putrefy and the smell became unbearable. The inhabitants of the area were unable to bury the rotting corpses so they built a fence around them to protect them from scavengers until their flesh decomposed and all that remained were bones. The prophet Ezekiel journeyed through the area and stopped there to contemplate when God revealed to him, "Ezekiel, do you want to see how I raise the dead?" "Yes, my Lord," he answered, and God brought all the decayed bodies back to life.

### Comment

The corresponding verses in the Book of Ezekiel come in Chapter 37 and say, "The hand of the Lord was upon me, and carried me out in the spirit of the Lord, and set me down in the middle of the valley which was full of bones. And caused me to pass around them and, behold, there were many in the open valley; and they were very dry. And He said to me, 'Son of man, can these bones live?' And I

answerd, 'O Lord God, You know.' Again He said to me, 'Prophesy to these bones and say to them, 'O dry bones, hear the word of the Lord' Thus say the Lord God to these bones, 'Behold, I will cause breath to enter you and you shall live. I will lay sinews on you and will bring up flesh on you and cover you with skin, and put breath in you and you shall live, and you shall know that I am the Lord."
Ezk. 37: 1-6

*Al-Mawdūdī* in his tafisr at 2:243 stated that this story refers to the Exodus of the Israelites when they refused to proceed–as God ordered them–to drive the Canaanites out of Palestine. God let them wander for forty years until one generation of the Israelites died.

# The Story of the Jewish Town
## whose inhabitants disgraced the Sabbath

**The Qur'anic version.**

"Ask them,[ the Jews of Medina], *about the town by the seashore that disgraced the Sabbath. On Sabbath day, an abundance of fish appeared, swimming near the surface of the sea, while no fish had showed themselves the rest of the week. Thus we tested them because they were transgressors.*" 7:163. "*You knew which of you had defied the Sabbath, so we told them, 'becomes apes, despised and rejected' *"2:65

**The story in detail** according to *Al-Ḥasan bin al-Fāḍil, Wahb* and *Ibn 'Abbās*:

This is the story of the people of the Jewish town of Elath[1] on the Red Sea. The people of Elath were fishermen, and God prohibited them from fishing or doing other work on their Sabbath, and they were to use that day as a day of worship. They would fish for six days, but fish had been scarce and the catch had been light until the Sabbath, when a plethora of fish bombarded the shoreline making it difficult to even see the water. The fishermen dug large pools close to the sea and connected them with narrow channels. On Friday afternoon the channels were opened and the fish swam into these pools and could not swim out as the water was too shallow. The fish were collected on Sunday. They would also circumvent the Sabbath prohibition by placing fish traps on Friday and collecting them on Sunday. Their fishing business boomed and they made money, but their hearts hardened as their sins became accepted. Their justification being that the prohibitions were meant for their ances-tors, as punishment for killing the prophets, something they felt was far removed from them.

---

[1]- The town of Elath, mentioned in 1King:26 was an Idumean city, at the gulf of Akaba and has never been a Jewish city. According to 1King Book, Solomon built a fleet of ships near to Elath, on the Red Sea, the land of Edom.

The town was divided into many factions. One respecting the Sabbath and warning others of their sin, another respecting the Sabbath but not objecting to their neighbors' dishonoring the Sabbath. A third group chose to ignore the Sabbath. The people who both honored the Sabbath and chastised those who did not, found that no one listened to them. They did not want to share a housing area with the dissenters, and moved away, building a wall to separate themselves from the rest of the city. They lived separately for a few years watching each other going to work, until one day, those that honored the Sabbath noticed that no one came out of the city for work. Concerned about what might have happened to the others, they climbed over the wall to see, and were shocked to find that all of them had been turned into apes. The apes recognized their human relatives and came to them crying, then left the town, wandering in different directions for three days, at which time they all died.[1]

**Comment**

From the beginning of the Qur'anic story, *"Ask them about...."* we realize that this story was known to the Jews of Medina, who were known for their respect of the Sabbath. We did not find this story in the Jewish writings, probably because it was an oral story rather than a written one, used by the rabbis to discourage the disgracing of the Sabbath. The Qur'an mentioned this story to remind the Jews of Medina and Muslims, as well, to respect religious teachings.

---

[1]- Taf-Tab, Taf-Bagh & Taf-Khaz and most books of tafsir at 2:65-66 and 7:163.

# 14     The Gospel

*We gave Jesus the son of Mary clear signs*
*and strengthened him with the Holy Spirit.*

*– Qur'an 2:87*

## Introduction

Muslims have much respect for Jesus and the Virgin Mary, and Jesus is considered to be one of the five most holy persons to walk the earth, along with Noah, Abraham, Moses, and Muhammad, the major prophets of Islam. Jesus is described in the Qur'an *"The Christ, Jesus, the son of Mary was a messenger of God and His word, which He bestowed on Mary, and a spirit which emanated from Him."* 4:171 Though Muslims believe that Jesus was born from a virgin, the major theological difference between them and most Christians is that Muslims do not believe in the divinity of Jesus but see Jesus as a great prophet. This belief is not unique to Muslims. Irenaeus, (late in the second century), talked about the Ebionites, an early Christian group living in the Jordan Valley and who survived until the end of the fourth century. They believed in one God, and believed Jesus was the Christ but human and not divine. Another major Christian group, the Arians, (from Arius 256-336, a priest of Alexandria), maintained that Jesus was created by God the Father, and was inferior to Him, but this teaching was condemned in 325 C.E. at the Council of Nicaea, and later in 381 in the Council of Constantinople as heresy. After that, Arianism disappeared from the Roman Empire but remained active outside the Empire. The Arian missionaries converted German tribes to Christianity during the three and four hundreds. When these tribes invaded the Roman Empire, they reintroduced Arianism which stayed active until the six hundreds, when the tribes were converted to orthodox Christianity. Arianism survived among some of the Lombards in Italy until the late seventh century.

The word 'Gospel / *Injīl*,' was mentioned twelve times in the Qur'an as the name of the holy book which was revealed to Jesus. The Gospels are, according to Christian definition, the holy books which describe the life and teaching of Jesus, and were written by the Disciples. Although the Christians of Yemen were sometimes critical of Islamic teaching concerning basic Christian theology, and debated Muslims regarding the divinity and genealogy of Jesus, they did not object to the Islamic concept of the Gospel. Perhaps this was because the idea of the "lost Gospel," the book which contains the sayings of Jesus, was known to them.

# The Gospel

## The Birth of Mary

Anna and her husband, Joashim /*Umrān*, were both people of God, and though Anna had passed her childbearing years without children, her maternal feeling were kindled when she saw a bird feeding her offspring.*She asked God for a child, and vowed that if Prot James 3:1-3 her wish were granted, she would give the child to the temple to be one of His servants. God accepted her prayer, and when she became pregnant, she rejoiced and renewed her vow: *"My Lord, I dedicate to You what rests in my womb to the service of the temple and Your worship, accept this of me, You hear and know all things."* When Anna delivered her baby girl she said to the Lord, *"My Lord, I gave birth to a baby girl, and name her Mary, and though traditionally only boys serve in the temple, I remand her and her offspring to Your protection from the evil one, the rejected."*3:35-36 Anna readied Mary and brought her to the temple where thirty priests, all descendants of Aaron, competed for Mary's care and teaching. The priests went to a creek and put their arrows in the water. The flowing water carried all the arrows but that of Zachariah's downstream.[1] His stood still, despite the rushing water, and it was determined that this was a sign that Zachariah should have custody of Mary. 3:44 Zachariah, who was the chief of the priests, took Mary home and raised her with the help of his wife Elizabeth, Mary's maternal aunt, until she became a young woman. At that time he had a special room built for her in the temple with a high door, reachable only by means of a ladder[2]. He brought

---

[1]- In Prot. Jas. the competition for Mary's care occurred when she was twelve years old. Zachariah, on instruction from an angel, assembled the widowers of the community and told them to bring rods which were taken to the high priest, and a dove came from the rods and flew onto Joseph's head. This was considered a sign and he took Mary, the Virgin of the Lord, under his care. 9:1.

[2]-In Prot. Jas. Mary's parents took her to the temple when she was three.

her food and drink every day, but when he entered her room, he saw
she had been provided with fruit that was out of season. When asked
where it came from, she told him, "It is *from God*, from His
Prot James 8:2 garden."3:37 *

As the years went on and Zachariah began to grow old, he
asked if anyone from the temple would like the honor of caring for
Mary, and once again, the person was chosen by casting arrows into
the river. Mary's cousin Joseph, a carpenter,[1] and dedicated to the
temple, then became her benefactor and continued to bring her food
and drink.

## The Annunciation

Mary and Joseph would walk together every day to a nearby
water source to draw water for the temple, and one day when she
Pro Jm 9:7 went alone* she saw the Angel Gabriel in the shape of a man. She
was afraid and said, "I *am seeking God's protection, the most gracious.
If you fear God honor that.*" And Gabriel responded, "I *am only a
messenger from your Lord to announce to you the gift of a holy son.*"
Mary asked, "*How can I have a son when no man has touched me and
I am not an unchaste woman?*" Gabriel answered, "*Your Lord said,
'It will be,' and it is an easy thing for him to do. Your son will be a
sign for all mankind and mercy from us.*" 19:16-21. "*Mary, God has
chosen you and blessed you among women of all nations,[2] so bow and
Lk 1:26-38 kneel to your Lord and worship Him devoutly.*"3:42-43 * Gabriel blew
his breath over Mary and she became pregnant with Jesus. As time
passed, Joseph realized that Mary appeared to be pregnant, and
though he tacitly denounced it, he refrained from accusing her when

---

[1]- There is no mention of Joseph in the Qur'an, only Zachariah is
mentioned in relation to Mary's care. When Islamic story tellers mention Joseph,
he is neither fiancé nor husband, but a pious man helping his cousin Mary. Mary's
birth story pub. by almost all tafsir books at 3:35; in Ara-Tha 344; Qis-Kath II:376.

[2]-The Devil touched every baby after his or her birth, which is why all
babies cry except for Mary and her son Jesus, because Anna said, at Mary's birth,
"I *remand her and her offspring to Your protection from the Devil, the rejected.*"
God protected Mary by a veil, and the Devil touched that veil instead. Hadith rep.
by *Abu Hurayra* and pub. by Sah-Bukh # 4548, Sah-Mus # 1619.

he remembered her innocence and piety. But as Mary's condition
became more and more obvious, he thought it best to ask her gently,
"Mary, though I have tried to ignore a certain subject it seems better
to discuss it; tell me, Mary, do plants grow without seeds, does a tree
grow without rain, and can a baby be conceived without a male?"
Mary told Joseph, "Did you not know that God grew the plants on the
day of Creation without seed, then seeds came from the plants? God
created the trees first, then made rain necessary for their life, and did
you not know that God created Adam and Eve from neither male nor
female?" Joseph agreed that he did know these things, and realized
that whatever happened to Mary was a divine intervention, and he
should no longer question her situation.[1]

As Mary's pregnancy progressed, she went to live with her
maternal aunt Elizabeth, who was herself expecting John. Elizabeth
welcomed Mary and told her, "I feel the baby in my womb is bowing
to yours."* Mary was close to giving birth, and Joseph, afraid she    Lk 1:39-44
might be accused of carrying an illegitimate child, took them on
a journey to Egypt.* When Mary, astride a donkey went into labor,    Mt 2:13-15
Joseph stoped under a dead palm tree near Bethlehem where the
angels crowded around them. When the labor pains became frequent
she said, *"Would that I had died before this, would that I had been
something forgotten and out of sight."* Gabriel answered from beneath
the palm tree, *"Grieve not, for your Lord has provided a rivulet
beneath you,"* and the Angel kicked the earth with his leg, water
flowed, and the dead tree blossomed with leaves and fruit. Gabriel
told Mary to *"Shake the trunk of the palm tree, and from it will fall
ripe dates, drink from the rivulet of water, eat the dates and be
satisfied."* 19:22-26 Mary did as the Angel instructed[2] while Joseph
built a hut and started a fire.[3]

---

[1]- Rep. by *Wahb*, pub. by Ara -Tha 343; Qis-Kath II:388.

[2]- In the Infancy Gospel of Pseudo-Matthew, the miracle of the palm
tree occurred on the third day of the journey into Egypt. This was the only gospel
to report this miracle, and accoding to the editor of "The Other Bible," this text
exists in Latin and was probably written and compiled in the eighth or ninth century.
Its sources are the Gospel of James and the Infancy Gospel of Thomas, and this
raises the question of the possible borrowing of this story from the Qur'an.

[3]- In most tafsir books at 3:42 & 19:22.

**Zachariah and his Son John**

Zachariah was a prophet and an important priest in the service of the temple, who was responsible for the proffering of the temple offerings. He and his wife Elizabeth were an elderly couple with no children of their own,* though they were entrusted with Mary's care, and they helped her to be the perfect young woman she appeared to be. When Zachariah realized that Mary, by the grace of God, enjoyed fruit even out of season, he knew God could bless them with a child, even in old age. He cried to his Lord in secret, *"My Lord, my bones are infirm and my heads glistens with grey, but never am I unblessed in my prayers to You, my Lord. [With no son] I am afraid my relatives will inherit from me, but my wife is barren. So give me an heir as from you, one that will represent me and represent the posterity of Jacob, and make him, My Lord, one with whom You are well pleased."* One day, while he was in his chambers to make an offering, the Angel Gabriel, clad all in white, presented himself before Zachariah, and said, "Zachariah, your prayer was answered, and I am here to *"give you the good news of a son whose name shall be John. None by this name have conferred distinction before."* At that time Zachariah was ninety-two and his wife ninety-eight years of age, and he questioned, *"But sir, how shall I have a son when my wife is barren, and I have grown quite decrepit from old age?"* Gabriel responded, *"So it will be, your Lord said, 'That is easy for Me, did I not create you when you were nothing?'"* And when Zachariah asked for a sign he was told, *"Your sign is that you shall speak to no man for three nights* and devote yourself to worshiping and obeying Me." Zachariah came out of his chamber, and gestured to the congregation to celebrate God's glory * every morning and every evening. Q 19:3-11

Lk 1:7 (margin)

Lk 1:11-12 (margin)

**The Mission of John the Baptist**

Elizabeth gave birth to a boy and they called him John. He grew up to be a very pious boy and he received his mission at an early age. He began to preach on the Sabbath as well as on holy days. His message was to worship God alone and no other deities—worshiping others was akin to providing slaves with a home and money for trade, then having these slaves work for another master. He also taught the importance of prayer; those who do not pray are no different from someone who asks for an audience with the king, but when presented before the ruler is so unfamiliar with the protocol that no favor will be granted. John further instructed the people of Judea to pay alms, as a prisoner in enemy lands contracts to pay and work in order to gain freedom. The Judeans were to frequently recite the name of God in order to protect them from Satan as a fort protects the inhabitants from outsiders. And finally, the Judeans were to fast, for fasting is like a garden that separates and protects from the enemy.[1]

### The Death of John the Baptist

John opposed the marriage of the King of Judea to a particular woman[2], and when this woman's mother heard of the opposition she vowed to rid herself and her daughter of the hated John. On the day of one of the king's parties, she dressed her daughter seductively in a red and black diaphanous silk dress, and had her wear ostentatious jewels and heavy perfume. Then she sent her to serve wine and

---

[1]- Pub. by Ara-Tha, the author did not attribute it to anyone. We find similar parables in the Mandaean writings attributed to John. "Worship God and no one else, worshiping others is like buying a slave but the slave gives his earnings to someone other than his master." "The significance of giving alms is like a man imprisoned by an enemy. They tied his arms and brought him to be beheaded, but he asked if he could ransom himself by making payments which they accepted and which he did." "The significance of fasting is like a man with a bundle of musk, all those around him enjoy the scent." From Tarikh al-Sabi'ah al-Manda'iyyin. Page 91,130.

[2]- The story of the woman who caused John's death has many versions. *Ibn Abbas* said she was the king's niece and John was preventing an incestuous marriage. *As-Siddi* maintains she was his stepdaughter, and *Ka'b* said she was the queen who had tried unsuccessfully to seduce John, and for his rejection of her she had him killed. Pub. in Ara-Tha 340 & Qis-Kath II:362. In Mark 6, the woman was Herodius, the ex-wife of Philip, Herod Antipas' brother. John was against her marriage to Herod, and Herodius had a grudge against him and wanted to kill him, but Herod would not because he feared John, a holy man. But on Herod's birthday, Herodius' daughter danced and beguiled him, and when he asked if there was anything she wished for, she asked for John's head. In Josephus Antiquities, there is yet another reason for John's death. King Herod Antipas feared the influence of John upon the Jewish people–perhaps he would lead an uprising against the king and the people would willingly follow his lead. To avoid future trouble, the king wanted him dead.

seduce the king but not to give herself to him until he agreed to give her anything she requested. Her scheme went according to plan, and when the king asked what she wished for, she demanded John's head on a plate. Though he tried to dissuade her, she stood firm and John was killed. On the spot where he had been killed, his blood kept bubbling no matter how much dirt was used to cover it. The sun lamented John's death for forty days by rising and setting red like blood. John, on Resurrection Day, will be the leader of the martyrs and will guide them to Paradise, and he will have the honor of slaying "the death," which will be symbolically presented in the shape of a white ram, and no one after that shall die.

Traditionally it has been accepted that John's head was buried in a tomb in the Omayyad Mosque in Damascus, which was originally a Christian cathedral.[1]

---

[1]- John (Yahya) holds a very special position in the Mandaean religion, and they consider themselves his followers. They believe that one of their holly books, "Adrasha ad Yahya," which is devoted to his life story and teachings, was written by John himself at the request of the Angel Gabriel. According to this book, John was not killed but died a natural death, "while John was busy baptizing his people Archangel Mendadhi approached him in the shape of a three year old child and asked him to be baptized, but John apologized because the sun was about to set, and according to the Mandaean tradition baptism cannot be done after sunset. But when John sat down to rest, God made him feel that he slept the entire night and changed the night into day, so John awoke refreshed and went back to the river where he saw the child waiting for him. The light's reflection from that child and the retraction of water underneath his feet made John think this was no ordinary child and asked him who he was. At that time, the fish chanted saying, 'bless your presence Angel Mendadhi, bless the place from whence you came, blessed and holy the place which you are going to.' This is followed by the chanting of birds. At that time Angel Mendadhi told John that he was entrusted to ascend with John's soul into Heaven. John was happy to know his mission on earth was to end and he was going to life immortal, and when the angel touched John's hand his soul was liberated from the prison of his body, leaving it on the bank of the river. John was 64 years old at the time of his death. From the Book of Yahya as translated by Lady Drower.

## The Death of Zachariah

When Zachariah learned that his son had been killed, he ran and hid on a farm, hiding in a tree that had called to him and opened its trunk, giving him a safe place to hide. The tree closed after he entered, but the Devil, *Iblīs*, appeared and grasped a piece of Zachariah's dress which he displayed to the king's army, thereby exposing the hiding place. The soldiers sawed the tree in half and killed Zachariah.[1]

## The Birth of Jesus

When Jesus was born, the idols from every corner of the world were thrown to the ground, and this frightened the demons because they did not know why this happened. They went to the Devil, *Iblīs*, who was sitting on a throne in the middle of a green lagoon. Seeing the demons all gathered together alarmed him, as he had sent them to every part of the world. The demons told him how the idols, whom they had entered and spoken through, had fallen, and how this would bring doubt to the mind of their idol worshipers. The Devil was puzzled, but realized something monumental had occurred. He asked the demons to wait until he could determine what had transpired. *Iblīs* took flight around the world and found the place where the baby Jesus had been born. But because so many angels were gazing upon the sight, the Devil was unable to have a glimpse of the infant. Trying to see him from the sky did not work either, for flying angels kept him away. Iblis returned to the demons, saying, "No man's birth before has caused us so much hardship."[2]

On the night Jesus was born, a new star appeared in the sky, and those people who knew its meaning went in search of the newborn. They passed by Herod the Great, King of Judea, who questioned them about their travels. They told him about Jesus and that they had gifts they were to give the baby. Herod thought it would

---

[1]- Rep. by *Ka'b*, pub. by Ara-Tha 341. A different story for Zachariah's murder is reported in Prot. Jas. which said he was killed at the entrance of the Temple and Altar by Herod's servants while John was still a baby, because he refused to tell them where John was hidden. His body then disappeared, but his blood petrified and Israel lamented for three days.

[2]- Rep. by *Wahb*, pub. in Ara-Tha 345.

be to his best advantage to have Jesus killed, and asked these people to inform him of the baby's whereabouts, as he had a gift to give as well. They found Jesus with the Virgin Mary and offered them gold, frankincense and myrrh and, as an angel warned them about Herod's plan, they returned via a different route.* Joseph, Mary, and Jesus continued toward Egypt where they stayed until news of Herod's death reached them and they were able to return home. *

Mt 2:1-12

Mt 2:14-15

## Jesus and the Miracles in Egypt[1]
### THE MIRACLES AT THE HOME OF THE EGYPTIAN PRIEST.

Joseph brought Mary and Jesus to a house belonging to an Egyptian priest who often housed poor and disabled people there. When the priest found that some money was missing, he did not blame any of his guests, but Mary felt sorry for the priest's loss. Seeing Mary's sadness, Jesus wanted to intervene and show the priest where his money had gone; Jesus assembled all the guests and placed a paraplegic man on the shoulders of a blind man and told the blind man to stand up. "But I am not that strong!" he protested. Jesus then asked how they were able to accomplish the same feat only the day before. When the others heard that, they proceeded to beat the blind man. The beating brought him to his feet, and then everyone was able to see how a blind man and a paraplegic man had conspired together and stole the money by using the legs of the blind man and the eyes of the paraplegic. The accusers confessed and the money was returned. The priest offered half of the recovered money to Mary, who refused it.

When the priest's son was married the priest hosted a large gathering attended by all of Egypt, and celebrated with enough food and drink for two months. But when the celebration was over and the priest ran out of wine, he received guests from Syria. Jesus heard of the priest's predicament and entered a room with two rows of

---

[1]- The trip to Egypt was not clearly mentioned in the Qur'an but Q 19:22 tells us that Mary went while pregnant to a "faraway place," which some mufassirun explained to mean Egypt. The stay in Egypt was brief because when she returned with Jesus still in the crib. This is one reason why 'the miracles of Egypt,' are generally not accepted by Islamic scholars, as well as not being mentioned in the Qur'an nor the four gospels and it is mostly mentioned by story tellers.

empty jars and as Jesus' hands passed over the spouts of the empty jars, they miraculously filled with wine.[1]

## THE KING'S PARTY

Jesus and the Virgin Mary were guests at a house in the country, and one day Mary saw that the host was sad and disheartened, and asked his wife the reason. She explained to Mary that the king and his soldiers visited each of his officers' homes and their turn was approaching; however, she and her husband felt that they were ill-equipped to host such a gathering, and could not provide enough food or drink. Mary assured the woman that they should not worry, and as they had been good to others, Mary would ask her son to pray for them, and there would be food and drink. But when Mary told Jesus of her request, Jesus said, "If I do what you want, there will be trouble." But Mary persisted and said, "We have to help that man who was so good to us." Jesus then said, "When the time comes, ask him to fill his jars and cooking pots with water, and let me know when this has been done." The host did so, and when Jesus prayed, the water in the jars changed into wine, and the water in the pots turned to meat. The king arrived, and when he tasted the wine he asked from which area it came. When the host named a particular wine growing area, the king said, "My wine also comes from that area, but tastes nothing like this." The host gave the king another fictitious region, but when the king demanded to be told the truth, the host confessed that he had a young boy who was granted whatever was wished for from God, and asked God to turn the water into wine. The king told his host that his son and heir had died several days before, and whoever could turn water into wine could raise someone from the dead. The king asked Jesus himself if he would help him, and Jesus responded, "If your son is raised from the dead, trouble will ensue." But the king told Jesus that all he wanted was his son's return, and he had no fear of the consequences. Jesus asked the king that if he and his son were reunited, would Jesus and his mother be able to travel freely? The king agreed, the king's son was resurrected with Jesus' prayers. But the people of the kingdom did not want the

---

[1]- The story of changing water into wine occurred, according to John 2:1-11, at the wedding in Cana.

son as the heir to the throne, and rallied against the king and his family. Jesus and the Virgin Mary left the kingdom.

### JESUS ACCUSED OF KILLING A CHILD

Jesus was playing with some other children when one boy jumped on another, kicking him with his foot and killing him. The slain boy fell in front of Jesus, who was splattered with his blood. Those seeing Jesus covered in blood accused him of the killing, and he was brought before a judge. Jesus denied the accusations before the judge, and when the Egyptians called for the death penalty, Jesus asked to see the dead boy so he might be asked who the actual killer was. "But he is dead; how do you expect him to answer?" In spite of their doubts, the dead boy was brought, and, as Jesus prayed to God, the boy returned to life. He was asked who had killed him, and after mentioning the name of the true killer, returned to death.[1] Jesus went to his mother, and they were followed by a large crowd. His mother admonished Jesus, saying, "Have I not prohibited you from this?" And Jesus said, "God is our protector and the most merciful."[2]

## Mary and Jesus Return Home and Jesus Preaches from the Crib

When Joseph returned home and Mary's family saw her with the baby Jesus in her arms, they said, *"Mary, we find this hard to believe, kinswoman of Aaron. Your father was not an evil man, nor was your mother a loose woman."* Mary gave no reply, but gestured to the baby as if asking him to explain. Her family questioned how an infant in a cradle could speak, when to their amazement the baby spoke and said, *"I am God's servant. He will make me a prophet and reveal the book to me. He has made me blessed and enjoined me in charity and prayer as long as I live. I must be considerate toward my*

---

[1]-In "Inf. Thom," when one of the children Jesus was playing with, fell from the second story and died, Jesus was accused of killing him, and when he was returned to life was asked, "Who killed you?" 9:1-3.

[2]- *As-Siddi* reported the miracle of the king's party, while *Wahb* reported the rest. These miracles have not been accepted by most Islamic scholars, and are published only in story books.

*mother and must not be domineering or hard to get along with. Peace be on the day I was born and the day I shall die, and on the day I will be resurrected."* 19:27-33 Mary's family then accepted her and her story.

## JESUS AND HIS TEACHER[1]

At the age of nine, Mary took Jesus to a teacher who began to teach him the alphabet. Jesus spelled out Alef (A), Ba (B), Geem (G), Dal (D), and asked the teacher if he understood the meaning of these letters. The teacher raised his stick as if to strike, when Jesus pleaded, "Teacher, do not hit me. If you do not understand, I will explain it." And he did so. Jesus connected every letter in the alphabet with a religious word or expression that began with the same letter in Arabic. The 'A' or Alef for "there is no deity but God." The 'B' or Ba for "the joy from God." The 'J' or Jeem for "the majesty of God," and the 'D' or Dal for "the religion of God." And Jesus continued through the alphabet. The teacher returned Jesus to his mother, saying, "Take back your son; Jesus has been taught without a teacher."

## JESUS AND THE DYE MASTER[2]

After Jesus left school, Mary sent him to different craft masters to learn their trades, the last of which was the dye master. The master had business to attend to out of town, and entrusted Jesus with the running of his shop. He left instructions as to which color should be applied to the different dresses, but Jesus chose to use one color on all the clothes. When the master returned and found all the fabric simmering togother in one dye pit, he was furious, and told Jesus he had ruined all the fabric. Jesus told the master to remove the cloth, and when this was done he found that each piece was dyed its intended color. The master was amazed and realized that he had witnessed a miracle from God, and he said to the people, "Come and see what Jesus has done."

---

[1]- One of the story tellers miracles, and most mufassirun did not mention it because it has no origin in the Qur'an. This story is mentioned in Inf. Thom. The alphabet is in Greek, Alpha to Omega.

[2]- Another non-Qur'anic miracle mentioned mostly by story tellers. Rep. by 'Ata, pub. in Ara-Tha 350; Taf-Khaz 3:52.

### The Mission of Jesus

At thirty years of age, God commanded Jesus to preach, and cure the sick, the blind, the mentally impaired, and to exorcize demons. He accomplished all of this, thereby earning the love of an ever-growing number of followers. Wherever Jesus stopped to preach, as many as fifty thousand sick or disabled persons gathered and asked for help. His cure was to pray, "God, You are the God of all Heavens and earth. There is no deity but You You are almighty on earth and Heaven. You are the king, the judge, the sovereign and Mt 6:9-13 the most powerful in Heaven and on earth."*

### The Miracles of Jesus after Mission

God gave Jesus support with the help of the Holy Spirit, and Jesus was taught divine knowledge. Jesus formed a bird from mud, and when he blew on it, by the grace of God, it became a living and Inf Tm 2:1-4 breathing bird. Q 3:49 * Jesus cured the sick and raised the dead. Lazarus was a dying man whose sister went to Jesus asking for help. When Jesus and the disciples reached Lazarus, he had been dead and buried for three days. Jesus was taken to his grave and said, "God, Jn 11:1-44 Lord of the seven heavens and seven lands,* I was sent to the people of Judea to preach and bring them to Your faith. I told them I can raise the dead with Your grace, 'Raise up Lazarus,'" and with that, Lazarus did rise from his grave. Jesus also raised the daughter of a tax collector after she had been dead one day[1].

### THE RESURRECTION OF EZRA THE SCRIBE[2]

In the old time, the Jews buried their dead in stone sarcophagi, and one was discovered bearing the name "Ezra the Scribe". The Judeans told Jesus to raise Ezra from the dead or be burned to death, and they began to gather firewood to prove their intention. They were unable to open the sarcophagus until Jesus had them spray it with water. Once it was opened, Ezra's remains were removed and

---

[1]- All these miracles are mentioned in the Qur'an, but the names and details have been adapted by early mufassirun from Christian sources. Pub. by Taf-Khaz 3:49.

[2]- Another non-Qur'anic story, most mufassirun ignore it. Pub. by Ara-Tha 354.

brought before Jesus, who lifted Ezra's shroud, sprinkled him with water, and said, "Ezra, by the grace of God, arise." Ezra sat up, and when asked by those gathered around him what he thought of Jesus, said, "I witness that Jesus is the servant and messenger of God." The people asked Jesus to allow Ezra to stay with them, but Jesus had him returned to his grave and he was dead once again.

### THE RESURRECTION OF SHEM[1]

Jesus and his disciples were discussing Noah and the ark, when someone asked Jesus to bring forth a witness to the flood. Jesus walked up a dirt hill where Shem, the son of Noah, rested in his grave. He took a fistful of dirt, struck the hill with a staff while calling the most holy name of God, and said, "Be alive, in the name of God." And Shem walked out of his tomb, his hair partially white, and asked if this was Resurrection Day. Jesus told him it was not, and that he had been called back by the most holy name of God to recount the story of Noah and the ark. When Shem had finished his story, and Jesus commanded him to return to the dead, Shem asked to be spared from the agony of death. Jesus asked God for this protection, which was given, and Shem returned to death.[2]

### THE WALK ON THE WATER[3]

Jesus and one of the disciples walked until they came to the sea, and Jesus said, "In the name of God in truth and certainty," and walked on the water.* His disciple saw this and, reiterating the same words, also walked on water. But when the disciple became proud and said to himself, "I walk on water as Jesus, the Spirit of God, does," he began to sink. Jesus snatched him from the water and questioned the disciple about what he had been thinking. When the disciple confessed, Jesus said, "Do not try to imagine youself where God did not intended you to be, Repent to God for your thought." The man did that.

Mt 14:25-33

---

[1]- Non Qur'anic story, pub. by Ara-Tha 354; Taf-Khaz 3:49.

[2]-In Jewish lore, Shem related to Eliezer, the servant of Abraham, the story of the animals in the Ark. There was no need to resurrect Shem because he lived long enough to be Abraham's teacher.

[3]- Non Qur'anic story, rep. by Ara-Tha 355.

## THE HEAVENLY FEAST

The disciples asked, *"Jesus, Son of Mary, can you send us a feast from Heaven?* Jesus responded, *"Heed God if you are believers."* *"We want to eat from it and know that what you have told us is the truth; we receive serenity in our hearts and we will be the witnesses for this occasion,"* said the disciples. Jesus prayed and said, *"Our Lord, send us down a table from Heaven that will hold a feast; from the first to the last of us, provide us with a sign, You are the best provider."* God answered, *"I shall send down such a feast, but any one of you who disbelieves afterward will be tormented and punished as no one before has been."* 5:112-115 The angels brought down a table laden with seven fish and seven loaves, surrounded by vegetables. Jesus gestured for the disciples to come and eat, when the food began to multiply, and in the end five thousand people had eaten from the table.[1]

## Jesus is Raised to Heaven

God revealed to Jesus, "Your life on earth is coming to an end." Jesus called the disciples together and prepared food for them. When they arrived for supper, Jesus served them food, washed their feet,* and preached to them. They disliked having Jesus wash their feet, but agreed to it when Jesus said, "Whoever rejects anything I do does not belong to me." After the Supper, Jesus said, "I served you food and washed your feet, although I am your teacher, so you do not look down upon each other but humble yourselves to one another and pray for me, so God may delay my departure." But when the disciples tried to pray for Jesus, God had sleep overtake them, and even when Jesus tried to wake them they were incoherent and unable to pray or intercede. Jesus realized that destiny had been determined, and said, "The shepherd will leave but the flock shall remain. One of you will reject me three times before the rooster crows, and one of

Jn 13:1-20

---

[1]-Some mufassirun connect this feast with the story of Jesus feeding four thousand people with seven loaves and seven fish, mentioned in Matthew.15:32-39, and in Mark 8:1-10. Others like Taf-Tab 5:115 said actually the miracle did not occur because the apostles had second thoughts when they heard the warning, and because it did not happen it was not mentioned in Christian sources.

you will reject me three times before the rooster crows, and one of you will sell me out for little money," and Jesus was then separated from the disciples.

As the Judeans searched for Jesus, they came upon Simon who three times denied he was one of the disciples. When Simon heard the rooster crow and remembered Jesus' words he cried.* The Mt 26:69-75 following morning another disciple named Judas learned that the Judeans were offering thirty drachmas if Jesus was found. Judas took the money when he brought them to Jesus * who was apprehended Mt 26:21-25 and bound with rope, struck with thorns, spat upon and then taken to be crucified. The Judean asked Jesus, "You used to raise the dead, give vision to the blind and cure lepers; why do you not untie the ropes?" At that moment the earth became dark and God sent angels to save Jesus; Judas was miraculously changed so he now appeared to look exactly like Jesus, and was crucified as the Judeans assumed he was Jesus.[1] Jesus did die after that but remained dead only three hours, when he was raised to Heaven and remained there for seven days.

Mary, the mother of Jesus, and Mary Magdalene, a woman whom Jesus had helped, saw the crucified man and broke into tears. Jesus returned to earth aftert the seven days on a mountain that was aglow with bright light. He met with his mother and Mary

---

[1]-The basic teaching in Islam about the end of Jesus' life on this earth is that there was no crucifixion. Those who thought they had crucified Jesus had actually killed the "similar," according to Q4:157-158. The story mentioned above is but one of different stories that have tried to explain the crucifixion of another. This belief is not unique to Moslems, but is shared by the Gnostic Christians. In one of their books, "The Apocalypse of Peter," discovered in Nag Hammadi, we read about Jesus telling Peter, "He who you saw being glad and laughing on the tree is the living Jesus, but he into whose hands and feet they are driving the nails is his fleshy part which is the substitute. They put to shame that which remained in his likeness. 81:4-19. In "The Second Treatise of the Great Sith," another Gnostic book from Nag Hammadi, Jesus said, "It was another ......who drank the gall and the vinegar. It was not I they struck with reeds; it was another, Simon, who bore the cross on his shoulders. It was another upon whom they placed the crown of thorns, but I was rejoicing in the heights over all the wealth of the archons and the offspring of their error, of their empty glory, and I was laughing at their ignorance." The similarity between gnostic and Islamic teaching in this respect is only superficial and not theological.

Mt 28:9-11 Magdelene* and told them what God had done. He also met with
Mt 28:18-20 his disciples and dispersed them to different parts of the earth.*[1]

God then raised Jesus to Heaven covering him with light, took away all his desire for food or drink and Jesus then joined the angels who surrounded the Holy Throne.

## The Second Coming of Jesus

Jesus is coming back and will return to the earth before the end of time, but before the second coming, the Antichrist will appear and fool people with false miracles. The antichrist can bring rain on command, and his followers will have good crops, while those who do not yield to his sorcery will suffer a drought. Should he pass by an ancient ruin, he can command its hidden treasure to follow him. He will have the ability to cut a man in half, then bring him back to life, once again in one piece.

During that time, God will have Jesus descend on the white minaret, east of Damascus. He will be holding onto the wings of two angels, gazing downward, and his sweat will drip from his forehead like precious pearls. Every non-believer for as far as the eye can see will die immediately by the power of his breath. He will find and kill the antichrist at the gate of "Ladd" in Palestine.

God will then send the Gog and Magog who, when passing by the Sea of Galilee, will drink its water until it is all gone. They will surround Jesus and the followers, who will retreat up a mountain and run out of food. Jesus will ask for God's help, and He will send worms which will bite the Gog and Magog in their necks, and by the next morning, all will be dead. When Jesus and the followers descend the mountain they will find the earth contaminated with dead bodies, and again pray for relief. God will send birds the size of camels to pick up the corpses and carry them away, and this will be followed by rain which will cleanse the earth.

Good crops will grow and flourish after that. The pomegranate fruit will feed many people, and its shells will shield them. A nursing she-camel will feed a tribe, a nursing cow will feed many families, and a nursing sheep will feed a large family. Peace will be on earth,

---

[1]- There is no standard Islamic story for what happened between the crucifixion of the similar and the final ascension to Heaven, this is one of many stories about this subject reported by Ibn 'Abbas, Muqatil, Wahb and others.

lions will lay down with the camels, the tigers with the cows, and the wolves with the sheep. Children will play with snakes, and no one will hurt each other.

God will then send a saving breeze, which will take the soul of every believer and only the wicked will remain. The Day of Resurrection comes with only the evil people left on the earth.[1]

---

[1]- The Islamic stories about the second coming of Jesus and the Antichrist are many, and some contradict each other.

# 15     Christian Stories

*You will find the most affectionate of them towards [Muslim] Believers, are those who say: "We are Christians." That is because Some of them are priests and monks; they do not behave so proudly.*

– Qur'an 5:82

## Introduction

The relationship between the long established Christian Church and the new Islamic faith was one of cooperation and support dating back to the early days of Islam. *Waraqah bin Nawfal*, the Christian uncle of the Prophet's wife, gave his support to the Prophet after his first vision of revelation, and assured him that he had received his mission from God. When the people of Al-Taif turned a deaf ear to the Prophet's teachings and had their children throw stones at him, it was a Christian slave who comforted him and brought him grapes to eat. When the Christian Byzantine army was defeated in its war against the Zoroastrian army of the Persians, the early Muslim community felt as if they had been defeated, and it took a divine revelation to reassure them and promise them that within a few years the Christian army would triumph in victory against the Persians. When the early Muslim community members in Mecca were persecuted and tortured, the Prophet told them to flee to Abyssinia, a Christian country, because, in the words of the Prophet, "It is a land of truth and no one there will suffer injustice." The King of Abyssinia granted the early Muslims asylum, which they took advantage of until it was decided they should return home. When the king died, he was eulogized by the Prophet who honored him with a special prayer service.

In this chapter, I will present three stories which were originally Christian but after their introduction in the Qur'an they became part of the Islamic narrative.  The Qur'an praises the sacrifices of the early Christians and raised their heros to the status of an Islamic martyr.

# The Acts of the Apostles

The only story in Islamic writings about the apostles is found in Q 36:13-30, and in its original version does not mention the names of the apostles, the town nor the date. It tells the story of three missionaries who went to a town and preached to its people, which most mufassirun maintain was Antioch. But the preaching was rejected by the townspeople, and when one of them tried to defend the missionaries, he was killed by his own people. The following is the expanded version according to *Ibn 'Abbās* and *Muqātil.*

This is the story of the town of Antioch when it was visited by two apostles with a third to follow, and they were all to preach the same message: to believe in the teachings of Jesus Christ and to worship God and not any other deity. But the people of Antioch rejected their message, and told the apostles, "You are only men like us, and there is no such thing as a revelation from God. You do not tell the truth."36:15 The apostles did not give up; they continued to preach, and said, 'Our Lord knows we are here on a mission from Him to serve you."36:16 The persistence of the apostles only served to irritate the people, and they warned them, "We believe you to be a bad omen. Cease your preaching, or you will be stoned and severely punished."36:18 These threats did nothing to deter the apostles, who responded by reprimanding the people of Antioch, "The omen is in yourselves, and you are the transgressors."36:19

As the tension grew and the danger for the apostles increased, a man named *Habīb*, a believer in God who lived at the edge of the city and worshiped secretly in a cave, came to their defense. Habib was a carpenter who gave half of his earnings to charity. He confronted the people threatening the apostles, saying, "My people, follow the message of these missionaries; they are asking for no reward from you and they are enlightened people."36:20-21 His people asked him, "Have you rejected our religion and now follow the teachings of these missionaries?"  And *Habīb* responded, *"Why should I not worship He who created me and to whom I will one day return? I will take no other gods but Him; these gods cannot intervene to help me. If God the most gracious should cause adversity for me, they cannot save me.  It is a great mistake to worship these gods; listen to me, I am a believer in the Lord of everyone."* 36:22-25  Although *Habīb* was successful in diffusing the anger against the apostles, the people then turned on him, and as they stoned him to death, he repeated the words, "God forgive them and show them the truth."  The martyred *Habīb* went to Heaven, and when he found what awaited those worthy enough to be accepted there, wished *"the people of my city would know how God granted me forgiveness and counted me among those held in honor."* 36:26-27

After *Habīb*'s martyrdom, God sent the Angel Gabriel to the city, and as he held onto the columns of the city gate, he sent a blast over the city, causing every inhabitant to drop dead.

### Comment

Mufassirun unanimously hold that Antioch was the town in the story, and this supports the idea that it was a known Christian story.  In the 'Acts of the Apostles,' the story which parallels the Islamic one is the story of the mission of Paul, Barnabas and Mark in Antioch to the north of Pisidia, and not the Syrian Antioch.  Sent by the Holy Spirit, Paul, Barnabas and Mark first went to Seleucia, then sailed to Cyprus, and after preaching there sailed to Perga in Pamphylia, and then on to Antioch in Pisidia.  Antioch had a large Jewish community which gathered in the synagogue on the Sabbath, and where the apostles were well received at their first sermon.  On the following Sabbath, an enormous crowd had gathered, and this popular reception made the priests of the synagogues very jealous; in retaliation they rallied the support of the city leaders against the apostles and incited the people who drove them from the city.  In the 'Book of the Acts', it is said that Mark left after Perga and went back to Jerusalem, and although the writer of 'Acts' talked about the persecution of the apostles in Antioch, there is no record of anyone that matches the description of *Habīb* as mentioned in the Islamic story.

## The Spread of Christianity in Southern Arabia
### (The People of the Ditch)

This Qur'anic story also does not mention either names or places. *"Woe to the makers of the ditch, of fire-suppliers of fuel who sat and watched as the believers were harmed, and ill-treated for no other reason than because of the belief in God, exalted in power and worthy of all praise."*85:4-8

Mufassirun maintain that these verses are describing the persecution which the early Christians of Najran in Southern Arabia suffered. The Qur'an praised these martyrs who were burned to death in a ditch, and threatened those who caused the persecution. *"Those who persecute the believers, both men and women, and do not repent, will suffer the torture of Hell, and the torture of the burning fire."*85:10 The suffering and torture of the Christians was so horrendous that the story was included in the most holy Islamic book, the Qur'an. The following story is an Islamic-Christian story mentioned in most tafsir books and many hadith books, reported by *Suhayb* and attributed to the prophet Muhammad, and describes how Christianity spread in pagan Najran.

The chief priest told the king, "I am worried that I might die with no one worthy to succeed me. Find an intelligent boy who I can teach and prepare to some- day take over my position." The king's courtiers found such a boy who, on his daily trip to see the priest, passed by a monk in a monastery. He would sometimes stop to talk. One day, the boy asked the monk whom he worshiped, and when the monk answered that he worshiped God, the boy became interested in his teaching and spent more time with the monk than with the priest. When the priest complained about the boy's lack of punctuality, the monk told the boy to say that his parents had delayed him, and to tell his parents that the priest was responsible for his tardiness. This was a satisfactory arrangement until one day when the boy passed by a group of people trapped by a lion. He picked up a pebble and said,

"God, if what the monk is telling me is true, I ask you to let me kill this beast, but if it is the priest that has the true teaching, let me not kill the lion." When he threw the stone at the lion and killed it, the people said that "this boy possesses a knowledge which no one before us has had." Having heard about the boy, a blind man approached him and said, "I will give you a vast sum of money if you return my vision," and the boy answered that he did not want any money, but did ask that if the man's sight was restored, would he then believe in the one that restored it? The man agreed, his vision returned, and he became a believer. The king heard about this miracle and had the boy, the monk, and the once-blind man brought before him and said, "Each one of you will be killed in a different way, and after doing away with the monk and the believer, he decreed that the boy should be thrown from a high cliff. Soldiers attempted to do just that, but found themselves hurtling over the side of the cliff while the boy remained on top. The boy went back to the king, whose next order was to have the boy drown, but when the soldiers tried to throw him into the sea, they were the ones who drowned while the boy survived. This time when he went before the king he said, "If you want to kill me, you must impale me; shoot me with an arrow, and say, "In the name of your Lord, you shall die." Once the king did that, the boy was dead, and when the people saw what had happened they said, "The knowledge which that boy possessed is superior, and we all believe in the Lord of that boy." The king's courtiers told him, "You panicked when only three people challenged you; what are you now going to do when all your subjects are opposing you?" The king ordered that many ditches be dug, and filled them with firewood, and announced, "Whomsoever does not return to our original religion will be thrown onto this fire." And twelve thousand people died in the fiery ditches.[1]

Though no names were mentioned in the hadith, Arab historians have called the boy *'Abdullah bin Thāmir*. *Ibn Ishāq* tells the story that, in the time of the second caliph, *'Umar bin al-Khaṭṭāb*, a man from Najran was digging in an ancient ruin and found *'Abdullah bin Thāmir*, in a sitting position and protecting his head

---

[1]- From a hadith of the Prophet rep. by *Suhayb*. Pub. In Taf-Bagh & Khaz 85:4

with his hand.  When they moved his hand, the area on his head that had been covered began to bleed, and the caliph ordered the people of Najran to return him as they found him, and cover him with dirt.

**Comment**
        There is uncertainty about when Christianity first came to Southern Arabia.  Greek sources claim that the Emperor Constantine sent Theophilus Indusin 345 C.E. to southern Arabia to preach about Christianity. Theophilus was successful, and he built churches in Aden, Zuphar and Hormuz.[1]  Syriac sources gave this honor to a merchant from Najran, whose name is *Hayyān* and who, at the time of the Sassanian king Yazdejird I, 399-420 C.E., was converted to Christianity when he visited the Christian Arabian city Al-Hira,[2] while Abyssinians sources gave this honor to St. Azkir.  Islamic sources gave that honor to two saints, one of them having a Greek name, Phemion, which is a corruption of Euphemion.  The second saint was a Syrian man named *Ṣāliḥ.* [3] But this story can not be dated.
        The persecution of the Christians of Najran happened in the first quarter of the fifth century when the Jewish king of *Himyar, Dhū Nuwās*, persecuted the Christians to stop the spread of their religion in Yemen. This continued until the Christian Abyssinians invaded Yemen in 525 C.E. and killed king *Dhū Nuwās*. This event was mentioned in Greek and Syriac as well as Arabic sources.

---

[1]- Philostorgius, Historia Ecclesiastica. III, 46.
[2]- Chronik von Seer, II, 149.
[3]- Tar-Tab II:120.

# The Seven Sleepers
# (The People of the Cave)

This Qur'anic story which is found in Q 18:9-26, is about a few young men, devout believers, whose numbers and names are not mentioned. These young men were true believers in a city of non-believers, and they fled from persecution, accompanied by their dog, to live in a cave. God had them sleep for hundreds of years, but when they awoke they thought they had been asleep for only a day, or perhaps less. And when one of the men left to find food, he was careful to not attract any unwanted attention. The Qur'anic story then jumps ahead to say that after the young men and their story were discovered, the people of the town realized that God's promises are real and there will be a Day of Resurrection. A shrine was built around their resting place by the believers who were in power at that time.

## The story according to *Ibn Isḥāq*

At the time of the Emperor Decius, in the city of Ephesus, Christians were persecuted unless they rejected their religion and followed the rituals of the Romans who made sacrifice to idols. Those who refused to abjure Christianity were killed, and their mutilated bodies were put on display on the gates of the town. A group of young believers from noble families was brought before the emperor and accused of being Christian. "What prevented you from honoring and giving sacrifice to our gods? You should set an example for other citizens," the emperor raged, and threatened to kill them all. Maxilmina, the eldest of them, said, "The Majesty and the Might of our Lord fills heaven and earth, we will never call another god, 18:14 and we will never accept what you have commanded us to do, no matter the con- sequences." The emperor had their fine clothes removed and told them, "I am leaving on a trip to another city, and will delay your sentence until I return. You are young men, and I dislike having to kill you. Perhaps if you have some time to rethink the matter you will come to your senses." And with that, they were released.  After consulting each other, the young men agreed that they should bring money from their fathers, giving some to charity and keeping the remainder for themselves, and hide in a cave in the mountains of Bingelos.  Once ensconced in the cave, now accompanied by a dog, they assigned the buying of food and necessities to one of them named 'Jamblichus', and then devoted themselves to fasting, praying and praising God.  Each morning Jamblichus disguised himself and went to the city to purchase what they might need and learn of any news that was pertinent to them.  This was their daily routine until the emperor returned, and when he learned that the boys were nowhere to be found, he summoned their fathers, who apologized and lamented the fact their children had disobeyed them, stole money, spent wildly, then disappeared into the mountains. Jamblichus heard the disturbing news, and upon his return to the cave with only a meager amount of provisions, the young men decided to put their faith in God.  They bowed to Him, then sat and contemplated what to do, when God put them with the dog into a deep sleep.  The emperor and his guards searched on horseback, and when he was informed they were hiding in a cave, the emperor ordered his men to enter the cave and bring out the boys.  But not one of the guards was able to gain entry, so it was decided to seal the entrance, thereby making the cave the young men's grave. Two believers, Pedros and Wanas, who worshiped clandestinely, inscribed the story including the boys' names and family history on two lead tablets, and secured and sealed them in a copper box with the hope that one day people would learn who had met their fate in the cave.

God kept the young men asleep for many generations, protected from the sun,  and had them turn in their sleep.  Many emperors came and went, and slowly the Christian faith spread throughout the empire until the emperor himself professed to be a Christian.  When Theodosius came to power, there came the question of the resurrection of the body, which split the Church apart, and the emperor was said to be in a quandary, and dressed in sackcloth, sat in ash and prayed to God for guidance.  A shepherd, tending his flock close to the cave, was caught in a heavy rain and tore down the blocked entrance to seek shelter during the storm.  The following day, when the sunshine illuminated the inside of the cave and the sleepers awoke, they believed they had only been asleep for a day or less.

When Jamblichus went to buy their daily rations, he was surprised to see a sign of Christian belief above the gates to the city, and upon entering he became further disoriented but continued on, until he found a shop selling what he was looking for. When he paid the store owner with coins minted during the reign of Decius, the owner thought he had found a hidden treasure, and said, "Show me where the treasure is hidden or I will notify the authorities." Jamblichus questioned whether Decius was not the emperor, and the merchant informed him that Decius had been dead for over a century, and that the current emperor was called Theodosius. This unusual conversation attracted a number of people, and eventually the youth was taken to the authorities, and from there to the emperor himself, who listened to his story. Theodosius had heard of the legend of the young men who hid in the cave at the time of Decius, and requested a meeting with the church elders to discuss the matter. One of the elders said he knew their names and their families' genealogy, and when Jamblichus was questioned about the names of his companions it was discovered that the two lists matched. The elders realized that the youth was telling the truth, and finally learned the real story of what had happened. The emperor said, "This is a sign from God that resurrection is real," and went with the people of the town and Jamblichus to meet and rejoice with the sleepers in the cave. The sleepers were still young and their clothes like new, and they explained to Theodosius how they had suffered under Decius, then said, "We are going to leave you in the protection of God; peace and God's mercy be upon you. May God protect you and your kingdom." The sleepers then lay down and died. The emperor covered them with his own dress, and ordered gold coffins for each of the young men, but that night the emperor had a dream in which the sleepers told him, "Do not place us in gold, we are from dust and to dust we will return." So they were put in wooden coffins, left inside the cave, and the emperor had a place of worship built at the entrance to the cave.

### The Story from Syriac Sources

While in Ephesus, the Emperor Decius demanded that everyone, including the Christians, engage in the practice of sacrifice for the worship of idols. While some Christians cooperated, others chose to suffer, but remained faithful to their beliefs. Depending on the source, either seven or eight young men, whose names also differ with different historians, are presented to Decius as Christians who refuse to make sacrifice. Hoping time will change their will, the emperor leaves, and after his departure the men make haste to Mount Anchilus where they hide in a cave. Diomedes (or Iamblichus) changes his appearance and goes to the town to purchase food, and there learns that Decius has returned and wants to see the young men. When they hear this they are disheartened, and after eating their meal, fall, by the grace of God, into a long and deep sleep. Decius' men cannot find them, and when their parents are questioned they apologize for their sons' behavior and readily tell Decius of the cave. Decius has the cave's entrance barricaded with large rocks, making the young men's egress impossible and their death inevitable. Three hundreds and seven years later, under Theodosius II, a conflict arose when Bishop Theodore denied the resurrection of the dead, which disturbed the emperor.

Adolius, the owner of the field where the cave was located, wanted to build a break for his sheep, and when the workers remove the stones from the cave's entrance to use it in the building, the cave was opened. Once awake, by God's grace, each young man thinks he has only slept for one night, and each encourages the other to risk martyrdom, and to return to Ephesus. It is once again Diomedes who is chosen, and when he approaches the city and sees a cross on the gates, becomes very confused and questions where he has wandered. Eventually he finds a shop, and when the merchant sees his coin from the reign of Decius, thinks, along with others gathered at the market, that this person holds the secret to hidden treasure. Diomedes is harassed for information until he is brought before a bishop and the governor, and is able to tell them his story. He asks them to come to the cave, and while hiking near the entrance two lead tablets are found—written at the time of the incarceration by Theodore and Rufinus—that detailed the incident and that were sequestered under the stone. These tablets are proof that Diomedes has spoken the truth. Soon afterward the emperor himself arrives. Either Maximilian or Achilledes, or others, explains to Theodosius that God had them sleep and then brought them back before Judgement Day to tell the truth of the Resurrection. The sleepers then pass away in death, and the emperor marks that spot with a shrine.[1]

## Comment

As to the exact number of sleepers, the Qur'an does not mention a number."*Some say they were three and a dog being the fourth among them. Others say they were five, the dog being the sixth, doubting the unknown. Yet others say they were seven, the dog being the eighth. My Lord knows best their number, it is but few that know their real case.*" 18:22 But *Ibn 'Abbās* said he is one of the few and their number is seven; most mufassirun accepted this number, but *Ibn Isḥāq* made them eight; seven or eight is the number in the Christian stories.

How long did they stay asleep? It is clear from Qur'anic verse 18:12 that there were at least two different Christian stories with two differing opinions as to how long they slept. "*Thus we roused them, in order to test which of the two parties was best at calculating the term of years they had tarried.*" The Christian sources vary regarding the number of years they slept from 146 to 353 years. In Q 18:25, 309 years was mentioned; "*They stayed in their cave three hundred years and some added nine years to that.*" According to *Qutāda* and *Maṭar Al-warrāq*, this verse is not presenting an Islamic view but citing what the Christians were saying. The Islamic view is: "*God knows best how long they stayed, with Him is the knowledge of the secrets of the heavens and the earth.*" 18:26. Other mufassirun maintain that the number 309 is the actual number of years they remained in the cave, but that the time that elapsed between Decius and Theodosius is not more than 146 years, this interpretation is not compatible with either that of *Ibn Isḥāq* or other Christian stories. *At-Ṭabarī* mentioned in his tafsir that this story was revealed to the Prophet Muhammad in response to indirect challenge from 'the people of the book,' through unbelievers of Mecca. The expression, 'the people of the book,' was used by Muslims in reference to either Jews or Christians, and although *At-Ṭabarī* mentioned that the Jews

---

[1]- Encyclopedia of Religion & Ethics, Edited by James Hastings.

were behind the challenge, it is more likely that it was the Christians, as it was a Christian story. The earliest Christian text to mention the story according to Noldeke, Ryssel and Heller was a Syriac text (poetic elaboration), dating back to the end of the fifth century and attributed to James of Serugh. It is thought that this is the story which the Prophet was challenged to recount. I do not think this story was well known before that but its revelation in the Qu'ran made it famous. It was then translated into many languages, including Ethiopian, Armenian, Coptic and Arabic. The story moved west and found its way into Byzantine literature, and is mentioned in Theophanes (758-816 C.E.), as well as in Pholius and in the Menaea, and was eventually translated into Latin, where it was copied and recounted through the ages, and is found in Anglo-Saxon, Medieval German, ancient Norse, Swedish, Italian, French and Spanish literature.

# Qur'anic references
## Who is where in the Qur'an "in suras and verses."

## Aaron / *Hārūn*
Praised by God    4:248; 6:84
Moses' brother and helper    19:53; 20:30; 25:35; 26:13; 28:34.
His mission with Moses    10:75; 20:70; 21:48; 23:45; 26:48;
                                            37:114,120.
Involvement in the worship of the golden calf    7:142,150-151;
                                                                    20:90-94.

## Abel and Cain / *Hābīl and Qābīl*    **5:27-31.**
## Abraham / *Ibrāhīm*
Abraham recognizes his Lord    6:76-79
Abraham argues with his father and his people    6:74; 6:80-83;
19:43-46; **21:51-56**; **26:69-77**; **37:83-87**; 43:26-27; 60:4.
Hymn #1    26:78-89.
Praying for his father's guidance    9:114; 19:47; 60:4-5.
Abraham and the idols    21:57-67; 37:88-96.
Abraham in the burning fire    21:68-70; 37:97-98.
Hymn #2    37:99-100.
Abraham debates with Nimrod    2:258.
Moving to the Holy Land    21:71; 19:48.
Leaving Hagar and son in the desert, hymn #3    14:35-41.
The sacrifice    37:101-108.
Abraham the Imam, praised by God    2:124; 4:125; 16:120-122.
How do you raise the dead?    2:260.
Abraham visited by angels    11:69-76; 15:51; 29:32; 51:24-34.
Abraham was foretold of the birth of his son 'Isaac' and a grandson
'Jacob.'    19:49-50; 21:72-73; 37:101.
Abraham and Ishmael building the Ka'ba    2:125-127; 22:26.
Abraham announcing the Hajj    22:26-29.
Hymn #4    2:128-131.

# Index

## Arabic references

*Akhbār Makkah; Al-Azraqī*
*(Tar-Mak) Dar al-Thaqafa,*
*Makkah.*              96, 98, 106.
*Al-Wafā; Ibn ul-Jawzī*    44.
*'Arāyis ul-Majālis; Al-*
*Tha'labī* (Ara-Tha)
15, 31, 32, 33, 37, 41, 43, 44,
45, 46, 47, 48, 51, 57, 58, 59,
82, 93, 102, 106, 107, 114,
115, 116, 117, 118, 119, 121,
122, 123, 124, 126, 127, 128,
131, 133, 134, 135, 139, 140,
141, 142, 143, 144, 146, 147,
149, 150, 151, 152, 153, 157,
158, 160, 161, 162, 163, 164,
165, 167, 169, 170, 171, 174,
175, 179, 180, 185, 186, 187,
188, 189, 190, 191,192, 193,
194, 195, 196, 197, 198, 204,
205, 206, 207, 208, 209, 210,
212, 214, 215, 216, 222, 223,
224, 239, 240, 248, 249, 260,
263, 265, 269, 270, 271.
*Bihār ul-Anwār;*
*Muhammad Bāqir al-Majlisī*
24.
*Diwān Umayya bin Abis-Salt*
28.
*Hayāt ul-Hayawān al-Kubrā;*
*Al-Dumayrī, Dar al-Kutub al-*
*'Ilmiyyah,* Bayrut, 1994.
57, 58.

*Al-Iktifā bi Sīrat ul-*
*Mustafā; Ibn ul-Jawzī*
98, 100, 104.
*Masnad Imām Ahmad*
36, 49, 93.
*Qisas al-Anbiya; Ibn Kathīr*
(Qis-Kath)
17, 31, 33, 48, 58, 179, 215, 240,
243, 260, 261, 263.
*Sahīh Al-Bukhārī* (Sah-
Bukh,)    *Al-Maktaba al-*
*'Asriyyah,* Bayrut,
8, 12, 14, 15, 45, 93.
*Sahīh Muslim* (Sah-Mus),
*An-Nīsābūrī* edition, edited
by M.N.D. *Al-Albānī, Al-*
*Maktab al-Islami,* Bayrut,
1972.
*Salwat ul-Ahzān; Ibn ul-*
*Jawzī*                    38.
*Sunan An-Nisā'ī*
12, 14, 36.
*Sunan At-Tirmidhī*
12, 13, 14, 36, 49, 160.
*Tafsīr Al-Baghawī* (Taf-
Bagh),    Dar    al-Ma'rifa,
Bayrut,1995
20, 23, 25, 35, 38, 39, 43, 48,
55, 56, 57, 58, 59, 60, 89, 90,
93, 94, 100, 102, 104, 105,
107, 117, 120, 121, 122, 126,
127, 128, 130, 131, 133, 134,
continue next page

# Hebrew Sources

# General Sources

**Apocalypse of Peter,** from "The Other Bible," p. 532-536, Harper & Row Publishers, 1984.
273.

**Apocalypse of Abraham,** from O.T.P. I 'p. 681-705'
91.

**4Baruch,** from O.T.P. II, 'p. 423-425'
251, 252.

**Chronik Von Seer**
283.

**Encyclopedia of Religion and Ethics**
288.

**Encyclopedia Judaica**
252.

**Josephus Antiquity,** from "The Complete Works of Josephus," Kregel Publications, 1981.
1, 55, 106, 142, 200, 263.

**Legends of the Bible (L.O.B.)** by Louis Ginzberg, The Jewish Publication Society, 1992.
165, 167.

**Legends of the Jews (L.O.J.)** by Louis Ginzberg.
30, 31, 36, 38, 42, 45, 60, 66, 90, 91, 94, 100, 127, 130, 141, 149, 160, 186, 189, 191, 192, 193, 209, 213, 223, 229, 236.

**Old Testament Pseudepigrapha (O.T.P.)** Edited by James Charlesworth, Doubleday, 1983.
67, 252.

**Philotorgius Historia Ecclesiastica**
283.

**Ps-philo**
106, 161, 189.

**Second Treatise of the Great Sith**, p. 117 "The Other Bible,"
273.